STUDIES ON KOSOVA

Edited by

ARSHI PIPA and SAMI REPISHTI

EAST EUROPEAN MONOGRAPHS, BOULDER
DISTRIBUTED BY COLUMBIA UNIVERSITY PRESS, NEW YORK
1984

Prepared for publication by Arshi Pipa

Printed in the United States of America

CONTENTS

iii

FOREWORD

Studies on Kosova is an elaborated version of papers read, in a summarized form, at the International Conference on Kosova. The Conference took place at the University Graduate Center, the City University of New York, on November 6, 1982.

The Conference represented a gathering of scholars with special interest in Yugoslavia and Albania.[1] The topic proposed for discussion was "The Question of Kosova: the Present Situation and Prospects for the Future." The morning session, chaired by Albert B. Lord, examined "Historical Considerations and Cultural Aspects." The afternoon session, chaired by Arshi Pipa, dealt with "The Economic and Political Situation."

The International Conference on Kosova was convened to discuss an intricate ethnic problem, which, due to its magnitude and explosive potential, may provoke serious troubles in the Balkans, thus destabilizing the status quo in Europe. Kosova, a Yugoslav federal unit bordering on Albania, is overwhelmingly inhabited by Albanians (77.5%). The unit is officially known as the Socialist Autonomous Province of Kosova. The degree of autonomy the ethnic Albanians (Kosovars) enjoy has been a hotly debated issue ever since the Province was constituted—originally as an Autonomous Region—as part of the Republic of Serbia.[2] Resenting Serbian tutelage, the Kosovars have been unhappy with this solution. In the Spring of 1981, during mass riots in the capital of the Province and other cities, the Kosovars demanded the status of a republic for Kosova. At the same time the Albanians in the Republic of Macedonia, who account for about 22 percent of its population, demonstrated against their own subaltern position with respect to Slavs. According to the latest official census, there are 1,754,000 Albanians in Yugoslavia, distributed among Kosova, Macedonia, Montenegro and Inner Serbia. The number of Albanians in the mother country is about 2,800,000. The prospect of an united Albania is a major concern for Yugoslavs. Were they to grant Kosova republic status, the next thing the Kosovars would do is to merge with Albania, the Yugoslavs think. The secession of Kosova would encourage an irredentistic movement among the Albanians of Macedonia and Montenegro while setting a precedent for nationalistic and religious groups who are hostile to the concept of federation. Granting republic status to Kosova might set in motion a chain reaction that could well end with the breakup of Yugoslavia itself. But a greater Albania would be unpalatable also to Greece, where a segment of the population has long been claiming Southern Albania ("Northern Epirus") as Greek territory. Kosova's merger with Albania—assuming that Serbia would agree to fully emancipate its province—could be a pretext for Albania's neighbors to start another Balkan war, similar to those in the 1912-1913 period.

Thoughts such as these were in the minds of the organizers of the Conference when they set about to convene it, choose its topic, the place of meeting, and define the procedures for holding it. Determinant for their undertaking was their conviction that an international scholarly conference would be a contribution to peaceful existence in the Balkans. For lasting peace cannot be built on deceptions and mirages. And the best service a scholar can do humankind is to pursue the truth.

Yet scientific pursuit is not always inspired by a desire for peace, and less than ever in our times, when science and technology are made to serve goals that only increase the chances for another holocaust. Our main effort was to secure contributors whose impartiality matched their intellectual competence.[3] The task was not easy, considering the limited means at our disposal. The Conference's obvious political implications were an added difficulty. We knew from the outset that our ethnic belonging and our own political views would leave us open to criticism. And we do not exclude that criticism of some aspects of our work may be justified. All we can say is that we have tried our best to abide by the criteria governing the kind of scientific research that cares for humanity and the destiny of our planet.

Our endeavor was rewarded by the response we received. Most of the participants in the Conference expressed a belief in the possibility of reaching a reasonable solution to the question of Kosova by dint of rational discourse and good will. It was generally thought that a dispassionate analysis of the question, conducted in a scholarly manner, would contribute to a better evaluation of the forces at work, and thus make it easier for the parties concerned to arrive at an equitable solution. The Conference was firmly committeed to avoiding any attitude derived from political affiliations and any form of hate or contempt for the nations involved.

* * * * *

Interest in Kosova, an area hitherto kept almost in complete darkness, grew with the increasing flow of information that reached the world after the Spring 1981 riots. The riots came as a surprise to many, including experts on Yugoslav affairs. The ensuing repression by special police forces and the army elicited comments in almost all the major newspapers and magazines in Europe, the United States and elsewhere.[4] The Kosova events were also discussed at several academic meetings held in the United States and England.[5]

The International Conference on Kosova was another such academic meeting, larger in size and broader in scope. Its international character was contingent on the relatively large number of participants from various countries,[6] as well as on the Conference's sponsorship by American and European learned centers.[7] The international composition of the Conference was intended to create a supra-nationalistic frame of mind, conducive to constructive proposals. The enduring enmity between Albania and Yugoslavia has turned Kosova into an ideological battleground between Albanian and Yugoslav nationalists. The Conference was meant to explore and possibly discover new ways leading to a solution of the question by reversing that trend. What we hoped to achieve was a sincere and honest dialogue between the two countries, with Kosova playing the role that best suits its geo-political situation—that of a mediator.

A fruitful dialogue between two hostile countries cannot be limited to politics alone. Politics as the crucible of social relations is emptied of much of its content when viewed in isolation from other aspects of life. Economic and cultural factors condition and shape politics, varying from country to country and from one epoch to another. Therefore, the papers on political science were placed last in the Conference's program, preceded by papers on history, language and folklore, economy and legislation. Such an order, we thought, would make political ideas more pertinent to the topic. They would not float among generalizations but be anchored on relevant ethnological information. Through this procedure we hoped to provide the outline of a method leading to tangible results. To that effect, of the manifold aspects of the questions, only some topics were proposed for discussion, those that were perceived to be treated in a competent manner.

Although the division of the volume into two parts corresponds to the original order of the papers read in the Conference, not every paper figures in this volume, and two of the articles appearing here have been solicited. Several papers did not reach us or came too late, and two of them were published elsewhere. That explains why the writings about the political situation are less numerous in this volume where emphasis has shifted to the historical-cultural analyses. To balance the two parts, an article by one of the editors was added.

*　*　*　*　*

The opening article introduces the reader to the history of medieval Albania, focusing on the concept of the state. According to the author, the evolution of the medieval Albanian state was nipped in the bud by the intervention of neighboring states, seeking to protect and expand their economic interests in an Adriatic area that has been, since antiquity, the gate for Western penetration into the Balkans. Kosova continued to be part of that area until the first decades of the fifteenth century. The next two historical articles demonstrate the presence of Albanians in parts of Kosova and Macedonia from the seventeenth century to the beginning of our century. The article on the Kosova maps shows that their drawing has been, more often than not, governed by political rather than scientific concerns. The article on Kosova dialects advances the thesis (hypothesis) that a distinctive phonetic property of those dialects is attributable to the impact on them of Slavonic, a phenomenon that is interpreted to signify the presence of Albanians in Kosova before the Slavic invasion of the province. The shorter linguistic article traces the etymology of the conservative South-Albanian (and Kosovar) form *e sh(ë)tunë*, 'saturday,' to Lat. *saturn-*. The two comparative essays on legendary and heroic folksongs investigate a folkloric institution that is shared by South Slavs, Kosovars and North-Albanians. The authors agree that the Serbocroatian and Albanian oral epic songs have been shaped by mutual exchanges occurring "in intervening territories, especially those of Albanian origin in the Sandžak."[8] The Pešter tradition of Albanian singers in Serbocroatian constitutes the link between Bosnian and Kosovar frontier cycles, according to the writer of the essay on that subject. And the author of the study on the Battle of Kosovo concludes that the Kosovar tradition of the songs about the battle is more or less independent from the Serbocroatian tradition. The last article in the first part is a contrastive comparison, based on the author's recent visits to Albania and Kosova, of the mores and customs in the two areas. The overall impression the reader receives from the volume's first part is that Albanians and Kosovars, while belonging to the same ethnic community, differ in quite a few cultural features.

The second part begins with an extensive study of Kosova's economy. The author describes its lag with respect to the economy of the rest of the country, and analyses the reasons for that lag. Industry has suffered from a discriminating federal credit policy, mainly responsible for the abnormal rate of unemployment, whereas progress in agriculture has been hampered by the fragmentation of arable land characterizing the private sector. Lack of qualified cadres is another negative factor. Yet the main cause seems to be political: Serbian tutelage fosters a sense of political impotence that foils initiative in the economic field. The contrast between Kosova's dependence and Albania's sovereignty is a principal point in the next article, which compares the economic systems of Albania and Kosova. One of the author's conclusions is that the Yugoslav economic system favors the country's richer areas to Kosova's disadvantage. The author of the next article explains the 1981 riots as the result of feelings of humiliation and anger accumulated during two generations. He invites the Yugoslav government to work for a compromise solution based on the recognition of the Kosovars' legitimate demand to be considered as equals. The same conclusion is reached in the extensive study of Kosova's constitutional status, based on official documents taken in chronological order. The patchwork of constitutional amendments to Kosova's status on a federal, republic, and provincial level witnesses an obdurate reluctance to grant Kosovars full equality. The author considers this attitude to be at variance with the principles of Yugoslav federalism and calls attention to the dangerous potential of such a political stance. On the contrary, the Yugoslav policy of protecting the rights of the Albanian population by granting the Province a *de facto* equality with the republics, though not a *de jure* republic status, seems successful to the writer of the following article. He acknowledges, however, the symbolic importance of the gesture, and laments the failure to establish a republic of Kosova from the outset. The last article is essentially a critical synthesis of the previous writings, supplemented by some personal ideas. The author's thesis is contained in a nutshell in the title of his article, which takes the lead from the overall conclusions inferred from the volume's first part. Not all the blame is laid with the Yugoslav authorities. Criticism works both ways, and concrete suggestions are made for a *modus vivendi* that would allow Kosovars to attain their goal.

The authors' views in the volume's second part often diverge. They concur, however, on the basic point, namely that the problem of Kosova can be solved only through rational dialogue between the interested parties. One of the writers advances the opinion that the dialogue could be mediated by representatives of Yugoslav and Albanian communities living abroad. We exclude that possibility as impractical. We think that the initiative will come from one of the involved parties, most likely the one that mostly feels the pinch of the created situation. We envisage the Kosovars as mediators. It is up to them to initiate negotiations with both their ethnic brothers and fellow citizens, thus bridging the existing gulf between Albania and Yugoslavia.

* * * * *

The holding of the International Conference on Kosova and the publication of *Studies on Kosova* would have been impossible without the contribution of the participants, financial aid from societies and individuals, moral support from academic institutions, and assistance from colleagues and friends who shared with us the organizational burden.[9] We express our gratitude to all of them. Our thanks go in particular to the colleagues who came from Europe, the institutes that sponsored the Conference, the members of the Albanian community who were generous with their donations,[10] the officials and personalities who sent letters and telegrams of congratulation,[11] and, last but not least, those who attended the Conference.[12]

The magnitude of the combined energies spent in organizing and holding the Conference makes us confident that the publication of its results will reach a larger audience. We think in the first place of those to whom this volume is addressed. The Kosovars need not be told how to manage their own affairs, which they know better than their advisers. Yet a detached and long-range perspective may prove to be a corrective to an insider's view that tends to focus on the *hic* and *nunc*. Our perspective of the Kosova problem underscores a dimension that has been, we think, over-looked. We envision the solution of the problem in an international rather than bilateral context. Yugoslavia is a country that maintains an uneasy balance in a long-divided continent. No one can foretell what would happen in Europe if that country were to disappear from the map or be drawn into the orbit of one of the two superpowers. Both have all but ignored the Kosova problem.[13] Our endeavor will not have been in vain if this volume succeeds in calling attention to the international implications of that problem.

The Editors

NOTES

1. Participants included eight political scientists (four specialists on Yugoslavia, three on Albania and one on the Soviet Union), three historians (two Balkanologists and one Byzantinologist), two economists (an expert on Albania and a specialist on Yugoslavia), two social scientists (an expert on Albania and a student of European minorities), two literary and folklore scholars (a Slavist and an Albanologist), and an art historian.

2. The article in this volume by Sami Repishti deals exhaustively with the concept of autonomy.

3. That scientific expertise can be marred by nationalism is best illustrated by Gerhard Grimm's article on the maps of Kosova. A telling case in this respect is that of the outstanding Serbian geographer, Jovan Cvijić.

4. According to the Albanian booklet, *Shtypi botëror mbi ngjarjet në Kosovë* (World Press on the Kosova Events), reports and articles appeared in some forty newspapers and weeklies published in various countries and continents. *Mbi ngjarjet në Kosovë* (On the Kosova Events) is a selection of articles that appeared in the Albanian press. The Yugoslav counterpart is *Šta se dogadjalo na Kosovu* (What Happened in Kosova). Scholarly

articles were published in *The World Today, Index on Censorship, Conflict Studies, Labor Focus on Eastern Europe* (England); *Orbis, East European Quarterly, Problems of Communism* (the United States); *Inprecor, Hérodote, Albanie* (France). A monograph by Jens Reuter, *Die Albaner in Jugoslawien,* provides a general picture.

5.   A first encounter took place in Asilomar, California, during the September meeting of the Western Slavic Association (a division of the American Association for the Advancement of Slavic Studies). A session of the AAASS Midwest Slavic Association resumed the discussion in its May meeting in Chicago. A Seminar on "The Albanians in Yugoslavia" was held at the University of London School of Slavonic and East European Studies on May 19, 1982, with Patrick F. R. Artisien, Branka Magaš, Arshi Pipa and George Schöpflin as participants. During the AAASS annual meeting in Washington, D.C. (October 16, 1982), a panel discussion composed of George W. Hoffman, Thomas Paulsen and Fred N. Neal reexamined the question.

6.   Among the twenty participants, ten were non-Americans: four from the Federal Republic of Germany, three from England, and one each from France, Belgium and Australia.

7.   The conference was sponsored by, among others, the University of Minnesota Office of International Programs, the Albanien-Institut in Munich, the Istituto di Lingua e Letteratura Albanese at the University of Palermo, the French and Italian Department at the University of Minnesota, and the Society for Albanian Studies in the United States.

8.   A. B. Lord, "The Battle of Kosova . . .". p. 82.

9.   Stephanie Kosmo was secretary of the Conference, Agim Karagjozi took care of the guests. Dr. Safete Juka was instrumental in establishing contacts with foreign colleagues. Hers is also the idea to hold a seminar on Kosova. Peter Prifti translated the article by A. Ducellier, Gretchen Monette that by M. Camaj. They and Dr. Christine Körner prepared summarized versions of some of the papers read at the Conference. Fehime Pipa and Diana Repishti organized the exhibition of books related to the topic of the Conference. Faye Powe helped edit several papers.

10.   Zef Shllaku and Agim Leka, M.D. deserve particular mention.

11.   Letters were received by Georg Stadtmüller, the well-known historian and Albanologist, founder of *Albanische Forschungen;* the distinguished Balkanologist L. S. Stavrianos, Professor of History at Northwestern University; Peter Bartl, Director of the Albanian-Institut in Munich; Philip

Porter, Director of the Office of International Programs at the University of Minnesota; Andrew D. Elias, M.D., President of VATRA, Antonino Guzzetta, Director of the Istituto di Lingua e Letteratura Albanese at the University of Palermo; F. R. P. Akehurst, Chairman of the French and Italian Department at the University of Minnesota, and Denis Deletant, Professor of Rumanian at the London University School of Slavonic and East European Studies.

12.   An estimated two hundred.

13.   Signs of governmental interest are beginning to appear in the United States. *Congressional Record* (June 7, 1983) published a speech by Senator Jesse Helms in which the Kosova events are attributed to "organizations influenced and controlled by the Soviet Union in Kosovo."

EDITING NOTES

For uniformity's sake, the following procedures were adopted:

1. Albanian proper nouns, which have a definite and an indefinite form, are given in the shorter indefinite form: *Mat,* not *Mati; Prishtinë* (sounded *Prishtīn*), not *Prishtinë*. An exception are names that have acquired international status: *Tirana,* not *Tiranë.*

2. Proper nouns are spelled as written in the languages to which they belong: *Dušan,* not *Dushan; Popović,* not *Popovich* (but *Pavlowitch,* the way in which the author by that name writes it).

3. Occassionally, when toponyms have different names in Albanian and Serbocroatian (this holds for Kosova), the Serbocroatian name is given in parentheses: *Pejë (Peć).*

4. To Serbocroatian *Kósovo* corresponds to Albanian *Kosóva.* It seemed appropriate to use the Serbocroatian name when the reference was to the province during the Middle Ages. The Albanian name is used in the definite form to keep it closer to the Serbocroatian name.

5. An Albanian of Kosova calls himself *Kosovar.* We have adopted the term to mean an ethnic Albanian, employing the term *Kosovan* for everyone living in Kosova, regardless of ethnic belonging.

6. The format for the bibliographical citation (publisher, place, and year of publication) was preferred on account of its greater similarity with the citation format used in some European countries, where the publisher is often omitted.

PART I

HISTORY, LANGUAGE, ETHNOLOGY

Alain Ducellier

GENESIS AND FAILURE OF THE ALBANIAN STATE IN THE FOURTEENTH AND FIFTEENTH CENTURIES

The disintegration of the Byzantine state, beginning at the end of the Eleventh Century, gave rise gradually, throughout its former territory, to youthful political entities made up of national minorities that had sought for centuries to affirm themselves, and whose individual aspirations resulted in giving the *coup de grâce* to the old Empire, already subject to many other disintegrating factors.[1]

If we look back to the Thirteenth Century, we see that Serbia, Bosnia, and Bulgaria had become real states, even though the centuries that followed witnessed the emergence, especially in the case of Serbia, of numerous autonomies, most notably that of Zeta-Montenegro.[2] While it is hardly possible to see her as a veritable independent state, Greece herself, being the Despotate of Morea, was for a century, until the Ottoman conquest in 1460, a political entity which might perhaps have given birth to an authentic Greek national state.[3] In this context, the case of Albania may seem astonishing, since this country was the only national entity to emerge from Byzantium which, in spite of the aspirations of her people and the often brilliant attempts of her princes, never succeeded in pouring her strong ethnic, linguistic, and cultural identity into the mold of a political structure. As is known, this failure persisted well beyond the Middle Ages, since there was no Albanian state before 1912.

To explain that failure, it is too easy to invoke the Turkish invasion, although obviously one cannot underestimate its importance. It suffices

3

to note that the Ottomans did not intervene in Albania until 1385, and their presence there did not become effective and stable until after 1415.[4] It is only from that date onward that the Turks could be considered as a negative factor in the process of the formation of an Albanian state. The brutal fact remains that whereas elsewhere the Turks disrupted and afterward destroyed previously established states, in Albania they found only a conglomerate of heterogeneous and rival princedoms. One can maintain, in what seems like a paradox, that when Albania almost succeeded in becoming a State, under the strong leadership of Skanderbeg, she owed that to a national resurgence the source of which was precisely the Turkish invasion. One must therefore search more deeply and further back for the causes of the Albanian failure.

We should not return to the vast problem of Albanian origins. Numerous recent works, especially those based on archeology, have proved in our view that certain zones, like that of Kruja, were inhabited by Albanians since the Eighth Century.[5] It is not without import to note that in what is presently Yugoslavian territory, at Mjele near Virpazar in Montenegro and in the vicinity of Ohrid in Macedonia, objects have been discovered that manifestly belong to the same civilization, which means that the same Illyrian-Albanian continuity characterizes at once present-day Albania and the regions immediately adjacent to her, at the head of which obviously stands Kosova.[6]

For our part, we believe we have shown that, from the Eleventh Century onward, a compact Albanian nucleus, known henceforth as Arbanon, extended between the central valleys of the Shkumbin and Devoll, which moreover did not exclude the existence of Albanian communities all the way to the seacoast, especially in the areas surrounding Dyrrachion,[7] as well as in northwestern Macedonia, where the Hellenic influence had always been superficial, and Slavic invasions had definitely not led to the disappearance of all preexistent elements.[8] Furthermore, when one considers that "proto Albanian" evidence very similar to that in Krujë has been found in numerous sites in the valleys of Ishëm and Drin, including Lezhë, Perlat, Bukël and Shurdhë and considering that there is no reason at all to think that the carriers of this culture disappeared later on, one must believe that Albanians inhabited at one and the same time the entire mountainous zone that extends from the plain of Tirana to the approaches of the basin of Shkodër.[9] Finally, the data gathered from the medieval necropolises of Birranj and Shtikë in the proximity of Korcë, lead one to believe that Albanians also occupied the high plateaus that comprise the upper reaches of Devoll and Osum.[10] Truly, with the exception of closed up towns that were still inhabited by a majority of Greeks and Romans, it is reasonable to admit that the majority of the inhabitants of present-day Albania and Kosova have, since that time, been Albanians.

What is important to underline here is that neither Arbanon, nor much less Albania as a whole, constituted a political entity in the Eleventh Century. Albania did not at the time have even administrative status, regardless of what has been said about it,[11] since she comprised merely the eastern part of the department ["thème"] of Dyrrachion.[12] Geographically, this means, of course, that populations of Albanian stock were deliberately apportioned among several administrative departments—Dyrrachion, Dalmatia, Thessalonica, Nikopolis—a system of division which would demonstrate its worth again, as it is well known, during the Ottoman epoch. Moreover, if a true Albania never did emerge from the imperial body before the Thirteenth Century, it was not solely on account of those constraints. The vigorous Albanian growth that characterized the Tenth and Eleventh Centuries does not appear to have ever been translated into any demand for autonomy. On the contrary, during struggles among Byzantines, Slavs, and Bulgarians in these parts, only the upper urban classes seem to have compromised themselves with the young neighboring states, while documents from that period insist on the loyalty of the local population as a whole, and especially that of Albanians, who are mentioned for the first time about the year 1040, as communicants of the same Orthodox faith.[13] In spite of the differences in the two epochs and attendant risks, one cannot help evoking pre-1878 Albania, which remained attached to the imperial Ottoman body for fear of being devoured by her neighbors, at the risk of afterward being accused of complicity with the enemy. Already in the Middle Ages, it was facile to view Albanians as the "Emperor's men," in order to deny them any right to a national space.

To explain this tight integration of Albania with the Byzantine world, it is necessary above all to take into account the geographical and political situation of this province in the context of the Empire. Thanks to her numerous and generally accessible valleys, Albania was the only area along the Adriatic coast that permitted easy access to the heart of the Empire.

From ancient times, the Via Egnatia—the continuation in the Balkans of the Via Appia—was the grand road that led from Rome to Greece.[14] At the end of the Eleventh Century and in the Thirteenth Century, hagiographic texts and early Venetian documents confirm that Greeks and Italians traveled from Dyrrachion to Thessalonica and Constantinople, and to mainland and peninsular Greek towns.[15] Quite naturally, this economic axis was also the easiest line of attack for all invaders coming from the West, which explains why Albania, beginning with the early Byzantine epoch, became an imposing fortified complex, carefully and constantly maintained, the efficacy of which was to be fully demonstrated at the time of the Norman attacks in 1081-1085 and 1108.[16] Hence, economically and strategically, to hold onto Albania was a matter of life and death for the Empire. One can understand why there was no question of letting Albania become a hostile political entity or even an autonomy. Nevertheless, it does not appear that the perpetuation of Albania as a Byzantine province was solely the result of a policy of force. We have already noted the "Byzantine loyalism" of the Albanians. But it goes without saying that this loyalty rested on an interest that was well understood. Unlike the Croats, the Diocletians, or even the Serbians, who were concentrated in uninviting or outlying areas, the Albanians had for centuries occupied a zone that was widely covered with rich commercial routes, which, moreover, were linked to a culture whose visible marks abound to this day, and in which they had participated for a long time.[17] Since it does not appear, on the other hand, that there was ever the least clash between Greeks and Albanians before the Thirteenth Century,[18] we must assume that the Albanian people, like many other minorities within the Empire, felt perfectly integrated in it, and had no serious inclination to break away from it. It is significant that even in 1203, on the eve of the breakup of the Empire, the people of Dyrrachion, lining up behind their duke, opposed the passage through their ports of the Archbishop of Bulgaria, giving as an excuse that the Emperor would be displeased if passage were granted. One cannot better underscore to what extent the greatly compromised power of the Emperor still seemed to the people of the province, even now, as a rampart against the pretensions of Slavic entities that had just regained their independence.[19]

Moreover, the connection between the Albanian "atony" and the vigor of the great trans-Balkan axis is confirmed *a contrario* by the initial appearance of an incipient Albania at the very moment when that axis was broken, toward the end of the Twelfth Century.

We have elsewhere demonstrated the evolution which, during the second half of the Twelfth Century, had enabled Arbanon to attain a semi-autonomous status.[20] As the *Partitio Romanie* of March 1204 testifies, Arbanon henceforth constituted a well defined part of the duchy of Dyrrachion, significantly named "provincia Dirrachii et Arbani."[21] Furthermore, it was about 1190 when the first "princes" of Arbanon, Progon and his sons Dhimitër and Gjin, appeared, even though Progon carried only the title of 'ἀρχων.[22] It must be noted besides that, from all appearances, Arbanon continued to recognize the authority of the Empire. In this respect, her case is hardly different from that of small autonomous units that appeared at that time in connection with a certain number of great families, especially in Greece.[23] This strong attachment to old structures is explained always in the same manner. Arbanon could not live except by participating in transcontinental commerce. This is well illustrated by the privilege granted to the town of Krujë by Manuel Commenus I, probably after his victories of 1165,[24] an essential point of which was exemption from payment of taxes upon entering and leaving Dyrrachion. It is not surprising, under these conditions, to find Arbanon in the anti-Venetian camp, following the Fourth Crusade, since the first result of the Venetian presence on the coast was to stifle the Albanian hinterland,[25] a development that caused Arbanon to remain loyally attached to the Greek princes of the Empire until the spring of 1252, when the Nicean reconquest naturally led Prince Gulam to recognize the authority of Jean Vatatzis.[26] It was undoubtedly with a sense of relief that Arbanon regained her former position within the Empire, and it is significant that the episode concluded with a renewal of the privileges to Krujë."[27] It is nonetheless certain that the centrifugal forces that operated during the three-quarters of a century of autonomy had done their job. Desiring to return to the Empire in order to regain her traditional advantages, Albania could not accept becoming once again a simple province. But that is what happened with the appointment in 1256 of a Byzantine Governor to Albania, while the princes of Arbanon disappeared definitively from the records.[28] Beginning in 1257, a general revolt placed Albania back under the authority of the Greeks of Epirus, but nothing is known of her status in the "Occidental Greek State."[29]

It is thus easy to explain the failure of Arbanon, the first sketch of an "Albanian state." Whether clinging to the Doukas of Epirus or to Laskaris of Nicaea, Albania continued to conceive of herself as the western extremity of an Empire, even though she developed a strong sense of autonomy. It was moreover a singular setback for the political structures and economic realities at a time when the Balkan transit was increasingly obliterated by Slavic and Greek separatism, and the commercial axis of the Adriatic that was dominated by Venice and Raguse became clearly more and more meridional.[30] Besides, Arbanon of the Thirteenth Century was not politically viable, since she encompassed only a very small portion of the area and population of Albania. In comparison with the imperial period, when administrative divisions were never a real obstacle to economic and human exchanges, Arbanon represented a regression in the process of unification of the Albanian people, the majority of whom were outside her borders, in the rich plains of central Albania and Kosova. Such a rump state was obviously not in a position to resist alone the expansion of the Slavic states. It could gamble on the Byzantine alliance only in the case of a weakening of the Empire, and would inevitably be absorbed anew by the latter during its last flowering in the middle of the Thirteenth Century.

But this failure can also be explained by other reasons, above all, cultural ones. First of all, it was probably during the Twelfth Century that the definite differentiation occurred between the Gheg linguistic group north of the Shkumbin, and the Tosk group to the south of that river. This is clearly indicated in 1210 by the choice of this valley as the northern border of the territories "conceded" by Venice to Michel of Epirus.[31] At the same time, Roman Catholicism, coming from Dalmatia, spread throughout northern Albania, while the south remained under the jurisdiction of the Orthodox Church. This was another divisive factor which could not but hinder the embryonic Albanian state. In particular, Dhimitër of Arbanon, who in 1208 had asked Innocent III to be instructed in the Catholic faith, coudl scarcely pretend to unify the "two Albanias" under his authority.[32] He had even less hold on Kosova, where Roman expansion was out of the question by this time. One cannot overemphasize these cultural ruptures, of which the consequences can still be perceived today at the level of the construction of a state.

This impossibility of taking charge politically was aggravated even more by the vicissitudes of the Thirteenth and Fourteenth Centuries, which made of Albania a dueling field for the political and economic ambitions of her powerful neighbors. The implantation along the coastal zone of Staufen Sicilians in 1257-1258, and above all of the Angevins starting in 1268, resulted in the breakup of relations between interior Albania and the sea, creating thus an artificial pseudo-kingdom of Albania, which could only be a bridgehead to Constantinople, and consequently never had any political reality.[33] Henceforth, Venetian and Ragusan merchants shunned the great seaports, especially Dyrrachion, where the Angevins multiplied taxes and monopolies. The decline of these old cities thus eliminated any possibility of building around them a coastal Albanian state, which up to then was by no means to be ruled out.[34] These disorders were magnified by the obstinacy with which Venice and Raguse set out thereafter to exploit the natural resources of the country—generally neglected before—for the benefit of transit commerce. These great merchants of the Adriatic who fled from the traditional ports, which moreover were cut off from the hinterland, naturally formed the habit of dealing with the grand local proprietors, the masters of the land, in respect to the uncontrolled coastal areas, especially in the great estuaries (the "fiumare") such as those of Drin, Mat, Ishëm, Shkumbin, Devoll and Vjosë. They were the personages who, beginning with the Angevin period, were designated as "barons" or "counts" of Albania, and who gave birth to multiple little Albanian "principalities" in the Fourteenth Century.[35] Thus it was that an Angevin document, dating from 1279, mentions the Blinishtis as being positioned in Mirditë, and the Muzakis as being without doubt already masters of Myzeqe.[36] Then, at the beginning of the Fourteenth Century, the list lengthened with the appearance of the Spatas, the Letis, the Skuras, the Matarangas, the Jonimas, the Aranitis, and finally the Thopias, all of them princes who were strengthened simultaneously by their economic relations with the mercantile republics, and by the privileges accorded them by the ever failing Angevin power, with a view to winning them over.[37]

From this moment on, some of these families manifested plainly their hegemonic intentions. On December 30, 1336, Andre Muzaki ventured to sign a veritable agreement with prince Louis of Duras, confirming the wealth he possessed in Durazzo and gaining free access to that city. Significantly, the Albanian dynast bore henceforth the title of "Despot of Albania," which his descendants took care not to forget.[38] At the same time, the Thopias, who were recently converted to Catholicism, had received from the Pope a "county" which extended from Mat to Shkumbin, and which the Angevins recognized in 1338.[39] Thereafter, the Muzakis and the Thopias became masters of all of "useful Albania," and did as they pleased in Durazzo as well. One could foresee that in the event of a conflict between the two families, one of them would seize the city and make it the capital of a true Albanian principality, thereby risking loss of all contact with Albanian elements in the mountainous zones and in Kosova.[40] But this would be to forget the many obstacles that had to be overcome. Beyond the fantasy Angevian kingdom of Durazzo, there subsisted until 1345 a Byzantine province of Albania, centered around Valona (Vlorë) and strengthened by having important relations with Raguse and Venice.[41] Above all, we are now in the period of the great Serbian expansion which, beginning in 1343, spread over Albania. Even though this expansion left behind only a small Slavic despotate, which, in Vlorë, replaced that of the Byzantines,[42] it was not inconsequential to Albania, even in terms of its failure. Upon the death of Stephen Dušan in 1355, the disintegration of his empire permitted the Balshas—the Slavic-Albanian lords of the Shkodër region—to secure for themselves the Zeta, the coast of Budva and Bar and the entire northern Albanian plain by the year 1362.[43] The matter now became a game for three, but it was an unequal game, above all, for geo-political reasons. The Muzakis were quickly condemned by their inability to secure for themselves a maritime façade.[44] And although the Thopias stopped the Balshas on the Mat in 1364, they were later encircled by their adversaries, who had spread to the east all the way to Prizren, and through marriages in 1372 secured Vlorë and Berat, which enabled them to extend their power to the Myzeqe. In this respect, the Balshas figure among the few rare Albanian princes who understood that building an Albania meant the unification of all Albanian lands, from the Akrokeraunian mountains and including Kosova. After them, only the Kastriotë understood this.

Nevertheless, while both princely families adorned themselves already with the titles of "Prince of Albania," it was Charles Thopia who ended up seizing Durazzo in 1383. Yet, it was the Turks alone who delivered him from his competitor, when they crushed the Balshas at Savra in 1385.[45] One can say that from then on there did indeed exist an Albanian state, whose influence extended from the delta of Drin to the delta of

Devoll. But the wars among the princes brought in their wake at least three formidable developments. Different from that of the Balshas, the principality of the Thopias retracted to the coastal zone. Furthermore, in order to preserve her economic interests, Venice intervened politically from 1363-1365, which is the time when she decided to support the Balshas.[46] Thereafter, her interventions would warp the play of Albanian forces, as will be clearly seen during the epoch of Skanderbeg. Finally, the Turks were now in Albania, and offered henceforth a tempting solution to all the dynasts who dreamed of ascending with the support of the Turks. In sum, the interaction of Venetian and Turkish forces, to which must be added the more discreet but not unimportant Ragusan interventions, resulted in a balance of power among the diverse principalities that amounted to an equality of impotence. For Venice and the Turks stood watch so that none among them dominated the others, since a unified Albania was as frightening to the Republic as to the Sultan. Objectively, both of them were almost always in accord on the question of undermining the foundations of Albanian principalities.[47] At the same time, Ragusan commerce, which was predominant in Albania, also contributed to the scattering of Albanian forces, since it supplied a great number of little Albanian princes with sufficient resources to maintain themselves vis-à-vis the others, yet never allowing any of them to become sufficiently wealthy to acquire predominance over the others.[48]

At this point in her history, one can grasp perfectly the elements that made of Albania the "business of others." Politically, the multiplicity of centers of power was an obstacle to the indispensible unification of the interior and coastal territories. Strategically, Albania was the key to the Adriatic, and Venice could not permit the birth of a state which would hinder her links with the Mediterranean. Economically, Albania was a rich land, a producer of salt, grains and wood. This made her a land well suited to a colonial economy, with as many suppliers as possible—nearly all of them along the coastal zone—in order to assure the perpetuation of high profits. Needless to say, the various princes could not sell to their clients except on condition of enslaving their peasantry more and more. It was not by chance, therefore, that the end of the Fourteenth Century witnessed the inception of a grave phenomenon, the Albanian migration to Greece, Italy and Dalmatia, which, by emptying the country of its substance, increased still more her atony and the mediocre equilibrium of her forces.[49]

All of these causes explain sufficiently the failure of a variety of potential Albanian political nuclei. The death of Balsha II at Savra sealed the
fate of the principality of Shkodër, whose province of Vlorë detached herself from it, and continued as such until 1417, when she was overpowered by
the Turks.[50] But this was only an apparent triumph for the Thopias who,
from 1386, carried anew the title of "Princes of Albania and Lords of
Durazzo,"[51] which indicated plainly their firm intention to create around
that great port a true state structure. It is worth noting, moreover, that
already in 1381, in the tri-lingual inscriptions at the monastery of St.
John-Vladimir near Elbasan, Charles Thopia looked for a dynastic justifi-
cation for his ambitions. In fact a bastard of a princess of Naples, he called himself, in Greek, "master of the the whole country of Albania and
nephew by blood of the King of France," and in Latin, "primus de domo
Francie."[52] But Thopia was seized by the throat by the Turks, and hardly
ruled over anything except the city of Durazzo. In 1386-1387, he was already seeking Venetian protection, and even went so far as to offer to sell
his city to the Republic in return for refuge on her territories.[53] Venice,
which did not want to clash directly with the Ottomans, and scarcely
savored being accused of contravening the clauses of the peace of Turin,
dragged the negotiations beyond even the death of the prince, who mediated at the beginning of 1388. It was his son, Georges, who sick and
increasingly unprotected, ended up ceding Durazzo to the Republic
in 1392.[54] As for the Balshas, they too were constrained in 1396 to cede
their main cities to Venice. In spite of efforts at reconquest by Balsha III
which he pursued until 1421, the Republic was now mistress of the basin
of Shkodër, and of the coast from Kotor to Lezhë, the whole of which
henceforth came to be known as "Venetian Albania."[55]

Albania thus became once again a mass of heterogeneous principalities
that were subjected more or less either to the Turks, or to her Lordship,
with territories directly administered by the latter, and zones that were
incorporated into the Ottoman Empire. Toward Turkish Vlorë and in areas
not ruled by Venetians, Ragusan commerce now took on the demeanor of
a monopoly, and quickly emptied Albania of resources already insufficient
for the population, a development which only increased the wave of emigration at the beginning of the Fifteenth Century.

At that time, it is difficult to see how the Albanian principalities could
exercise political independence. Powerful families like the Balshas or the

Dukagjins, menaced by Venice, leaned occasionally on the Turks,[56] while others, like the Jonimas, begged the favors of the Republic, for which moreover they were badly paid.[57] As for Raguse, she did all she could to maintain the splits, in particular by arming, but always in moderation, some of the dynasts like the Dukagjins, to whom she supplied a piece of artillery in 1417.[58] Hence the many fratricidal and futile wars, of which we shall give but one example. In 1411 or 1412, Nikita Thopia, lord of Krujë, was taken prisoner by the Muzakis, and it was only through the intervention of Raguse, which was concerned about her wheat, that he was released in 1413. The Thopias moreover fell very low. Following his liberation, Nikita demanded of Venice the "provision" that she was obliged to pay him annually, but was told in response that such payment was due only in consideration of services rendered, which was not the case in this instance, since the "count" had come out of prison.[59]

It was nevertheless at that time that there emerged the principality which gave rise to the last Albanian political experience, that of the Kastriotë. Starting from the highlands between Mat and Drin, Gjon Kastrioti, the father of Skanderbeg, was probably the master of the coast and both sides of the Ishëm estuary by 1417. From then on, he was in control of the great market of Suffada, which enabled him to export the products of his land to Venice and especially to Raguse, two cities whose citizenship he acquired in the same year, 1413, while wisely remaining a vassal of the Turks.[60] Thereafter, the Kastriotë pursued a constant policy of expansion toward the sea which culminated, about the year 1450, in the incorporation of the Cape of Rodon and its region to the domain of Skanderbeg.[61] While we do not know the conditions under which it happened, the expansion occurred—no doubt in a contemporary manner— in the direction of the upper Drin and the plain of Kosova. In 1420, the year when Gjon Kastrioti concluded a real commercial treaty with Raguse, he was able to grant to his partner free travel over his lands, from the coast all the way to Prizren. This certainly indicates a grand political and economic design, since the new Albanian state, endowed with a maritime façade and a Macedonian hinterland, was able henceforth to make profitable use of the country's two traditional sources of wealth: the exploitation of the natural products of the coastal zone, and control of the trans-Balkan commerce that had timidly emerged by this time. It was moreover, with a view to sustaining this progression that Skanderbeg built, though

without much success, a fleet at the ship-building facilities of Ishëm.[62]
However, the foreign presence that was now established in Albania limited
in a singular manner the initiative of the prince. While Venice was not able
to annihilate him, she intervened in 1424 and 1428 in order to limit his
salt trade, which was a source of dangerous profits for her.[63] At the same
time, the Turkish danger became increasingly pressing, so that Gjon Kastrioti could not avoid participating in the great Albanian revolt of 1432-
1436. This was an inorganic aggregate of uprisings against the Ottoman
implantation and administration, an aggregate the lack of unity of which
was ill concealed by the figure of Gjergj Araniti.[64] The prince was obliged
to relinquish nearly all of his domains, except the territories "in the vicinity of Lezhë" which, we are given to understand, still belonged to him in
1438, the year of his death.[65]

The prince Gjon Kastrioti was assuredly a powerful dynast, whose field
of action extended beyond the Albanian domain, inasmuch as he was able
in 1426 to bequeath a village and a church to the Athonite monastery of
Hilandar, for, being lord of Kosova, he naturally comported himself as
the successor of Serbian sovereigns.[66] After his fall, his prestige was not
without import in the elevation of his son Gjergj, the future Skanderbeg.
It is noteworthy that by the 1430s the name of Kastrioti had assumed
"national" significance in Albania.

When he rebelled against the Turks, toward the end of 1443, Skanderbeg had two clear and complementary intentions. Claiming the heritage
of the Balshas, he intended to make of his domain the principal Albanian
territorial unit.[67] Then at the Lezhë convention of March 1444, he succeeded in reuniting all Albanian lords in a common struggle against the
Ottomans, with an army to be placed under his supreme command, and
financed by a common treasury funded by the various princes of the
country, in accordance with their means. Clearly, this means that for
Skanderbeg, the work of unification, which was undertaken by the Balshas
and resumed by his father, and which finally led to the regrouping of
North Albania and Kosova, had to be extended to the center and to the
south of the country, the end goal of which was to give birth to an Albania
that was to be the mistress of all her land and of all her people. Initially,
to be sure, it was a question of establishing, around a rich and strategically
well-situated principality, a confederation of princes whose total independence was not brought into question, since the single task at hand was to

boot the Turks out of the country.[68] Nonetheless, it goes without saying that from this moment on, Skanderbeg understood the need for true Albanian unity, in view of the anti-Ottoman struggle. Little by little, between 1444 and 1447, he comported himself clearly as a sovereign, relieving incompetents of their command, intervening directly in the domains of others, appointing to sensitive positions men who were personally loyal to him, even if they did not have high family lineage, and going so far as to confiscate the lands of lords of doubtful loyalty. But Skanderbeg never had the means necessary for such a policy, and defections began early, owing to the absence of any true organic bond among the princes, which gave them license to quite the League in reaction to "encroachments" by Skanderbeg. Their discontent, moreover, was ceaselessly fanned by Venice and by the Turks. In 1447, the Spans and the Dushmans withdrew. Then, in 1450, it was the turn of the Aranitis and the Dukagjinis, the former drawing close to Venice, and the latter to the Sultan.[69] Again in 1455, in the midst of war against the Turks, Moise Golemi, commander of the Albanian border forces went over to the enemy, which entailed the repulse of Skanderbeg before Berat, the key to central Albania.[70]

It is thus true that while the creation of the League of Lezhë was the only real attempt in the Middle Ages to unify the country, and the devotion of the masses was generally strong and enthusiastic,[71] the League was never more than a loose political structure, without any centralized organization. We do not know whether the League had ever had even a minimal administrative framework, except in the military domain. As for its chief, to whom foreign texts generously attribute the title of "Prince of Albania," he was never more than the Commander-in-Chief of the League, and his interventions outside his domains were always feats of strength devoid of any legitimacy.

Of course, it is not enough to invoke the individualism of the Albanian princes to explain this failure. And it is not even enough to cite the deleterious actions of Venice and the Turks, who knew so well how to profit from the internal divisions in the country. It goes without saying, in fact, that apart from the interest of the Sultan, Venice felt immediately threatened by the young "Albanian unit," which was from the beginning hostile to her presence on the coast. The Venetian-Albanian war of 1447-1448 was made inevitable by the clear annexationist aims of Skanderbeg over her possessions, including Dagno, Durazzo, Scutari and even Antibari.[72]

In 1458 also, Skanderbeg affirmed that he was going to recruit soldiers within the possessions of Venice, even against the will of the Republic.[73] From then on, until his death in 1468, Skanderbeg had to confront constantly the overt or covert malice of the Venetians, who did not hesitate to ally with the Turks against him. Moreover, confronted with his hostility, he never had any meaningful support from abroad. The Hungarians of Janco de Hunedoara were not able to do anything for him.[74] Alfonso of Aragon, to whom the Albanian hero had become a vassal in 1451, only sent him derisive forces in 1455. And the aid of Rome was in general confined to encouraging words and a few miserable subsidies.[75]

Attacked by determined enemies and badly supported by its allies, the incipient Albanian state was the plaything of profound forces which had divided the country for centuries. The heroism of Skanderbeg and his troops was of no avail against the economic exploitation of Albania that culminated in the middle of century. For Venice and Raguse, as well as for the Catalans, the Anconitans and soon the Florentines, the little princes and the Turkish beys were much more reliable partners than the offensive principality of the Kastriotë' Good evidence for this is the intense traffic which, in the middle of the century, linked the central estuaries and, above all, the region of Vlora to Raguse and to Venice. The commercial benefits that had formed the basis of the fortune of the Kastriotë in 1415-1420, henceforth enriched primarily their rivals or their enemies, contributing thereby to an accentuation of the divisions of the country.[77] In addition, after 1460, western merchants, especially the Ragusans, rediscovered the virtues of a unified state in the Balkans. Thanks to the Turkish invasion, caravan traffic to Macedonia resumed, with the Turkish port of Vlorë as the point of departure. And though Prizren and Prishtinë became important stages on the route, where Albanian traders participated in the transactions, it was with the blessings of the Ottoman authorities that was organized an entire Ragusan-Florentine commercial and financial network, whose unity an Albanian State would have broken, collecting custom dues for itself.[78] From then on, in spite of her national sentiment and heroic efforts, an independent Albania could only be an obstacle to the origins of the new trans-Balkan network.[79]

The failure of the Albanian medieval state was not due to a fundamental incapacity to become a nation and afterwards a state. Beginning with the Fourteenth Century, documents testifying to a community of language and customs in Albanian territory,[80] and the struggles in the period that were led by Skanderbeg, demonstrate plainly that the national sentiment was henceforth capable of surrmounting the religious and linguistic divisions already mentioned, even though the Republic of Venice, the Pope and the Sultan, intentionally or not, fanned conflicts in the domains. What prevented Albania always from becoming a political reality was the fact that she belonged to an economic network whose system of command was out of her hands. An outpost for an Empire until the Thirteenth Century, a land of colonial exploitation in the Thirteenth and Fourteenth Centuries, she combined afterward those two functions, beginning with the Ottoman invasion. For the Sultan and the western powers understood very well that it was in their interest to assure the supply of profitable market commodities, and to maintain rigorous freedom of movement between the Adriatic and the interior of the Balkans. Needless to say, such goals could not be reached except by keeping Albania in a state of disunity and dependence. And this is well illustrated by the new administrative system of the Turks, which definitely established after 1480 and reviving former Byzantine conceptions, divided the territory and population of Albania into at least four areas, which, among other things, cut off Kosova from the western provinces of the country, and even from the nuclei of Albanians inhabiting the fringes of Montenegro and Macedonia, from the Lake of Shkodër to the Pejë region.[81]

* * * * *

NOTES

1.   Regarding this vast problem, see H. Ahrweiler, "Erosion sociale et comportements excentriques à Byzance aux XIème-XIIIème siècles"; N. Oikonomides, "La décomposition de l'Empire Byzantin à la veille de 1204 et les origines de l'Empire de Nicée: à propos de la 'Partitio Romanie'"; A. P. Každan, "Tsentrostremitel'nie i tsentrobeznie sily v vizantijskom mire" (1081-1261 g.), report at the XVth International Congress of Byzantine Studies, Athens, 1976.

2.   S. Ćirković and I. Božić, "Crna Gora i doba oblasnih gospodara." *Istorija Crne Gore,* t. II, Titograd, 1970, pp. 1-133.

3.   D. Zakythinos, *Le Despotat grec de Morée,* t. I, Paris, 1932; J. W.

Barker, "The Problem of Appanages in Byzantium," *Byzantina* III, 1971; A. Ducellier, "Les 'principautés' byzantines sous les Paléologues; autonomismes réels ou nouveau système impérial," *Actes du Congrès de la Société des Historiens médiévistes,* Bordeaux, 1979.

4.   S. Pulaha, "Luftrat shqiptaro-turke në veprat e kronistëve dhe historianëve osmanë të shekujve XV-XVII," *Studime historike,* 1968, I, part, pp. 126-127.

5.   See especially Skender Anamali, "De la civilisation haute-médiévale albanaise," in *Les Illyriens et la genèse des Albanais,* Tirana, 1971. The rest of the contributions in this volume are worth consulting.

6.   A. Ducellier, "Les Albanais ont-ils envahi le Kosova?" *Albanie* (1981): 10-14, where one will find the major references to previous works.

7.   A. Ducellier, "L'Arbanon et les Albanais au XIème siècle," *Travaux et Mémoires,* III, Paris, 1968, pp. 354-357; K. Luka, "Toponimia shqiptare në Kangën e Rolandit lidhun me disa ngjarje të vjetëve 1081-1085," *Studime historike* (1967) 2: 127-144.

8.   A. Ducellier, "Les Albanais," p. 12.

9.   S. Anamali, "De la civilisation," pp. 192-193.

10.   Ibid., p. 193ff.

11.   For details of the discussions which oppose us to Mme. H. Vranoussis, see A. Ducellier, "Nouvel essai de mise au point sur l'apparition du peuple albanais dans les sources historiques byzantines," *Studia albanica* (1972) 2, esp. p. 305.

12.   J. Ferluga, "Durazzo e la sua regione nella seconda metà del secolo X e nella prima del secolo XI," *Byzantium on the Balkans,* Amsterdam, 1976, pp. 239-240; A. Ducellier, *La Façade maritime de l'Albanie au Moyen Age; Durazzo et Valona du XIème au XVème siècle,* Salonica, 1981, pp. 92-110.

13.   A. Ducellier, "L'Arbanon," p. 357-358; concerning a definitely erroneous interpretation which turns the αφβανῖτης into Croats, see M. Tadin, "Les Arvanitai des chroniques byzantines," *Actes du XVème Congrès International des Études Byzantines,* Athens, 1976.

14.   A. Ducellier, *La Façade maritime,* pp. 75-77.

15.   A. Ducellier, "L'Albanie entre Orient et Occident aux XIème et XIIème siècles, aspects politiques et économiques," *Cahiers de Civilisation Médiévale* (1976) 1, pp. 6-7.

16.   A. Ducellier, *La Façade maritime,* pp. 9-45.

17. A. Ducellier, "L'Arbanon," pp. 359-360; Dh. Shuteriqi, "Mbi disa çështje t'Arbërit dhe mbi emrin Shqipëri," *Buletin për Shkencat shoqërore* (1956) 3, p. 192; also by the same author, "Aranitët, emri dhe gjenealogjia," *Studime historike* (1965) 4, pp. 4-8.

18. A. Ducellier, *La Façade maritime,* pp. 210-211.

19. Ibid., pp. 122-123.

20. A. Ducellier, op. cit., p. 98; A. Carile, "Partitio Terrarum Imperii Romanie," *Studi Veneziani,* VII, 1965, p. 220.

21. With regard to Krujë belonging to Arbanon at the end of the XIIth century, see Thallóczy-Jireček, "Zwei Urkunden aus Nordalbanien," *Illyrisch-Albanische Forschungen,* Vienna, 1916, I, pp. 130-131.

22. Dh. Shuteriqi, "Një mbishkrim i Arbërit (1190-1216)," *Studime historike* (1967) 3, passim (it concerns an inscription found at Gëzid, in Mirditë, and originating from the Monastery of St. Mary of Trifandina); it will be noted that the title of "panhypersebastos," which prince Dhimitër still carried at the beginning of the XIIIth century, is supplementary proof of attachment to the framework of the Empire. (See, A. V. Solovjev, "Ein Urkunde des Panhypersebastos Demetrios," *B.Z.,* 1934, p. 304.)

23. A. Ducellier, "Les Principautés," p. 182.

24. Barcelona, *Archivio general de la Corona de Aragon,* Reg. 2623, f. 118-119v; Thallóczy-Jireček, "Zwei Urkunden," pp. 147-151.

25. A. Ducellier, *La Façade maritime,* pp. 132-135. The clearest act of the prince of Arbanon is his privilege in favor of the Ragusans (see Solovjev, loc. cit.).

26. Acropolitēs, Bonn, p. 98.

27. Thallóczy-Jireček, "Zwei Urkunden," p. 149.

28. A. Ducellier, *La Façade maritime,* pp. 168-171.

29. A. Ducellier, op. cit., pp. 171-173; however, there is no proof that the revolt was directed by Gulam, as D. Nicol writes in *The Despotate of Epiros,* Oxford, 1957, p. 162.

30. A. Ducellier, *La Façade maritime,* pp. 182-186; also by the same author, "Les mutations de l'Albanie au XVème siècle (du monopole ragusain à la redécouverte des fonctions de transit), *Études Balkaniques,* Sofia (1978) 1: 55-56.

31. Tafel-Thomas, *Urkunden,* II, pp. 120-123; P. Lemerle, "Trois actes du Despote d'Epire Michel II concernant Corfou," *Hellenika,* IV, p. 407; Nicol, *Despotate,* p. 31. A. Ducellier, *La Façade maritime,* p. 143.

32.   Shuteriqi, "Një mbishkrim," p. 147; Thallóczy-Jireček-Šufflay, *Acta Albaniae*, I, No. 133; Ducellier, *La Façade maritime*, pp. 138-139, and 206-208.

33.   G. M. Monti, "La dominazione napoletana in Albania: Carlo I d'Angiò, primo re degli Albanesi," *Rivista d'Albania*, I, 1940, p. 1; B. G. Leonard, *Les Angevins de Naples*, Paris, 1954, p. 107; A. Ducellier, *La Façade maritime*, pp. 262-274.

34.   The most salient fact is the semi-disappearance of the Venetians and the Ragusans from Durazzo during the Angevin rule; see A. Ducellier, op. cit., pp. 281-288.

35.   A. Ducellier, op. cit., pp. 293-299.

36.   *Reg. Ang.* XVIII, f. 92, October 11, 1279; it concerns Johannes Musac and Carnesius and Gulielmus Blenisti; A. Ducellier, *La Façade maritime*, pp. 294-295.

37.   *Acta Albaniae*, I, No. 563 (1304); M. Šufflay, *Srbi i Arbanasi*, Belgrade, 1925, p. 58; A. Ducellier, *La Façade maritime*, pp. 338-339.

38.   *Acta Albaniae*, I, No. 808; A. Ducellier, *La Façade maritime*, p. 339.

39.   *Acta Albaniae*, I, no. 816; A. Ducellier, *La Façade maritime*, pp. 339-340.

40.   A. Ducellier, op. cit., p. 340.

41.   Ibid., pp. 346-357.

42.   Ibid., pp. 485-489.

43.   Ćirković-Božić, *Istorija Crne Gore*, II, pp. 17-18 and chart p. 32.

44.   A. Ducellier, *La Façade maritime*, p. 485.

45.   The seizure of Durazzo by the Thopias was, at any rate, after January 1383 (Radonić, *Dubrovačka Akta i Povelje*, I, No. LXV, p. 115); on the Savra, see the notices published by Sp. Lambros, *Neos Hellenom-nemôn*, VII, 1910, No. 77 and 78, p. 145.

46.   A. Ducellier, *La Façade maritime*, pp. 477-478. Again in January 1385, Venice accorded arms to Balsha II (Venezia, *Misti del Senato*, XXXIX, f. 123).

47.   A. Ducellier, "Les mutations de l'Albanie," p. 79; also by the same author, "La façade maritime de la principauté des Kastriotë," *Studia Albanica* (1968) 1: 119-121.

48.   A. Ducellier, "Les mutations de l'Albanie," pp. 57-62.

49.   A. Ducellier, "Les Albanais au XIIIème siècle; nomades ou

sedentaires," *Byzantinische Forschungen,* vol. VI, Amsterdam, 1979, pp. 34-35.

50.   A. Ducellier, "Les mutations de l'Albanie," p. 62; W. Miller, "Valona," in *Essays on the Latin Orient,* rééd', Amsterdam, 1964, p. 437; K. Jireček, "Valona im Mittelalter," *Illyrisch-Albanische Forschungen,* I, p. 182.

51.   Venezia, *Commemoriali,* VIII, f. 116, August 16, 1386.

52.   Th. Popa, "Të dhana mbi princët mesjetarë shqiptarë në mbishkrimet e kishave tona," *Buletin i Universitetit Shtetëror të Tiranës* (1957) 2: 186-195, with photographs and transcription of three inscriptions.

53.   A. Ducellier, *La Façade maritime,* pp. 492-501.

54.   Ibid., pp. 501-502; Luan Maltezi, "Përpjekjet dhe synimet e Venedikut për pushtimin e Durrësit (1386-1392)," *Studime Historike* (1977) 2:,153-61.

55.   I. Božić, "Le système foncier en 'Albanie vénitienne' au XVème siècle," *Bolletino dell' Instituto di Storia della Società e dello Stato,* V-VI, 1963-1964, pp. 65-66.

56.   I. Božić, "O Dukadjinima," *Zbornik Filosofskog Fakulteta u Beogradu,* Belgrade, VIII/1, 1964, pp. 386-427, and especially pp. 402-406.

57.   A. Ducellier, "La Façade maritime de la principauté des Kastriotë," pp. 120 and 123.

58.   Dubrovnik, *Consilium Rogatorum,* III, f. 62v; A. Ducellier, *art. cit.,* pp. 121 and 124-125.

59.   Venezia, *Misti del Senato,* L, f. 18v.

60.   Fr. Thiriet, "Quelques réflexions sur la politique vénitienne a l'égard de Georges Skanderbeg," *Studia Albanica,* (1968), 1, p. 89; A. Ducellier, *art. cit.,* in note 57, p. 126.

61.   D. Radonić, *Djuradj Kastriot Skenderbeg i Arbanija u XV veku,* Belgrade, 1942, No. 2, p. 2 (February 25, 1420); A. Ducellier, *art. cit.,* pp. 126-127.

62.   A. Ducellier, *art. cit.,* p. 127.

63.   Ibid., pp. 122-123.

64.   S. Pulaha, "Luftrat shqiptaro-turke," *art. cit.,* pp. 137-140.

65.   A. Ducellier, *art. cit.,* in note 57, p. 128.

66.   Radonić, *Djuradj Kastriot,* No. 3 and 4, pp. 2-3.

67.   K. Biçoku, "Quelques aspects des rapports entre Skanderbeg et

Venise," *Studia Albanica* (1968) 1, p. 98 (text of *Raccolta Foscarini,* National Library of Vienna, cod. 6215, f. 9v).

68.   A. Buda, "Gjergj Kastrioti-Skënderbeu dhe epoka e tij," *Actes de la Seconde Conférence des Études Albanologiques,* I, Tirana, 1969, pp. 33-4; S. Pollo and A. Puto, *Histoire de l'Albanie,* Roanne-Paris, 1974, pp. 84-85.

69.   K. Biçoku, *art. cit.,* p. 99.

70.   Pollo-Puto, *Histoire de l'Albanie,* p. 93.

71.   A. Buda, "Gjergj Kastrioti," pp. 30-31.

72.   K. Biçoku, *art. cit.,* pp. 98-99.

73.   Radonić, *Djuradj Kastriot,* No. 141, p. 85 (Se me voleti dar a passar con la vostra benedicion, io passero, e se non me darete, io providero meglio che poro"; K. Biçoku, *art. cit.,* p. 100.

74.   Fr. Pall, "Skanderbeg et Janco de Hunedoara," *Studia Albanica* (1968) 1, pp. 103-117; Radonić, *Djuradj Kastriot,* No. 93 and 94, pp. 53-54; C. Marinesco, *Alphonse V, roi d'Aragon et de Naples et l'Albanie de Scanderbeg,* Paris, 1923, p. 97. The author's appreciation of the king's aid is plainly exaggerated.

75.   For a more correct idea of Papal aid to Skanderbeg, see St. Naçi, "A propos de quelques truchements concernant les rapports de la Papauté avec Skanderbeg durant le guerre albano-turque (1443-1468)," *Studia Albanica* (1968) 1, pp. 73-86.

76.   A. Ducellier, "Les mutations de l'Albanie," pp. 70-76.

77.   Ibid., pp. 76-78.

78.   Ibid., pp. 78-79.

79.   Such a conclusion is corroborated by considering the development of the financial Ragusan-Florentine network, after 1460, which rested entirely on the agreement with the Turks, and especially with the local representatives of the Sultan (A. Ducellier, "Le rôle des Florentins et des Italiens du Nord dans le commerce transbalkanique au XVème siècle," (*Proceedings of the Vth "Symposion Byzantinon" of Strasbourg,* 1982, forthcoming).

80.   Especially noteworthy is the testimony of Symeon Symeonis in 1322, and of Pseudo-Brochard in 1332, on the language and customs of Albanians; A. Ducellier, *La Façade maritime,* pp. 435-437.

81.   S. Pulaha, "Krahinat perëndimore dhe qendrore të sanxhakut të Shkodrës në fund të shekullit XV," *Studime historike* (1971) 2 and 3, pp. 43-73 and 115-138, and the introduction by the same author to his work, *Defteri i Regjistrimit të Sanxhakut të Shkodrës i vitit 1485,* Tirana, 1974, t. I, p. 9 sq.

Peter Bartl

KOSOVA AND MACEDONIA AS REFLECTED IN
ECCLESIASTICAL REPORTS

Kosova and Macedonia, like the other areas of European Turkey, were situated "in partibus infidelium." Therefore, they fell within the domain of the Catholic missions administered by the Propaganda Fide (Congregation for the Propagation of the Faith), which had been founded at Rome in 1622. The Propaganda Fide required its dignitaries engaged in missionary work to submit regular reports about conditions in the areas within their jurisdiction. Many of these reports have been preserved in the archives of the Propaganda Fide, yet few of them have been published.[1] These reports vary greatly in their value as historical sources; many of them contain material that is not restricted to the religious affairs of the areas under consideration, as will be shown in the discussion that follows.

Kosova and Macedonia, areas currently predominantly or at least largely settled by Albanians, were, according to the linguistic usage of the Church, part of Serbia. In his ecclesiastical report of 1703 Archbishop Vinzenz Zmajević includes the following observations on the geographical boundaries of Serbia:

> S' estende in lunghezza otto giornate, e quattro in larghezza. Dall'
> Oriente ha per confine divisivo dalla Bulgaria gl'ultimi monti di
> Montenegro sopra Scopia, detti Monte Emo, e tirando a dritta linea
> verso meriggio, arriva il fiume Drino, che la separa dall'Albania, e

dalle Diocesi di Durazzo, d'Alessio, e Sappa, tenendo verso occidente
il dorso del fiume Castranichio, o Valbona, e li Monti Super.ri di
Pulati, arriva ad altro fiume Drino, che la divide da Erzegovina, e
nella parte dalla Bossina, e continuando il corso di d.to fiume, giunge
al Danubio verso settentrione, che la separa dall'Ungaria, perfet-
tionando il giro per linea dritta alli sud.ti monti di Monte Negro.[2]

Until the middle of the seventeenth century the Archbishop of Antivari
(Bar) also served Serbia. In 1656 Skoplje became the first Catholic archdiocese in Serbia; this archdiocese existed until 1921. It must be admitted
that Skoplje was the residence only of the first archbishop, Andrea Bogdani, since his nephew and successor, Pietro Bogdani, transferred his residence to Janjevo (southern Prishtina) in 1680.[3]

The ecclesiastical reports all follow a rather similar format. First they
emphasize the difficulties surrounding the journey: The missionaries had
to arm themselves.[4] They had to steal into many a town secretly, under
cover of night.[5] Groups of bandits, conditions bordering on civil war,
and epidemics of the plague limited ecclesiastical visits to the winter or
necessitated changes in the itinerary.[6] The reports continue with a more
or less detailed description of the journey. They generally end with a summary that includes a statement of the number of Catholic parishioners
in the areas visited and a list of the needs of individual parishes—money
or items for religious services.

Naturally, it was very important to the Propaganda Fide that the exact
number of Catholics living in the various communities be determined. The
ecclesiastical visitors rarely succeeded in furnishing such precise figures:
Usually the numbers were rounded off; often only the number of households or families was indicated. Baptismal records were seldom kept in
Kosova and Macedonia. Families of more than one religion also contributed to the indecisiveness of the figures. To gain a tax advantage, the
head of a household would convert to Islam while his wife and children
remained Catholics. In certain cases the ecclesiastical visitors included
such families; othertimes, they did not because the Church denied the
sacraments to the wives of apostates.[7] According to the reports examined,
the number of Catholics in Serbia as well as in the Archdiocese of Skoplje—
was as shown in the table on the facing page.[8]

CATHOLIC HOUSEHOLDS AND INDIVIDUALS

Parish	1610	1623/24	1633	1637	1638	1638/39	1641/42	1703	1784	1791/92	1820	1853
Prizren	30/	/200	50/	/540+	22/325		40/400	7/31		23/167	68/650	150/1200
Gur[9]				/550+			80/550					
Shegjeç[10]				/550+								
Zym[11]								13/213			35/226	60/648+
Zogaj[12]								8/120		18/218	13/108	
Gjakovë				/550+	20/150		26/	9/27		57/720	25/324	75/560
Peć (Pejë)								11/33			8/39	16/90
Janjevo	120/	/400	/500	/680		85/650	85/530	19/87		47/330	53/428	143/987+
Novo Brdo	40/	40/	/700+	/366+		49/430+	80/540+					
Trepča	40/	50/200	/300	/350		25/350	30/200	/30				
Prokuplje	12/	20/		/120			20/80					
Skopska Crna Gora		/4000	/800	/600		86/560	80/540	22/123	34/	36/351	56/549	107/1060
Skoplje		15/50	15/	/45		.8/51	9/51	9/52		4/		/ca. 12
Kratovo		40/160	40/	/220		38/358	35/200.	2/28				
TOTAL					4260		521/3522	772/5296			612/6005	1026

* The number in front of / indicates households, the number after indicates individuals.
+ Includes neighboring villages within the jurisdiction of the parish.

The reports show that the number of Catholic parishes in the archdiocese of Skoplje declined from eleven to six during the period being considered, while at the same time the number of Catholic parishioners increased. It is interesting to note which parishes were abandoned: Of the parishes Novo Brdo, Prokuplje, Trepča, Skoplje, and Kratovo only Skoplje was functioning in 1703. All these parishes were part of "Serbia Superiore" according to the division made by Gjergj Bardhi, Archbishop of Antivari. The language of this area was "Illyrian," that is, Serbian.[13]

Could that be a factor in the demise of these parishes? Are we to assume these Catholics were Albanian immigrants, who were gradually assimilated into their Slavic surroundings? According to the evidence of the ecclesiastical reports this assumption would be valid, if at all, only in one instance—for Kratovo. When the Archbishop of Antivari visited Kratovo in February 1639, he found that all thirty-eight Catholic families had emigrated from Dibra in Albania, but they already understood "Illyrian." The priest was also an Albanian by the name of Dom Nikollë Kolesi. Aside from his native Albanian he understood very little Slavic.[14] Two years later, in April 1642, the same visitor noted that many immigrants had adopted the Slavic language and even had good control of Turkish.[15] The latter raises some doubt about the Slavonization of the Albanian Catholics of Kratovo, a doubt strengthened all the more by the ecclesiastical report of Vinzenz Zmajević written in 1703. There one reads: "havendo apostato tutti li maschi, e rimaste sole poche femine." From the figures it can be seen that there were still two Catholic families, about whom nothing more is heard later. Here a process of Islamization was undoubtedly at work, not Slavonization or even a conversion to the Orthodox Church. The very use of the word "apostato" argues that Slavonization was improbable.[16]

The fate of the Catholic communities in Novo Brdo, Prokuplje, Trepča, and Skoplje is even more uncertain. In Novo Brdo and Trepča the end of mining seems to have led to a decline in Catholicism. In 1623/24 Pietro Mazrreku reports that thirty years earlier these towns were rich in gold and silver deposits, which had attracted Catholics from Albania, Bosnia, and other places.[17] As early as 1633 Trepča could no longer support a priest.[18] In Novo Brdo the last priest is mentioned in 1642.[19] Here economic factors may well have caused a decline in Catholic Christianity.

In Prokuplje the core of the Catholic community consisted of a Ragusan colony of merchants. In 1610 the colony included twelve families who supported a priest and a chapel.[20] Later they were joined by ten Catholic families who had emigrated from Pulati.[21] The community was mentioned again in 1642, but nothing is known of its fate after that.

In Skoplje the Catholic community was very small from the time of the earliest ecclesiastical reports. Nevertheless, until the end of the eighteenth century it had its own priest, while in 1703 even administered to Kratovo and "Montenegro" (Skopska Crna Gora).[22] In the nineteenth century there were only about a dozen Catholics still in Skoplje. These "agents of Skutarian merchants" were probably Albanian.[23]

What was the nationality of the Catholics living in the Archdiocese of Skoplje? This question is not easy to answer because the ecclesiastical visitors showed no particular interest in it. They were concerned with "Christians," that is, with Catholics; religion, not nationality, was important to them. Bardhi is an exception to this generalization. He divided the diocese as a whole into "Serbia Superiore" and "Serbia Inferiore." In "Serbia Superiore"—Prokuplje, Novo Brdo, Trepča, Janjevo, Skopska Crna Gora, Skoplje, and Kratovo—the Catholics spoke "Illyrian." In "Serbia Inferiore"—Prizren, Gur, Shegjeç, Gjakovë—all the Catholics spoke "Epirotan," that is, Albanian.[24] That was somewhat of a simplification, as has already been shown through the example of Kratovo and Prokuplje. In principle, however, this rough division applies as far as the Catholics are concerned until the end of the eighteenth century, as the reports of Mazrreku in 1784 and 1791/92 demonstrate. Thus Mazrreku, who in spite of his name maintains that Albanian was not his native language, preached in Albanian for Zym, Zogaj, Gjakovë, and Prizren and in Slavic for Peć and Skopska Crna Gora.[25]

It goes without saying that the ecclesiastical visitor was obliged to record the number of Catholics as precisely as possible, but often he noted in addition the number of people belonging to other religions. With such information the ecclesiastical reports become sources for the religious and ethnic relations in Kosovo and Macedonia, and their value increases proportionately. Let us continue in the order established in the table of Catholic parishes:

Prizren consisted of 8,600 households in 1610 according to Marino Bizzi's report; of these slightly more than 30 were Catholic. The report contains only one additional observation: The Schismatics, that is, the Orthodox Christians, far outnumbered the Roman Christians; at the same time, they retained only two of their original 80 churches![26] Mazrreku is more precise in his report of 1623/24: The population of the city included 12,000 Turks, "quasi tutti Albanesi di natura scaltriti"; in addition to 200 Catholics 600 Serbs lived there. (In contrast to his customary usage Mazrreku here uses the term "Serviani," not "Scismatici.")[27] The report of Bardhi offers the following figures for 1638: In addition to 22 Catholic households the city had 34 Orthodox and 3,000 Moslem households.[28] The figures shift somewhat from 1641/42: While the number of Catholic households rose to 40, almost double what it was, the number of Orthodox households increased even more, to 80; at the same time the number of Moslems remained unchanged at 3,000.[29] The next figures do not appear until the last ecclesiastical report, that of 1853. Besides 150 Catholic households the city had 800 Orthodox households with 8,200 people and 6,570 Moslem households. Gypsies accounted for 603 households or 3,020 people.[30]

For the parishes of Gur, Shegjeç, Zym, and Zogaj, which are listed next in the table, the reports include only Catholic residents. Once again the report of 1853 is an exception: It mentions 4 Moslem households living near Zym.

Gjakovë included 20 Catholic, 20 Orthodox, and 320 Moslem households in 1638 according to Bardhi.[32] In the report of 1641/42 the number of Orthodox households was 16, Moslem households 250.[33] In 1853 Urban Bogdanović records 75 Catholic, 80 Orthodox, and 4,000 Moslem households for Gjakova. Gypsies numbered 300 households.[34]

For Peć (Pejë, Ipek) little has been written in the various reports. Bogdanović is the first to report on Peć where in 1853 he found 16 Catholic, 500 Orthodox, 3,000 Moslem, and 135 Gypsy households.[35]

Prishtinë, although not a parish, had 20 Catholic households for a total of 100 people according to the report of Mazrreku in 1623/24. In addition numerous "Turks"—especially those who owned a timar—and many Serbs also lived there.[36]

Janjevo, the locality with the largest proportion of Catholic inhabitants in the archdiocese, had in addition to its 120 Catholic families 200 Orthodox and 180 Moslem households in 1610.[37] For 1638/39 Orthodox households numbered 140, Moslem 120.[38] By 1641/42 there were 180 Orthodox and 120 Moslem households; the town had two mosques and two Orthodox churches.[39] Finally, for 1853 the report speaks of 15 Moslem and 10 Gypsy households.[40]

Novo Brdo had in addition to 40 Catholic households, 60 Orthodox, and 100 Jewish and Moslem households in 1610; the mines were still in operation at this time.[41] In 1638/39 the count stood at 80 Orthodox and 120 Moslem households.[42] By 1641/42 there were 50 Orthodox and 120 Moslem households; the town included four mosques.[43]

Trepča had a total of 500 households in 1610, including 40 Catholic and 200 Orthodox.[44] In 1638/39 it had 80 Orthodox and 20 Moslem households.[45] For 1641/42 the record shows 40 Orthodox and 100 Moslem households.[46]

Prokuplje with its 1,500 inhabitants in 1610 was the home of a Ragusan colony of merchants, which could afford to support a priest.[47] For 1633 Mazrreku indicates there were 600 Moslem households.[48] For 1641/42 his report mentions 300 Moslem and 30 Orthodox households.[49]

Skoplje included a total of 40,000 households in 1610 according to Marino Bizzi.[50] Mazrreku offers a more detailed statement about the population in 1623/24' "E' habitata da Turchi, la maggior parte sono Albanesi di Natione, i altri Asiatici." Jews, Serbs (specifically "Serviani"), and a few Greeks could be found there too.[51] By 1638/39 Skoplje numbered 23,000 Moslems, 120 Jewish, 328 "Schismatic" (probably Serbian-Orthodox) and Greek households.[52] For 1641/42 the count was 22,000 Moslem, 200 Greek and Serbian Orthodox, and 150 Jewish households.[53] In his ecclesiastical report of 1703 Vinzenz Zmajević cites 20,000 households consisting of Moslem, Jews, Greeks, and Armenians. The city had 50 mosques; of these 27 were "Maestosa struttura."[54] In the eighteenth century the population of Skoplje must have been drastically reduced because only 12,000 households are mentioned for 1791. These were occupied mainly by Moslem and Orthodox Christians.[55]

For *Kratovo* the first statistics are available for 1638/39: In addition to the 38 Catholic households, all Albanian, there were 40 Jewish, 100 Orthodox, and 300 Moslem households.[56] In 1641/42 there were 120 Moslem and 40 Jewish households.[57]

The figures reported in the ecclesiastical reports may not always be exact. They probably rely for the most part on information the local priest furnished to the visitor. They are probably correct, nevertheless, as a general indicator. The religious and, in part, the ethnic composition of the parishes of Kosovo and Macedonia as depicted in the ecclesiastical reports can be summarized as follows: From the beginning of the seventeenth to the middle of the nineteenth century the population of Prizren, Gjakovë, and Skoplje was almost exclusively Moslem, and the majority of these Moslems were of Albanian descent. In Peć, Novo Brdo, Trepča, Prokuplje, and Kratovo the Moslem element certainly predominated, but there was also a strong Orthodox segment of the population. Janjevo had an Orthodox majority, but the Catholic and Moslem population was sizable. The parishes of Gur, Shegjeç, Zym, and Zogaj in Has near Prizren were strictly Catholic and Albanian.

The ecclesiastical reports also contain accounts of Albanian expansion and settlement, as one would expect, primarily in connection with the Catholic Albanians. There seems to have been a steady influx of new residents for the period being studied. Mazrreku writes in 1623/24 that a short time before ten Catholic families from Albania had moved to Prishtinë. Similarly ten Catholic families left Pulat to settle in Prokuplje.[58] In 1638 six families with twenty people emigrated from Pulat to Prizren.[59] Fifteen Albanian families from Dukagjin—120 people in all—settled in Suha Reka (Suva Reka), a village near Prizren.[60] In 1638 Bardhi found two families with a total of 36 family members who had recently emigrated to the village of Dobrush from Dukagjin.[61] All the Catholics in Kratovo were Albanian immigrants from Dibër.[62]

Even the later ecclesiastic reports tell of Albanian migrations. Thus in 1792 Matteo Mazrreku reports that Catholics had moved to several villages surrounding Gjakovë from the mining districts in the Diocese of Alessio.[63] In the village of Romanzi (?) there were sixteen Catholic households with 139 people who had come from Albania one year earlier. They were "gente veramente salvatica, rozza, senza veruna civiltà, e tanto erano poveri, e senza l'abiti, che le loro carni tutte si vedevano, ma altretanto erano superbi, e caminavano orgogliosi, come se fossero vestiti di veluto, e seta."[64] In Janosh, another village near Gjakovë, the Catholics—twenty-six households with 191 people—had left Albania forty years earlier.[65]

The Catholics from Albania emigrated to the predominatly Moslem Kosovo and Macedonia for various reasons. The ecclesiastical vistors mention: emigration to avoid a vendetta, as in the village of Dobrush;[66] emigration for economic reasons as in the villages surrounding Gjakovë. Mazrreku tells of these villages in 1792 that they had experienced an influx of Catholics from Albania, ". . . venuti per motivo della fame dalle Montagne dell'Albania."[67] A third, and probably very important, reason for emigration is noted by Zmajević in 1703—namely compulsory emigration. He reports on the villages surrounding Gjakovë: "Le ville sud.e sono colonie delli albanesi montagnuoli, olbigati dalli Turchi alla trasmigrat.ne, e per levar ad essi l'occasione di rubbare, e per popolare il paese, che era distrutto dalle guerre."[68]

The ecclesiastical visitor did not limit himself to noting the state of Catholic Christianity; he was also charged with preserving the very existence of Christianity in regions where other religions prevailed. The survival of Christianity was threatened primarily by Islam which could attract converts by offering advantageous tax status or civil rights. The ecclesiastical reports therefore address the problem of Islamization and a phenomenon not specifically Albanian, but most often encountered among Albanians, crypto-Christianity.

The Albanians adopted the Islamic religion primarily for economic reasons, to escape the poll tax. The conversion was purely superficial at first: The converst assumed Moslem names and occasionally went to a mosque if there happened to be one close by. In private they continued to adhere to Christian tenets. In addition, it was only the head of the household who changed his faith, while his wife and children remained loyal to their old faith. Almost all ecclesiastical reports contain evidence of the transition from Christianity to Islam. For example, in 1623/24 Pietro Mazrreku writes that during the previous four years more than 3,000 people from 200 (!) Albanian villages in the vicinity of Prizren had converted to Islam.[69] In 1633 the same visitor reports that the process of Islamization had begun in Has, a mountainous area west of Prizren. Only five parishes with approximately 4,000 parishioners remained of the original fifty![70] Mazrreku makes the further interesting observation that the Islamization of the Albanians from Has was initially purely external, but that the converts had now begun to go to the hodja and to have themselves circumcized.

> . . . Has confinante con la Servia quest'e habitato da infinito numero d'Albanesi sudditi del Turco in maniera, che si come li Ducaginesi

> non si vogliono chiamar vassali del Turco ne per titolo di vassalaggio
> ne per debito di tributo, cosi questi sono stati tanto mal trattati che
> moltissimi, o quasi tutti (come s'e accennato altrove) si sono fatti
> Turchi con mutar il nome solo senz'haver amimo di renegar col
> cuore, ma hanno cominciato andar attorno li Hoggie, cioe i Sacer-
> doti de Turchi con il Circoncisore per circonciderli.[71]

In 1627 Bardhi reports that most of the 550 Catholics of Gjakovë and
its surroundings were women, while most of the men had converted to
Islam. Catholic women who were married to "Turks" requested the sacraments from their priests, but the priests had to deny the request.[72] The
priests found themselves in a difficult position as a result of this prohibition, as Bardhi reports in a detailed report one year later. Since the Christian women married to apostates could no longer receive the sacraments
and were essentially excluded from the Christian community, they were
forced by their husbands to convert to Islam. Sometimes the apostates
even compelled the priests to baptize their sons.[73]

In the cases described above the conversion to Islam was genuine, even
if certain Christian customs perserved for a long time. But it also happened,
and not just in rare cases, that the conversion to Islam remained a formality. This option—crypto-Christianity—was naturally available only in areas
not in the immediate vicinity of the Ottoman administrative centers.

Crypto-Christians are mentioned for the first time in 1703 in Vinzenz
Zmajević's "Notitie universali dello stato di Albania." Zmajević was, of
course, reporting on the Dioceses of Antivari, Skutari, and Durazzo, not
on Kosova and Macedonia.[74] In the more recent ecclesiastical reports included in this study references to crypto-Christians in Kosova abound. In
1784 Mazrreku met five crypto-Christians families in the Parish of Zogaj.
He convinced them to acknowledge their Christian faith in public, even
in the presence of officials, and promised to help if they were burdened
with higher taxes.[75]

In 1792 he experienced similar success with a crypto-Christian family
in Mejë near Gjakovë.[76] However, this public acknowledgement of silent
adherence to one's old faith was not always without danger, as the report
sent by Archbishop Matteo Krasniqi to the Propaganda Fide testifies.
The report tells how Islam was forced upon the population of Rugovë
(above Peć) in the year 1815. Three families tried to resist: The heads of

the households adopted Moslem names but continued to attend mass in the city. They were brought to trial and executed in public on November 13, 1817.[77]

The last report included in this study also contains interesting observations on crypto-Christianity; the Ragusan Urban Bogdanović wrote this account in 1853. He is the first to record statistics on the extent of crypto-Christianity in the archdioceses: According to his report there were 128 crypto-Christian families in the villages near Prizren.[78] In the vicinity of Peć the number was 165,[79] while Skopska Crna Gore had 30.[80] Bogdanović estimated the total number of crypto-Christian families in the Archdiocese of Skoplje to be 500.[81]

Some of these crypto-Christians in Peć and Gjakovë openly declared their Christianity in 1845. Thereupon one man from each family was thrown into prison and released only after being detained for two months and paying a fine of forty "borse di piastre turche" (one borsa = twenty-five Roman scudi).[82] The crypto-Christians from some villages in Skopska Crna Gore, who likewise declared their faith at the instigation of their priest, D. Antonio Marković, were not treated as leniently. Together with their priest they were imprisoned in Skoplje and then exiled to Bursa; there was a total of twenty-five families with 138 people.[83]

One other topic which concerned the ecclesiastical visitors was the problem of "abuses"—old folk customs incompatible with the teachings of the Catholic Church, which persisted among the Catholic Albanians despite the efforts of the clergy. In Kosova the priests were primarily concerned with one custom which supposedly originated with the Albanian emigrants from the Dioceses of Sappa, Alessio and Pulat, namely with the custom of trial marriage. Despite repeated complaints from the ecclesiastical visitors, it seemed impossible to stamp out the practice. The report of 1820 depicts the situation most explicitly:

> L'unico, non leggiero abuso, di cui l'Arcivescovo si lamenta, e sul quale chiede consiglio all'EE.VV. come debba diportarsi si restringe ad alcuni villani venuti dalle Diocesi di Sappa, Alessio, e Pulati, ed e che essi non si congiungono subito in vincolo Matrimoniale, ma a capo di due, o tre mesi i vecchi, e gli giovani a capo di un'anno, e piu. I primi dicono: Se sono le donne perturbatrici, e litigiose le ripudiamo per conservare la pace della famiglia, gli secondi poi

dicono: Se ci riescono sterili non ci servono, perche noi le prendiamo per fecondare, e moltiplicarci con la prole. Soggiunge l'Arcivescovo di aver molto procurato di estirpare quest' abuso mettendo anche mano a rigorose pene, ma non gli e riuscito, perche quei villani adducono sempre per ragione essere questa loro antichissima consuetudine.[84]

The relationship between "Turks" and "Christians" is another topic frequently discussed in the ecclesiastical reports. Here "Turks" generally implies Moslem Albanians, while "Christians" naturally means Catholics. In general, the assessment of the Moslems is not unfavorable. As early as 1703 Zmajević writes that the Moslems in Serbia have a more gentle disposition (genio piu mite) than their colleagues in Albania.[85]

The reports seldom mention explicit obstacles impeding the practice of the Catholic religion. Only Bardhi's report of 1641/42 states that in Gjakovë mass had to be celebrated in a cellar (cantine sotto terra) instead of in church "per sospeti de Turchi, e tempi cativi."[86] In other cases the hospitality and protection offered by the "Turks" are emphasized, especially that of Ottoman dignitaries. For example, in 1784 a certain Sumber Beg protected the Catholics in Krusha (north of Prizren).[87] In Lubkovo, a half Orthodox/half Moslem village in Macedonia, a "Sig.r turco potente" supported three Catholic Albanian refugee families in 1791.[88]

An exception is Matteo Mazrreku who judges the Moslem Albanians, especially the apostates, quite negatively in his ecclesiastical report of 1791; he reveals little of his own Christianity when he characterizes the Moslems as a "razza maledetta."[89] He prays: "Ab albanensibus libera nos Domine."[90] He may have had a personal reason for doing so. Nevertheless, Mazrreku's report is interesting because it points out the significant role of the Albanians in the Ottoman Empire by the end of the eighteenth century. Mazrreku presents the Albanians as if they were about to bring the entire Turkish Empire under their power:

La più maligna, o furba razza di uomini non vi è in questo mondo delli albanesi, e la più debole e codarda nel confessare la S. Fede di Xto; e la razza più, che si multiplica sono li albanesi rinegati, giacche di una famiglia in pochi anni si fanno cento case, e hanno empito non solam.te ogni cantone di tutta la nostra Servia, ma ancora sono in molta abbondanza fino in Costantinopoli.

They all had important posts in the army, courts, and administration. While one hesitated before to call oneself an Albanian or to speak Albanian, now one barely spoke any Turkish or Slavic; rather, everyone tried to prove his Albanian origin and to speak Albanian. Ottoman officials did not dare to take action against Albanian bands because Albanians were dominant at court and in the army.[91] According to Mazrreku, Albanian Moslems had usurped the lands and stolen the cattle of Christians in Skopska Crna Gora.[92]

The ecclesiastical reports, some of which are maintained very subjectively, as the example above shows, contain various other material: Among other things they describe internal and external political events from the perspective of the civilian population being affected by them. They report in great detail about the highwaymen, who made traveling so difficult and dangerous. At the end of the eighteenth century the reports contain numerous accounts of the activities of Kara Mahmud Pasha Bushatlliu of Skutari. These show a side of Mahmud Pasha which never appears in the official historial writings. In Kosova his troops plundered, ravaged, and killed. In Prizren and Prishtinë the local authorities were driven out and replaced with Mahmud Pasha's followers. The palaces of those driven out were burned down.[93] The ecclesiastical visitors also protested repeatedly against the "guerre civile" which local Ottoman rulers waged among themselves, thereby inflicting great suffering upon the population.[94] As Bogdanović reports, the Sublime Porte had to send a Serasker to Rumelia in 1845 to disarm the Moslem population; he was not very successful.[95]

The ecclesiastical reports also contain some descriptions which sound absolutely unbelievable, for example, the story of the Ottoman Beg Salahor, which Mazrreku includes at the end of his report for 1784.[96] This Ottoman Beg "consigliere secreto del gran Signore" came to Prishtinë to settle a few disputes. He sent for the ecclesiastical visitor, with whom he conversed in Latin and revealed the following to him: "Ego sum Catholicus Ap.licus Romanus, sum Frater Regis Gallie, sum Administrator Bulgarie, sum Legatus Moscovie, sum consiliator a Secretis Imperatoris Ottomanici."

Mazrreku seems to have believed him because he writes that he could tell even from the accent that the noble gentleman from Constantinople was a Frenchman.

The discussion which Mazrreku claims to have had with the Orthodox in Skoplje in 1791 also seems unbelievable to me.[97]

The ecclesiastical reports, which have not yet received sufficient attention in historical research, are a very useful source for the internal history of European Turkey, even if they are admittedly not without errors. They are significant primarily because they describe conditions and events not from an official point of view, but from the perspective of the "common man," who suffered under those circumstances. Certain processes, such as Islamization or migration, as well as historical geography can scarcely be studied without these reports.

* * * * *

NOTES

1.   The first ecclesiastical report was published by Franjo Rački, "Izvještaj barskoga nadbiskupa Marina Bizzia o svojem putovanju god. 1610 po Arbanaskoj i staroj Srbiji," in *Starine* 20 (1888): 50-156; excerpts from various reports related to Albania can be found in Fulvio Cordignano, "Geografia ecclesiastica dell'Albania dagli ultimi decenni del secolo XVI alla metà del secolo XVII," *Orientalia Christiana Periodica* 36 (1936): 229-294. A complete series of ecclesiastical reports from Albania was published by Injac Zamputi, *Relacione mbi gjendjen e Shqipërisë veriore dhe të mesme në shekullin XVII.* 1-2 Tirana, 1963 and 1965 (hereafter Zamputi I/II).

2.   Peter Bartl (ed.), *Quellen und Materialien zur albanischen Geschichte im 17. und 18. Jahrhundert.* II München 1979: 126. (Hereafter Bartl, *Quellen* II).

3.   Relazione sullo stato attuale dell'Archidiocesi di Scopia fatta da Fr. Urbano Bogdanovich 1853 = Archivo storico della S. Congregazione 'de Propaganda Fide' (hereafter APF), SC Albania 34, f. 1017 v.

4.   Relazione della Visita della Diocesi di Scopia nel Regno di Servia 1784 = APF, SOCG 872, f. 136.

5.   Ibid., f. 137.

6.   Visita della Diocesi di Scopia in Servia dell'anno 1791 = APF, SOCG 895, f. 70.

7.   Relazione Giorgio Bianchi 1638 = Zamputi II 100.

8.   The following reports were consulted: Marino Bizzi 1610, Pjetër Mazrreku 1623/24, Pjetër Mazrreku 1633, Gjergj Bardhi 1637, 1638, 1638/

1639, and 1641/42 (all of these are included in Zamputi (1-2); Vinzenz Zmajević 1703 (included in Bartl, *Quellen* II); Matteo Mazrreku 1784 = APF, SOCG 872, f. 127-149 v.; Matteo Mazrreku 1791/92 = APF, SOCG 895, f. 70-83 v., 93-102 v.; Matteo Krasniqi 1820 = APF SOCG 922, f. 310-320, 326-336 v.; Urban Bogdanović 1853 = APF, SC Albania 34, f. 1016-1033.

    9.   Location unknown, see Milenko S. Filipović, *Has pod Paštrikom.* Sarajevo, 1958: 23.

    10.   In the documents Scegeçi, in Zamputi used in its Albanian form Shegjeç. Location unknown, see Filipović, 23.

    11.   In the documents Simbi or Zumbi, currently Zjumi/Zymi in northern Prizren.

    12.   In the documents Zogagni, location cannot be determined, near Gjakovë.

    13.   Zamputi II, 96.

    14.   Ibid., 172, 174.

    15.   Ibid., 266.

    16.   Bartl, *Quellen* II, 130.

    17.   Report of Mazrreku 1623/24 = Zamputi I, 342.

    18.   Report of Mazrreku 1633 = Zamputi I, 434.

    19.   Report of Bardhi 1641/42 = Zamputi II, 262.

    20.   Report of Bizzi 1610 = Zamputi I, 176.

    21.   Report of Mazrreku 1623/24 = Zamputi I, 344.

    22.   Bartl, *Quellen* II, 129.

    23.   Report of Bogdanović 1853 = APF, SC Albania 34, f. 1019v.

    24.   Report of Bardhi 1637 = Zamputi II, 98.

    25.   Report of Mazrreku 1784 = APF, SOCG 872, f. 137 v., 138, 139, 141v., 144.

    26.   Zamputi I, 168, 170.

    27.   Zamputi I, 335.

    28.   Zamputi II, 100.

    29.   Zamputi II, 254.

    30.   APF, SC Albania 34, f. 1026.

    31.   Ibid., f. 1027.

    32.   Zamputi II, 98, 100.

    33.   Zamputi II, 258.

    34.   APF, SC Albania 34, f. 1026.

35.   Ibid., f. 1025 v.
36.   Zamputi I, 340, 342.
37.   Zamputi I, 172.
38.   Zamputi II, 170.
39.   Zamputi II, 264.
40.   APF, SC Albania 34, f. 1025.
41.   Zamputi I, 174.
42.   Zamputi II, 172.
43.   Zamputi II, 262.
44.   Zamputi I, 176.
45.   Zamputi II, 170.
46.   Zamputi II, 260.
47.   Zamputi I, 174, 176.
48.   Zamputi I, 436.
49.   Zamputi II, 258.
50.   Zamputi I, 178.
51.   Zamputi I, 338.
52.   Zamputi II, 174.
53.   Zamputi II, 262.
54.   Bartl, *Quellen* II, 129.
55.   APF, SOCG 895, f. 76.
56.   Zamputi II, 174.
57.   Zamputi II, 266.
58.   Zamputi I, 342, 344.
59.   Zamputi II, 100.
60.   Ibid.
61.   Zamputi II, 168.
62.   Zamputi II, 172, 174.
63.   APF, SOCG 895, f. 95v.
64.   Ibid., f. 97.
65.   Ibid., f. 98.
66.   Zamputi II, 168.
67.   APF, SOCG 895, f. 95v.
68.   Bartl, *Quellen* II, 133.
69.   Zamputi I, 336.
70.   Ibid., 434.
71.   Ibid., 444.

72. Zamputi II, 98.
73. Zamputi II, 100.
74. Bartl, *Quellen* II, 21, 25, 29, 99, 106, 115, 131.
75. APF, SOCG 872, f. 139-139v.
76. APF, SOCG 895, f. 96v.
77. APF, SOCG 992, f. 319-320.
78. APF, SC Albania 34, f. 1024.
79. Ibid., f. 1026.
80. Ibid., f. 1025.
81. APF, SC Albania 34, f. 1027v.
82. Ibid., f. 1018v.
83. Ibid., f. 1018v-1019.
84. Ristretto sulla Relazione della Diocesi di Scopia nel Regno di Servia = APF, SOCG 922, f. 312v.
85. Bartl, *Quellen* II, 128.
86. Zamputi II, 256.
87. APF, SOCG 872, f. 137v.
88. APF, SOCG 895, f. 72v.
89. Ibid., f. 83.
90. Ibid., f. 81v.
91. Ibid., f. 73v.
92. Ibid., f. 73v.
93. Ibid., f. 93-93v.
94. APF, SOCG 922, f. 326.
95. APF, SC Albania 34, f. 1018v.
96. APF, SOCG 872, f. 146-147.
97. APF, SOCG 895, f. 76-77.

been systematically investigated. In his comprehensive work, *Maps and Politics*,[1] Henry Robert Wilkinson limited himself to Macedonia. We will attempt to answer the following questions: What progress has been made in the representation and the investigation of ethnographic relationships of the Kosova region? Were the research results influenced by extra-scientific factors and what image did the European public gain as a result of the ethnographic maps?

The choice of a beginning point for our investigation is based on the fact that for the first time in 1730 a map was printed on which ethnographic relationships, including those of Southeastern Europe, were represented. The creator was the otherwise not further distinguished Gottfried Hensel[2] of the firm of Homann Erben in Nuremberg. On his "Europa polyglotta"[3] he used the beginning of the Pater noster in the different languages to designate the settlement areas of the individual peoples. A handwritten flourish "Slavonia" with the Church-Slavic form of the prayer extends approximately from Istria to the Balkan Mountains. From the Adriatic coast near Dubrovnik to the middle Danube stretches the name "Illiri," which is obviously supposed to refer to the Albanians. The Albanian form of the Pater noster is, however, not entered, because the cartographer did not know Gjon Buzuku's "Meshari" of 1555.

The cut-off point of our investigation at 1913 coincides with the Peace of Bucarest, which marked the nearly complete eviction of the Ottoman Empire from Southeastern Europe and the political redistribution of the liberated regions among the conquering powers of the First and Second Balkan Wars. The conditions for a scientific investigation of the ethnic relationships had changed just as greatly as a result, as had the possibilities of the new owner, the Kingdom of Serbia, of changing the situation through political and administrative measures. I must also impose a restriction upon myself, one which derives from the subject matter itself. Only printed maps were examined. There is reason to believe that the governments in Vienna, London, and Paris had access to handwritten maps or maps with handwritten entries, which were different from publicly accessible maps. These were, however, not easily obtainable from Munich and they could not have influenced the picture of the ethnic relationships in the public sector. The map collection of the Bavarian State Library, which unfortunately lost a part of its collection during World War II, and the collection of the Central Bavarian State Archive, which contains the official cartographic documents of the former Bavarian Foreign Ministry, form the basis of my investigation, together with the maps reproduced in the secondary literature. This study could conceivably be continued in the future by colleagues, who are active in locations in other large map collections (London, Paris, Leningrad, Moscow, Vienna).

If one surveys the mass of map material available in Munich, one does best to proceed with the following categories: 1. Maps, whose cartographers knew the Kosova region personally; 2. Maps, whose compiler relied on the most diverse documents, but who were unable to form a picture of the relationships directly on location. Their products depend both on the documents available to them as well as on the ability to evaluate critically the primary material. Independently of these distinctions, one must also ask why ways were sought and found for representing the ethnic relationships on maps.

For a long time after the close of the Middle Ages, European cartographers held fast to the custom of naming the peoples of their own period by names handed down from antiquity.[4] Up into the middle of the eighteenth century, state and population boundaries were as a rule equated. Only in the nineteenth century did a sharpened awareness of the ethnic differences of inhabitants of the same state develop. Pavel Safarik, the outstanding linguist and literary scholar of the Slavs, was the first to point out the non-Slavic population (Hungarians, Turks, Albanians, Rumanians) living within the boundaries of the settlement areas of the Southern Slavs—by drawing lines of demarcation and using colored inks.[5] Three years later, in 1847, the multitalented natural scientist, Ami Boué, published an ethnographic map of European Turkey, on which he used colored areas to distinguish the different ethnic elements from each other.[7] The disadvantage of this was that, due to their proximity, small and very small minorities were no longer recognizable.

The Austrian consul, Johann Georg von Hahn, introduced a new practice when he used one or more identification letters (a = Albanians, S = Serbians, B ≠Bulgarians) placed by locations on large scale maps to designate the ethnic constituents which he had determined by personal observation or investigation.[8] It was likewise an Austrian consul, Carl Sax, who two years later published a small ethnographic map of Bosnia, on which the percentages of the respective populations were indicated by colored diagonal lines in five degrees of shading so that full coloration was achieved only when the ethnic make-up of the whole population was unmixed.[9]

The Bulgarian D. M. Brankov (pseudonym for Dimitur Niser) used a new method in 1905. He divided the individual Turkish *kazas* (districts) into squares and indicated the make-up of the population by using smaller squares in different coloration.[10] The advantage of this was that the number ratios became quite clear. This method provided no information, however, about the local distribution of the population groups within the administrative unit. The method used later of representing the ethnic constituents as segments of a circle corresponding to the respective percentage share was only a visual improvement over the previous method.[11] To be sure, not all cartographers adopted these procedures; rather there were always relapses into already scientifically surpassed methods of representation. One must concede, however, that the procedure used is related also to the scale utilized. With the choice of a large scale, coloration showing ethnic distribution can also mirror the actual relationships rather correct. However, for all index maps, (as in atlases), a certain scale could not be exceeded.

The oldest criterion for the determination of ethnic groups were languages. Hensel's map has already been mentioned. There was the difficulty, however, that in southeastern Europe, to a considerable extent, persons lived who spoke more than one language, i.e. their native tongue, and who could not easily be assigned to a particular group on the basis of linguistic features. One should recall here the social group of the far distant trade merchants who, whether Greeks, Armenians or Aromunians could speak Turkish, Italian, Bulgarian or Serbocroatian more or less fluently. For the investigator of ethnic relationships, this means that he must command several south European languages well enough to win the trust of his informants on the one hand, on the other hand to be able to determine whether they, for whatever reasons, were always telling him the truth or not. Except perhaps for Gustav Weigand, the Leipzig Romanist,[12] scarcely another Balkan ethnographer has fulfilled this prerequisite.

Within the Ottoman Empire, what mattered was not nationality, but religion. For this reason, there is often, for example, talk of "Greeks" in less informed reports of travelers, when in reality what was meant were confessors of the Orthodox faith. When language was the criterion, then Slavs were meant; and when nationality was considered, one meant the

Bulgarians, Serbians, or Montenegrins. Religious maps do not provide further assistance for the question of ethnic constituency of the population. There were differences between members of the same church during the period of nationality struggles, for example in Bulgaria.

Since national allegiance is ultimately a question of personal confession, censuses would be a worthwhile source of information. In the Ottoman Empire there was a census in 1834; its goal, like that of subsequent population counts of 1844, 1856, 1864 and 1873, was designed more to determine the male Muslim population than to count the Christians.[13] While regular population counts took place in Serbia from 1866, and in Bosnia after the occupation of 1879, this source of information was lacking for Montenegro until 1898. But even with censuses correct by European standards, one should bear in mind, that the nationality of the individual (and therefore as a rule, that of his entire family) can have been influenced by external pressure of by opportunistic considerations.

The determination and the cartographic designation of "national" schools and their students represented an additional source of information for our region, when one considers that the parents professed a tacit allegiance to a certain national group, when they sent their children to a particular school. One must certainly ask, how many schools were available, and whether in not a few cases the parents did not place the education of their children higher than "national" allegiance. In the areas still under Turkish administration, the establishment of schools for Christian children depended above all on whether the necessary financial means were raised by the already existing Christian states (Serbia, Bulgaria, Greece). Here, the children of Albanian parents were disadvantaged by the fact that an Albanian state came into existence only shortly before the First World War. Finally, one also sought to use certain modes of behavior as determining elements for ethnic classification. The Russian journalist, Peter Nebol'sin, who, as a correspondent for the St. Petersburg *Novoe vreme,* had lived for a long time in Serbia and Bulgaria, believed to have observed, that only the Serbians used to curse God. Today we know that such "national" traits are by no means characteristic for a people for a longer period, but spread very quickly to their neighbors.

Had it been possible for one of the ethno-cartographers to live for several years in the Kosova region, to learn the languages spoken there well enough to become sufficiently acquainted with the way and life of thinking of the inhabitants, then there would have been a chance of determining ethnic relationships with a measure of reliability. Actually, even the persons who knew the land were in the region under investigation as a rule only for a few days or weeks. No one was in a position to revisit at greater intervals—let us say of 10, 20, 30 years—the region which had already once been studied, in order to catalog the changes which had taken place in the meantime, especially from the viewpoint of the emergence of national feelings in the second half of the nineteenth century.

Seventeen ethnographic maps originated between 1847 and 1913. Their authors can be considered knowledgeable about the area. Among these, there are eleven maps drawn after journeys, which had led at least into the direct vicinity of the Kosova region. The series begins with the already mentioned Ami Boué, not an ethnographer in the strict sense, but a very experienced geographer who traversed the entire region of European Turkey on various routes,[15] accompanied by translators who spoke the local languages. He already determined that the western portion of the Metohija was "largely Arnautic" (inhabited by Muslim Albanians) and that in the Kosova Plateau, above all in its western part, Serbian villages were mixed with Albanian villages.

As French consul in Scutari, Hyacinthe Hecquard studied intensively the north Albanian mountain tribes and sought to determine the population figures for the Pashalik of his seat of office. For 1858, his map shows the seats of residence of the Albanians above Plava up to Bielopolje.[17] At about the same time, the French geographer, Guillaume Lejean[18] began his Balkan trips. He published his ethnographic information in a map in 1861.[19] According to it, the settlement area of the Albanians extended from the North Albanian mountains to Novi Pazar and almost to Leskovac, interrupted to be sure between Pejë and Prizren by a closed Serbian settlement area. Johann Georg von Hahn, already mentioned and no "Austrian railway engineer,"[20] published a map in the same year, on which he designated ethnically only those locations he himself had visited. If he was later criticized that he had not been able to determine the settlements of the Serbians due to his inability to speak Serbian,[21] his critics suppressed consciously the fact that Hahn was accompanied by the Czech officer, Frantisek Zach, who, as instructor at the military academy in Kragujevac, had a perfect command of Serbian. The journey of the two British philanthropists, G. Muir Mackenzie and A. P. Irby, whose map came out in 1867,[22] brought essentially no changes to the body of knowledge up to that time. Only in a few places was the Serbian-Albanian mix-area reduced in favor of the area settled solely by Serbians. When Carl Ritter von Sax, who has also been mentioned, published his "Ethnographic Map of European Turkey"[23] at the time of the Berlin Congress, official Turkish data and the information of his Austrian consul colleague were available to him in addition to his own observations. For him the Albanians were clearly the dominant ethnic element in the Kosova region.

A revision in favor of a wider diffusion of the Serbians, above all around Priština, was undertaken by the Serbian geographer and long-time general consul in Skopje, Vadim Karić.[25] He dissolved the closed settlement areas of the Albanians east and west of Kosovska Mitrovica into Serbian-Albanian mix-areas. The Austrian publicist of Montenegrin extraction, Spiridion Gopčević, went even further; he drew a Serbian settlement as far as Macedonia—at the expense of the Albanian (and Bulgarian) country inhabitants.[26] Michel Heim has already in 1966 demonstrated, that Gopčević consciously deceived the readers of his travelogue concerning the circumstances of the trip and deliberately falsified his ethnographic data.[27] On this basis, the map commissioned by the "Srpske Velikošolske Omladina" in 1891[28] extended the closed Serbian settlement area up to the mouth of the Vardar and up to Serres. The Albanians have in the Kosova region and in Macedonia only an isolated existence on this map. The Italian officer Eugenio Barbarich corrected this false picture in 1905 on his map back in favor of the Albanians.[29] He, however, repressed the Serbian and Bulgarian settlements in western Macedonia all too severely. Finally, between 1906 and 1913, the important Serbian geographer, Jovan Cvijić, drafted three ethnographic maps on the basis of his own travels and the compilation of existing material. The 1906 map preserves approximately the picture presented by the preceding serious research.[30] The map of 1909—i.e., after the Austrian annexation of Bosnia and Herzegovina—shows a noticeable increase in the number of Serbian settlements in eastern Macedonia and has them occupy the entire north coast of Lake Scutari.[31] Four years later, Cvijić shows Serbian settlements even south of Lake Skutari. Albanian settlements in eastern Macedonia have disappeared.[32] These incisive changes were made without the author having himself undertaken new field research or without others having presented corresponding maps. One does not do the outstanding scholar an injustice, if one notes, that in these maps of 1909 and 1913 the national interest of his native country took precedence over scientific objectivity.

Of six further maps, appearing in striking frequency between 1877 and 1911, it cannot reliably be determined whether their authors travelled in the Kosova region. In any case they were well acquainted with the relationships on the central Balkan peninsula. The engineer, F. Bianconi, had supervised Turkish railway construction in this region. His map[33] corresponds to the one by Sax. The map, finished in the same year by the Rumanian historian Nicolae E. Densusianu, breaks up the Albanian settlement area through inclusion of Vlach settlements, yet preserves on the whole the extent of the Albanian settlement area.[34] Even the Frenchman, A. Synvet, employed as professor at the lycée in Istanbul, offers no basic changes as regards the Albanians. He confuses his readers, however, when he distinguishes between Albanians and Muslims, but fails to indicate whether religion or national allegiance was for him the decisive factor.[35] The Englishman, Henry Noel Brailsford, gained excellent knowledge of the country due to his position as journalist and politician. His 1906 map does not show demarcation between Albanian and Serbian settlements from Mitrovica to Skopje.[36] Nor does the map of the Russian Slavist, Timofej Dimitrievich Florinskij, which appeared in the same year, show any essential changes at the expense of the Albanians.[37] Only the 1911 map of British publicist, Robert Seton-Watson, active on behalf of the southern Slavs, adopts for the most part the Serbian point of view.[38] Here the assertion that many contemporary Albanians were in fact Albanianized Serbians who had undergone this change of national allegiance against their will played an essential role in the argumentation of Cvijić and his predecessors.

European ethnographers at the turn of the century were thoroughly aware of the significance that a reliable determination of the population relationships in southeastern Europe would have had for science and politics. At the 12th International Orientalist Congress in Rome (1899), the Rumanian historian, Vasile Urechia, offered a reward of 500 francs for the best method of arriving at a "definitive" population map of southeastern Europe.[39] The participants at the congress accepted this suggestion unanimously. That Antonio Baldacci and Kurt Hassert, who took part in this congress, suggested an ethnographic map with a scale of 1:1 million, as Vinzenz Haardt von Hartenthurn asserts,[40] is not to be found in the acts of the congress. Whether the matter was discussed further at the Italian geographers' congresses in 1901 in Milan and 1902 in Naples,[41] I could not verify. In any case, as of 1913, these maps had not been published and so the decisions of the Bucarest Peace were not made on the basis of recognized data about the national constituency of the population.

If one surveys the many ethnographic maps not based on knowledge of the country, then a confusing picture results. Seven charts, which appeared between 1821 and 1843, were investigated. They precede the beginning of serious research, which starts with Ami Boué's travels. With the noteworthy exception of Pavel Josef Safarik, their authors were content to fill the area of southeastern Europe with the names of the Serbians, Vlachs, Albanians, etc., or to indicate quite roughly through various colors the heterogeneity in population. How unclear the relationships on the Balkan peninsula were to the investigators is evidenced by the fact that F. A. O'Etzel enters the "Illyrians" beside the Serbians, but separates them from the Albanians.[42] Another example is Gustav Kombst,[43] who inscribes "Illyricum" in the Kosova region, but uses the same color for the entire area from present day Albania to Istria.[44] Between 1870 and 1899, six ethnographic maps were included in major atlas works in Germany, France and England. The quality of the map compilers such as Ernst Debes, Richard Andree, George Gerland, Gustave-Léon Niox is just as striking as the increase in knowledge and in the manner of its presentation. To be sure, the scale was so small ($< 1:6$ million) that differences in the ethnographic entries could just as well be attributed to the need for generalization as to the various documents.

In comparison with this, many more maps were published as independent publications or as illustrations to a scientific monograph, occasionally in greater scale. Their factual information content is therefore generally greater. Nonetheless, they remain as a whole dependent on a more or less critical trust in the previously discussed maps of those who knew the area. Whereas two Russian and two German publications (the latter by Czech authors) document the spread of the panslavic feeling of community, the four German or Austrian examples testify to the soundness of the cartographic method. Deserving mention here is Heinrich Kiepert's map of 1876,[45] which served as a source of information for the deliberations of the Berlin Congress.[46] Only relatively late maps were edited which certify either the national-Rumanian position,[47] or the pro-

Albanian one of Italian authors.[48] Since one can assume that none of the
interested observers of the southeastern area had available all ethnographic
maps, formation of public opinion presumably have been based above all
on atlases and on maps which had been published several times. For example, the map by Synvet mentioned above was a source for the map
published anonymously by the British publisher Edward Stanford.[49] Another example is the 1913 map of Cvijić, which was included as "point
de vue serbe" by the Carnegie Commission in its investigation report.[50]

In summary, one can say, that external political influences prevented
the information of unprejudiced science concerning the ethnic situation
in the Kosova region from being utilized for an appropriate solution to
the problem. In view of this, it must be conceded that political will almost
always is stronger than scientifically grounded insight.

* * * * *

NOTES

1.   *Review of the ethnographic cartography of Macedonia.* Liverpool
1951.

2.   Johann Gabriel Doppelmayr, *Historische Nachricht von den Nürn-
bergischen Mathematicis und Künstlern.* Nuremberg, 1730.

3.   *Linguarum genealogiam exhibens una cum literis scribendisque
modis omnium gentium.* Nuremberg, 1730.

4.   See, for instance, Clément de Jonghe, *Nova totius terrarum orbis
geographica ac hydrographica tabula.* Amsterdam 1644, reproduced in *Die
Karte als Kunstwerk. Dekorative Landkarten aus Mittelalter und Neuzeit,*
ed. by the Bavarian State Library, Unterschneidheim 1979, illustration
60.

5.   *Slovanský zemevid.* Prague, 1842.

6.   See *Autobiographie du Docteur médecin Ami Boué,* Vienna,
1879.

7.   *Ethnographische Karte des Osmanischen Reichs europäischen
Teils und von Griechenland.* Gotha, 1847.

8.   *Croquis des westlichen Gebietes der bulgarischen Morava.* Vienna,
1861.

9.   "Skizzen über die Bewohner Bosniens," *Mitteilungen der k. geographischen Gesellschaft Wien,* 7(1863), pp. 93-107.

10.   *Carte des populations chrétiennes: Bulgare, Grecque et Koutso-vlacque en Macédonie,* Paris, 1905.

11.   See "Die nationale Zusammensetzung verschiedener Städte in Böhmen und Mähren-Schlesien in vorhussitischer Zeit," *Sudetendeutscher Atlas,* edited by Emil Meynen. Munich, 1955, leaf 8.

12.   A biography of this outstanding scholar has not been written yet; see the most recent sketch by Karl-Henning Schröder, *Biographisches Lexikon zur Geschichte Südosteuropas* 4 (1981), pp. 454-55.

13.   Franz Ritter von Le Monnier, "Die Volkszählungen in Europa mit besonderer Rücksicht auf die Zählungsepoche 1878-1881," *Deutsche Rundschau für Geographie und Statistik 5(1883), p. 203.*

14.   *Die Bulgaren in ihren historischen, ethnographischen und politischen Grenzen.* Berlin, 1917, p. 49.

15.   Ami Boué, *Recueil d'itinéraires dans la Turquie d'Europe. Détails géographiques, topographiques et statistiques.* 2 vols. Vienna, 1854.

16.   Ami Boué, "Die Ethnographie der europäischen Türkei und des westlichen Kleinasiens, geographisch dargestellt auf meiner Karte der Türkei," *Amtlicher Bericht über die 21. Versammlung deutscher Naturforscher und Ärzte.* Graz, 1841, p. 124.

17.   *Histoire ou description de la Haute Albanie ou Guégarie.* Paris, 1858.

18.   See P. Levot, "Guillaume Lejean. Sa vie, ses travaux, ses voyages," *Bulletin de la société académique de Brest, IIe série* 8 (1883), pp. 129-257.

19.   *Carte ethnographique de la Turquie d'Europe et des états vassaux autonomes/Ethnographie der europäischen Türkei.* Gotha, 1861 (Supplementary issue 4 of *Petermanns Mitteilungen*).

20.   Wilkinson falsely assumed this because Hahn had published on the railway construction in Turkey. See Gerhard Grimm, *Johann Georg von Hahn (1811-1869). Leben und Werk.* Wiesbaden, 1964. (*Albanische Forschungen* 1.)

21.   Spiridion Gopčević, *Makedonien und Altserbien.*, Vienna, 1889, p. 47, note 1.

22.   *Map of the South Slavonic countries.* London, 1867.

23.   *Mitteilungen der k.geographischen Gesellschaft Wien.* 21 (1878).

24.   Ibid., see the explanations on pages 177-183.

25.   *Srbija, opis države, zemlje i naroda.* Belgrad, 1887.

26.   "Ethnographische Karte von Altserbien und Mazedonien," *Petermanns Mitteilungen* 35 (1889), pp. 57-68.

27. *Spiridion Gopčević. Leben und Werk.* Wiesbaden, 1966 (*Albanische Forschungen* 4.)

28. *Etnografska karta Srpskih zemalja.* Belgrad, 1891.

29. *Carta etnografica della regione Albanese.* Rome, 1905.

30. *Politiko-etnografska skica Makedonije i Stare Srbije.* Belgrad, 1906.

31. *Carte ethnographique de la nation Serbe.* London, 1909.

32. "Ethnographische Karte der Balkan-Halbinsel," *Petermanns Mitteilungen* 59 (1913), table 22.

33. *Ethnographie et statistique de la Turquie d'Europe et de la Grèce.* Paris, 1887.

34. *Les Roumains du Sud. Carte éthnographique de la Macédoine, Thessalie, Epire et l'Albanie.* Paris and Bucarest, 1877.

35. *Carte éthnographique de la Turquie d'Europe.* 2nd edition. Constantinople, 1877.

36. *Macedonia. Its races and their future.* London, 1900 (reprint: New York, 1971).

37. "Etnografičeskaja karta Slavjanstva," *Slavjanskie plemja.* Kiev, 1906 (Izvestija universitetskija 1906, issue 12).

38. *The Southern Slav Question and the Hapsburg Monarchy.* London, 1911 (reprint: New York, 1969).

39. *Actes du douzième congrès international des orientalistes,* vol. 1 (Florence, 1901), p. CXXX.

40. *Die Kartographie der Balkan-Halbinsel im 19. Jahrhundert.* Vienna, 1902-1904, pp. 346-47. (*Mitteilungen des k.u.k.militärgeographischen Instituts,* 21-23); similarly see Jovan Cvijić, *Questions Balkaniques.* Paris, 1917, p. 73, note 2.

41. These acts of the congresses were not accessible to me.

42. *Völkerkarte von Europa.* Berlin, 1821.

43. Compare his *Erinnerungen aus meinem Leben.* Leipzig, 1848.

44. "Ethnographic map of Europe," *The national atlas of historical, commercial and political geography.* Edinburgh, 1843.

45. *Ethnographische Übersicht des europäischen Orients.* Berlin, 1876.

46. *Die Bulgaren,* (see note 14), p. 43.

47. Constantin Noë, "Carte éthnographique de la Macédoine, de l'Albanie, de la vieille Serbie et de la Thessalie," *Les Roumains, Koutso-*

vlaques, les populations Macédoniennes et le crise Balkanique. Bucharest, 1913.

48.   Arturo Galanti, "Carta etnografica della penisola Balcanica," *L'Albania. Notizie geografiche, etnografiche e storiche.* Rome, 1901.

49.   See "Les études éehnographiques sur la Turquie," *Le Messager d'Athènes* No. 3 (January 27, 1877), p. 14.

50.   *Enquête dans les Balkans.* Paris, 1914, around p. 449.

Martin Camaj

ON THE TYPOLOGY OF THE DIALECTS OF KOSOVA

In accordance with the latest data, the dialects of Kosova can be classified synchronically into five groups:

- The dialect group comprising Rrafshi i Dukagjinit (Gjakovë, Pejë, and Prizren), designated as the Central group;
- The northern dialects encompassing Mitrovicë, Vuçitern, Prishtinë, as far as Drenicë;
- The southern dialects extending from Ferizaj, Kaçanik, Gjilan to Mali i Zi i Shkupit;
- The dialect of Kumanovë (Macedonia) as well as that of Preshevë and Bujanovac (Serbia);
- The southern dialect group bordering on Albania (in the districts of Kukës and Tropojë[1]. This division seems to be strongly influenced by administrative reasons.

A. V. Desnickaja[2] has treated linguistic, historic, and ethnographic studies up to 1968, attempting thereby to give a sketch of the dialect type of Metohija. A few years later Desnickaja concluded that it is based on an autonomous dialect type: "The eastern variants of Northern Gheg diverged as a result of the connexion of Kosova-Metohija to inner-Balkan areas which were economically independent from the Adriatic coast."[3]

Of course it is very important to consider certain extra-linguistic features of a geographic, economic, and political nature, but we do not as yet

possess the linguistic and dialect materials needed for an accurate charact-
erization of the language situation in Kosova. To date Balkan lingustics has
changed little as regards research methods. The new components of the
written norm have received little attention. In this connexion, it may be
remarked that language contact and language mixture display other features
and processes which cannot be studied according to the laws of language
development typical of natural languages lacking a written norm. The
earlier language development (with regard to dialect) today influences
a) Tosk variants of the written norm, b) the Serbo-Croatian written norm,
and c) the dialects and languages which are exclusively spoken.

The introduction of innovations in the colloquial speech of Kosova
shows up clearly in the areas of syntax and morphology, where calques
of Serbian origin are evident.

In order to conceive of a more ancient stage of Eastern Gheg, one is
well-advised to take the older language material into consideration. This
is of particular importance in a diachronic study of these Albanian language variants. Such is, in my opinion, the study of Carlo Tagliavini,[4] based
to a great extent on the findings of Jokl,[5] Lambertz,[6] Mladenov,[7] and
others. Not to be overlooked is the valuable documentation provided by
Georg v. Hahn[8] and the linguistic elements found in *Cuneus Prophetarum*
of Pjetër Bogdani.[9]

The most recent studies of the Kosovar scholars[10] and the collected
folkloric corpus demonstrate that, despite the numerous variants, Kosovar
constitutes an independent dialect branch of Albanian. Until very recently,
the Gheg koine of folksongs and epic as well as the written norm caused
levelling. Elements of Eastern Gheg, on the other hand, also penetrated
the written variants in the western part of this linguistic region via the
folklore and the colloquial spoken language. Isolation because of the border is out of the question.

1) *Components of Eastern Gheg.* At the turn of the century the trend
among Albanologists was to divide Gheg into regions by means of horizontal lines: 1) *Southern Gheg* (Tiranë, Durrës, Elbasan), 2) *Middle Gheg*
(Mat, Dibër, and Mirditë), 3) *North Gheg* (Shkodër with the outlying
plains and mountains). The continuation of the parallels to the East beyond national boundaries would have included zones 2) and 3) and also
parts of the Albanian language regions in Kosova and Macedonia. But the
viewpoint of Maximilian Lambertz, the most enlightened Albanologist of

his day, has continued into the present. Accordingly, Northern Gheg is divided vertically. Later this proved to be appropriate chiefly for methodological reasons, seeing that Eastern Gheg is considered to be an autonomous branch.

The following factors have contributed to the development of Eastern Gheg:

- *Northern Gheg proper* (the dialects of Malësia e Madhe);
- *Northeastern Gheg* (the so-called dialect of Dukagjin in the broadest sense including Shkodër and the regions beyond the Drin);
- *Middle Eastern Gheg* (the dialect of Dibër);
- *Eastern Gheg proper* (synchronically the dialect group of the regions of Fusha e Kosovës and Rrafshi i Dukagjinit, diachronically a dialect underlying it as an ancient substratum, today difficult to reconstruct).

At an earlier stage the first two dialect types were not so much identified with distinct territories as with the speakers of the various tribes. *Northern Gheg* was spoken by the tribes: Hot, Grudë, Kelmend, Kuç, and others; *Northeastern Gheg* by the tribes: Berishë, Thaç, Krasniq, and others, on the one side, and by the tribes Shosh, Shalë up to Vûthaj and Gusîjë, on the other. In this language type, which can be designated as the tribal dialect (Alb. *fis* 'tribe'), the brilliant forms of the epic lay (*kangë kreshnike*) developed. Northeastern Gheg preserves its characteristics in a few dialects in the area of Dukagjin's retreat[11] and also partially in the aforementioned work *Cuneus Prophetarum* of Pjetër Bogdani. As the koine of folksongs, this dialect type is also considered a part of the Gheg written tradition, and particularly, as regards morphology. Because members of this speech community constantly wandered into Kosova, Northern Gheg may also be regarded as an important component of the dialect type, especially that of Rrafshi i Dukagjinit.

Middle Gheg is unfortunately inadequately researched. It is not closely bound with particular tribes, but strictly defined geographically. Characteristic of the dialect branch of Dibër, Mat, and Mirditë is the diphthongization of long or accented vowels, as *i>ai~ei* (*mirë>mair~mëir* 'good'). In the city of Dibër the old imperfect *−nj−* (*shkonje* instead of *shkojshe* 'I went') has survived to the present. It is a little known fact that the works of the early writer Pjetër Budi (1566-1623) of Mat contain elements of this dialect type. Although conservative and stable within its own territory, the dialect of Dibër is unstable in contact with other dialect types. This was undoubtedly the dialect spoken by the Albanian national hero Skanderbeg.

2. Tracing the substratum of Eastern Gheg. Methodologically, it is correct to distinguish the linguistic peculiarities of the three first-named dialect groups, which were introduced to Kosova in the course of migrations from the West in the last century. Remaining characteristics could be regarded as native elements. This alternative, however, remains closed to us, until the entire corpus of dialect material of this area is collected and placed at the disposal of scholars. Thus we are constrained to base it on well-known linguistic phenomena, i.e.

1) Tendency to denazalization and rounding (labialization) of the vowels;

2) Absence of palatalization of *l, k,* and *g,* which has led to the shifting of the present palatals *q* and *gj* to the front, i.e. occlusion;

3) Manifestation of morphological pecularities under the influence of loss of palatalization.

There can be no doubt that Kosova and Rrafshi i Dukagjinit (Metohija) are at the center of these phenomena.

As to 1): *â>o* (rounded and slightly nazalized): *zâni>zoni* 'the voice', *bâ>bo* 'made', *kângë>kong* 'song', *âmbël>omel* 'sweet'. The phenomenon has been generalized (as has oral *a*) in the sequences *a+n, a+m,* as *kanë> kon* 'they have', *kam>kom* 'I have', *duhan>duhon* 'tobacco', *agsham> agshom* 'dusk'. According to Tagliavini and other researchers such as Peter Skok, the rounding of *a* in a non-nasal environment has also occurred. This is disputed by Mulaku, however, chiefly for the area under investigation by him.[12]

Another widespread phenomenon seems to be the transition of *o* in unaccented position to *a,* as *obórr>abórr* 'yard', *opét>apét* 'again', apparently as the assimilation to the rounding of the accented *a,* which tends to become rounded.

As to 2): the old Albanian consonant clusters *kl, gl* are represented in the Kosovar dialect as *k, g* :

I. *kl>k: klumësht>kûmsht~kûsht* 'milk, whey', *klanj>kaj* 'I cry', *klenë>kânë~kon.*

II. *gl>g: gluha>guha* 'the tongue', *glatë>gat* 'long', *glû>gû* 'knee', *globë>gobë* 'fine, penalty,' *glofkë>gofk* 'hole', etc.

As is known, these sound groups developed as follows: *kl, gl > klj, glj > ki, gi > q, gj,* and continue to function in some places to the present as isophones for the differentiation of dialects; all of these stages are attested in the written norm as well.

It is beyond all doubt that the Kosovar phenomenon predates the palatalization; this opinion is shared by Tagliavini and Çabej. Moreover Desnickaja and some Kosovar linguists, including Ajeti, are of the opinion that *l* in this combination is lost after the completion of palatization.

This occurred not only in the sound combination *kl* + vowel, *gl* + vowel but also in the combination vowel + *lk* as

III. *ulk>*kosov. *uk* 'wolf', otherwise in common Albanian *ujk; ndulk> nduk~nuk* 'to ripen', otherwise in common Albanian *ndulk ndujk,* in which *l* is retained or palatalized, *tujg* in Malësia e Madhe (cf. 1, Northern Gheg proper) where the combination *nd>t,* as *ndesh>tesh* 'I meet' is found.

Surely this phenomenon is an internal Albanian sound change, even if the impetus is external; it ultimately depends on depalatalization or lack thereof, so that

Another effect of the same phenomenon is the fronting of the existing palatals, *q (qen* 'dog') and *gj (gjumë* 'sleep') to palato-alveolar affricates *c* and *xh.* This happened chiefly in the Northeastern Gheg territory.

As to 3): Such a phonetic and phonological transposition also had an impact on the morphology of the Kosovar substratum:

I. The definite form of nouns in *-k, -g* is not marked by the addition of *u,* but *-i,* as *mal-i* 'mountain'. There was no further danger that *-i* would palatalize *k* and *g,* as **miki* pl. *miq* 'friends', **zogi* pl. *zogj* 'birds'. Cf. the following sg.:

common Alb. *mik* (indef.), *miku* (def.);
Kosovar *mik* (indef.), *miki* (def.);
common Alb. *zog* (indef.), *zogu* (def.);
Kosovar *zog* (indef.), *zogi* (def.).

II. Plural formation without palatalization:

Common Alb. sg. *ka* 'ox', pl. *qe* ;
Kosovar sg. *ka,* pl. *ke.*

Of course later other cases of depalatalization occurred analogically, including *qepë>kep* 'onion', *qerr>kerr* 'sledge', and most probably the shifting of *nj* (palatal nasal) > *n* (nasal), as *njizét>nizét* 'twenty', etc.

3) *Effect of Language Contact.* It is my firm conviction that these sound changes cannot be explained without citing the influence of other Balkan languages on Kosovar territory, the native sound laws of Albanian being insufficient. Conceiveably, this linguistic development took place before the Turkish occupation, etc., as a result of the contact of the Albanian-speaking community with speakers of Serbian, which, like Bulgarian, has no nasal vowels, and likewise failed to carry out palatalization in similar positions. The structure of these medieval Serbian dialects is not known exactly, as Ivić has indicated.[13] On the other hand, one can point with certainty to a few characteristics of this language which are most certainly Serbian. It is known with certainty that the dialects of the Serbian linguistic area tend to vocalize syllabic *l* in final position, in combination with a semi-vowel, etc. It is precisely in this phenomenon that the Kosovar Albanian word *uk* parallels the word *vuk* 'wolf' (from common Slav. *vblk*) which shares a common primitive root.

Many questions of a theoretical and empirical nature related to language contact and mixture are readily explained if one casts off the prejudices of the various schools and judges the cases individually. Different results appear from the observed language contact of the south Montenegrin with the north Albanian dialects, on the one hand, and of the Arbëresh (Italo-Albanian) of southern Italy on the other. One, however, is particularly noteworthy, viz. that the "donor languages," so to speak, (those that influence other languages) in certain phases of contact act indirectly rather than directly on the recipient language. The recipients do not receive the exact letter for letter correspondence from the donor, but instead are motivated by an external impetus to innovate language processes, which lead to convergence or assimilation with the donor language. In the contract of two languages a third phenomenon arises that can be differently related to the two languages. And thus it happens that an Albanian dialect branch underlies the contemporary dialect substratum of Kosovo, a dialect branch which exhibits unique phonetic and morphological features which cannot be explained without considering the ancient contact with other languages and language forms of the area.

* * * * *

NOTES

1. L. Mulaku, "Über die albanische Mundart von Kosovo," *Akten des Internationalen Albanologischen Kolloquiums.* Innsbruch, 1977, p. 567.

2. A. V. Desnickaja, *Albanskij jazyk i ego dialekty.* Leningrad, 1968. (Albanian translation: *Gjuha shqipe dhe dialektet e saj.* Prishtinë, 1972).

3. A. V. Desnickaja, "Die historischen Grundlagen der Dialektgliederung des Albanischen," *Akten des Internationalen albanologischen Kolloquiums.* Innsbruck, 1977, p. 573.

4. C. Tagliavini, *Le parlate albanesi di tipo Ghego orientale (Dardania e Macedonia).* Rome, 1942. Cf. also the Albanian translation in *Studime gjuhësore I (Dialektologji).* Prishtinë, 1979, pp. 105-150.

5. N. Jokl, "Vorlaufiger Bericht des Privadozenten Dr. Norbert Jokl über seine nordgegischen Dialektstudien," *Anz. d. Akad. d. Wiss. Wien, phil.-hist. Kl.* 52 (1915), Nr. XIII, pp. 68-74.

6. N. Lambertz, "Bericht über meine linguistischen Studien in Albanien von Mitte Mai bis Ende August 1916," *Anz. d. Akad. d. Wis. Wien, phil.-hist. Kl.* 1916, Nr. XX, pp. 122-146.

7. S. Mladenov, "Bemerkungen über das Albanische in Nordmakedonien und in Altserbien," *Balkan-Archiv,* 1 (1925), pp. 43-70.

8. G. v. Hahn, "Reise durch die Gebiete des Drin und Vardar," *Denkschriften d. Akad. d. Wiss. in Wien, phil.-hist. Kl.* 15 (1867).

9. P. Bogdani, *Cuneus Prophetarum.* Patavii, MDCLXXXV.

10. Cf. the articles in *Studime Gjuhësore I (Dialektologji),* edition of the Instituti albanologjik i Prishtinës, Prishtinë, 1979, as well as a great number of volumes on folk literature (prose and verse), including Anton Çetta, *Prozë popullore nga Drenica,* I, II, Prishtinë, 1972.

11. Cf. among others W. Cimochowski, *Le dialecte de Dushmani.* Poznan, 1951.

12. L. Mulaku, *Govor albanaca Bajgorske Šalje.* Prishtinë, 1968, p. 65.

13.   P. Ivić, *Die serbokroatische Dialekte (ihre Struktur und Entwicklung).* The Hague, 1958. (Cf. especially "Über die Entwicklung der Mundarten des Kosovo-Resava Dialektes," p. 243.)

Eric P. Hamp

sh(ë)tunë

In order to explain this troublesome name for the weekday Saturday, Petar Skok proposed a progression (see Tagliavini, *l'Albanese di Dalmazia,* with its excellent summary of earlier work at p. 262) *sambata* > **shëmbëtë* > **shumbëtë* > *shtun(d)ë.* This begins reasonably, but the assumed metathesis is poorly motivated, complex, and imperfect. One might perhaps expect on this argument **shëtum(b)ë* or **shëpun(d)ë* or **shútëmbë,* etc. Moroever, conservative Tosk (e.g. Arvanítika dialects), which does not generally reduce *nd,* has *shëtunë.* Therefore Geg *e shtunde* (see S. Dobroshi, *Fjaluer,* Prishtinë, 1953) must be secondary, and *sambata* seems even farther removed than might at first appear to be the case.

True, *saturn-* should give **shëturrë;* cf. *furr(ë)* < *furnus.* Furthermore, **satuvV-* would give Tosk **shëtur-(ë).* Yet the first syllable and the accented vowel of *satúrn-* come closest of all to explaining the configuration of *shëtunë.*

The problem, then, is to explain the final consonantism of *shëtunë.* Spitzer's accusative **shëtutnë* is eminently reasonable, since we must clearly start from a cluster in order to produce a Tosk -*n*-. There is no likely basis for an earlier **-dn-*, **-sn-*, or perhaps (though I suspect quite impossibly) **-kn-*, which are the sole technically acceptable clusters for such an outcome.[1] It is clear to that Spitzer's explanation as **shëtut-* < **septm-tos* is forced, ignores the normal count of days in the week and fails to explain the stressed syllabic.[2]

63

If we assumed that both *satúrn-* and *sambáta* coexisted in early Albanian, a crossing of these could yield **satúta;* i.e. *satú-* could have been
superimposed on *sámbata,* the Balkan form, bringing with it its stressed
syllable. Perhaps too **-ta* (in whatever final form it then took) could have
been misanalyzed as being a reduced form of *ditë* 'day', as seen in *sot ~
sod* 'today'; but see my remarks on this phonological development in
Revue roumaine de linguistique 18, 1973, 333ff. on the subject of *gat.*
However, all of these considerations are very speculative and far-fetched,
especially if they are simply to rescue Spitzer's purely hypothetical
*shëtut-.

The only realistic phonological possibility then appears to be **-nn-*,
and we are led to see, after all, **satúnn-* as the most probable pre-form.
This would have an early accusative **shëtún-në.* The Albanian evidence
forces upon us a regionalism of Balkan Latinity *saturn-* > *satunn-.* As is
well known, the normal expectation in Latin is to find the cluster *-rn-*
preserved. Thus *e sh(ë)tunë* is an important acquisition to our knowledge.[3]

* * * * *

NOTES

1.   Other related clusters which will not yield the required output
here are illustrated by:
pë, pë-ri < **petmo-* : *gjumë* < **supno-*
amë < **odmā*   : *lum* < **lub(h)no-* : *lëng* < **lougno-.*

I discuss these and related matters elsewhere.

2.   See, for detail, my discussion elsewhere of *shtatë* in relation to
the fate of the IE syllabic nasal.

3.   It bears on Kosova, by rejecting the primacy of *e shtundë.*

Albert B. Lord

THE BATTLE OF KOSOVO IN ALBANIAN AND SERBOCROATIAN ORAL EPIC SONGS

From September 1934 to September 1935, I was with Milman Parry in Yugoslavia, with the exception of a few weeks in Greece in the Spring of 1935. In November 1934, Parry collected epic songs in Novi Pazar in South Serbia, and during the summer of 1935 in Bijelo Polje in Montenegro, which had once been in the Sandžak of Novi Pazar. Many of the singers from whom Parry collected at those times were Moslems of Albanian origin; some of them were bilingual in Serbo-Croatian and Albanian. Some of the singers in Novi Pazar came into that market center from the plateau of Pešter, which has a large Albanian population. Its market places are Rožaj on the south, Novi Pazar, Duga Poljana, and Senica on the north and east.

In May of 1950 I collected again in Novi Pazar, to some extent from the same singers, although our chief Albanian singer from the thirties, Salih Ugljanin, was by that time dead.[1] In the 1960s, with David Bynum, I returned to those areas. We collected in Duga Poljana, Senica, and in the center of Pešter at Karajukići Bunari, and at Rožaj. A number of the singers with whom we worked during those years, as before, were of Albanian origin. I have never collected in the Kosovo-Metohija region, but in 1937 I collected in the northern Albanian mountains from Kastrat to Kukës and returned to Lesh.[2]

This is a sketch of my contacts with living Albanian singers of epic songs in Yugoslavia and Albania.

There are three groups of songs of the Battle of Kosovo that I wish to consider in this paper. The first is the "classical" Serbian (or Serbo-Croatian) group, known to most Yugoslavs and stemming from the Karadžić collection, vol. II, and other similar collections. The second group consists of the Albanian texts, of which there are only four or five, the earliest of which is that published by Elezović in 1923. The third group includes songs of Kosovo sung by Moslem singers, especially in the Sandžak of Novi Pazar, and represented by two texts from Salih Ugljanin, one collected by Schmaus and the other by Milman Parry.

Schmaus studied the last two groups first by themselves and then in relationship to each other and to the "classical" group. He came to the conclusion that the Albanian songs derived from the Serbo-Croatian songs of the Moslem singers of the Sandžak. I want to suggest a somewhat different solution to the problem of their inter-relationship, with all due respect to the extraordinary learning and insight of Alois Schmaus. I have myself an unpublished Albanian text which I collected in Tropojë in 1937, and I have included it and Ugljanin's text in the Parry Collection in my investigation; neither of these was available to Schmaus in 1936 when he wrote, or at least published, his key article.

The first task is to sketch what I, and others, mean by the "classical" Kosovo songs, or the main events in the "classical" drama. They would include the following songs in Vuk II:

> 44. Car Lazar i carica Milica (O boju kosovskom) from Tešan Podrugović (204 lines). This tells of the conversation between Lazar and Milica in which she asks for one of the Jugovići to stay home with her. She asks them the next day as they leave, but all refuse to stay behind. Lazar leaves his servant Goluban with her. He takes Carica Milica back to the house, then mounts and leaves himself for Kosovo. The second part of the song tells of two ravens flying from Kosovo and alighting on the tower of Lazar. Milica asks them for news of the battle, and they report. Then the wounded Milutin arrives and reports to Milica of the death of the several heroes, Miloš' killing of Murat, the death of Lazar, and the betrayal of Vuk Branković.

45. Propast carstva srpskoga. Sent by Mušicki to Vuk. From a blind woman in Srem (93 lines). Sveti Ilija in the form of a falcon flies from Jerusalem to Lazar and asks whether he prefers a kingdom of this world or one in heaven. He chooses the latter. The Turks attack Kosovo. The commanders of the Christian forces move their contingents. The poem ends with the betrayal of Vuk Branković and the death of Lazar.

46. Musić Stefan. From an unknown singer, probably from Srem (169 lines). Fearing Lazar's curse, Stefan arrives late at Kosovo. He meets the maid of Kosovo who shows him Lazar's helmet. He enters battle and is killed.

47. Smrt majke Jugovica. From an unknown collector in Croatia (84 lines). This song is not pertinent, as it has no equivalents in Albanian or elsewhere.

48. Carica Milica i Vladeta Vojvoda. From blind Stephanija (53 lines). Milica is walking in Kruševac; Vladeta Vojvoda rides up. She asks if he has come from Kosovo and if he has seen Lazar. He has not seen him, but he has seen his horse; the Turks are pursuing it. She then asks about the nine Jugovići, and Jug Bogdan. She learns that they are dead. She asks about Miloš; Vladeta had seen Miloš leaning on his lance, but it had broken and the Turks were attacking him. By now he has perished. Vladeta had not seen Vuk Branković.

49. Komadi od različnijeh kosovskijeh pjesama. From his father (154 lines). There are five fragments. First (17 lines): Murat came to Kosovo and sent a letter to Lazar. "One country cannot have two masters; you must either send the keys and tribute for seven years, or come to Kosovo and we will decide the issue by swords." Lazar received the letter and wept. Second (16 lines): Lazar swore, "Whoever does not come to Kosovo, may nothing from his hand bear fruit, neither the grain in the field, nor the vine on the mountain." Third (63 lines). The Last Supper and Miloš's commitment to kill Murat. If he returns alive, he will capture Vuk Branković, tie him to his lance, and carry him to Kosovo. Fourth (63 lines): The spying of the Turkish army by Kosančić Ivan. Miloš asks what he found, and Ivan reports. He tells Miloš also where the tent of the Sultan is. Miloš asks him not to give the true report to Lazar. Fifth (15 lines): "Who was

that good hero who cut off twenty heads with one stroke?" "That was Banović Strahinja," etc.

50. Kosovka djevojka. Sent to Vuk by Mušicki from a blind woman of Grgurevac (136 lines). The figure of the maiden of Kosovo who seeks on the battlefield news of her betrothed and his friends and learns from a dying warrior that they have perished is found in multiform in Bogišić 2 but not in the Albanian songs.

51. Jurišić Janko Vuk wrote this down in 1815 in Karlovici from a Bosnian merchant (123 lines). Jurišić Janko screams in prison, and Car Sulejman asks him why. He says he wants to be ransomed, but Sulejman will not do so, but asks Janko about certain heroes. He identifies Marko Kraljević, Ognjane, his sister's son, and the third himself. Sulejman asks what kind of death he prefers. Janko is given an old horse and an old sword, and released to be chased by the Janissaries. A young Turk meets him; Janko pulls the sword, kills him, takes horse and sword and kills the Turks. (Not really a Kosovo song.)

52. Obretenije glave kneza Lazara. Sent to Vuk by Mušicki from a blind woman of Grgurevac (87 lines). When they cut off Lazar's head, a young Turk, son of a Serbian slave woman, took his head and placed it in a spring, where it lay for forty years. One day some caravan drivers going from Skoplje to Niš and Vidin spent the night nearby, built a fire and were thirsty. They went to the spring, and saw a light in it. One of them took out Lazar's head. His body was still lying, uncorrupted, where he had been killed. While the drivers were drinking and not looking at the head, it went off on its own accord to join with the body. The drivers reported this to the church. There were services, and Lazar was finally buried in the church he had himself built, Ravanica.

These are Vuk's "classical" Kosovo songs, to which is sometimes added "Branović Strahinje," which, however, does not really belong there, except that the action takes place in Kosovo.

To Vuk's Kosovo songs should be added those in Bogišić's collection of songs from older manuscripts. Nos. 1 and 2 are *bugarštice* dating from the eighteenth century. They are indeed the only Kosovo songs in Bogišić. No. 1 contains 252 lines, and is the earliest complete epic song of Kosovo. It is not clear whether it is oral traditional or literary.

No. 1 begins with the story of Bušić Stjepan's departure for Kosovo
and his farewell to his wife. He arrives at Lazar's court, and there
comes upon a conversation between Milica and Miloš. Milica reports
on a dream in which the stars fell from the sky to the black earth,
the moon turned black, and the clear sky was split into four pieces.
Miloš interprets this dream as ominous for the Hungarian lords who
have just arrived. Milica asks him to ask Lazar to leave one of the
Ugovići with her when he goes to Kosovo. He refuses, and in a bad
humor Milica asks Lazar for this favor. Lazar too refuses her request.
Lazar then mounted and went to Kosovo and encamped by the river
Marica. There follows the Last Supper scene. Miloš says he will not
betray Lazar on Kosovo but swears he will go to the sultan's tent
and stab him. Miloš then calls his servants, Ivan Milan and Nikola
Kosovčić, to saddle his horse. He goes to the Turkish camp, is an-
nounced to the sultan, who asks him to kiss his knee and right foot.
Miloš stabs him, mounts, and flees. The Turks pursue, but cannot
harm him. A voice from heaven tells them that he wears armor, and
suggests that they should put their swords underneath his horse.
Miloš's right leg is cut off and he takes his spear and uses it as a
crutch. He cries out for help from Lazar. Vuk Branković hears him.
Lazar says he thinks he has heard Miloš's voice (shades of Roland!).
Lazar mounts and goes to help, but the Turks capture him, and Vuk
Branković flees. Lazar and Miloš are brought before the sultan, who
is still alive. The sultan orders that when he had died, Lazar is to be
beheaded, and then Miloš. The sultan is to be buried at Kosovo, with
Lazar at his feet and Miloš at his right hand. When Miloš heard this,
he asks the sultan to bury him at his feet and Lazar at his right. The
sultan agrees. So it was done.

This is the first song with a full connected story. Bogišić No. 2 has 67
lines and is in stanzas with a refrain, a clearly different song from its predecessor.

Milica is walking and comes upon Miloš Dragilović lying in a lake of
blood. He asks whom she had sent to Kosovo. She says she sent
Lazar and Miloš. She does not recognize him at first. He tells her
that Lazar is dead, and asks her to take a kerchief from his pocket in

which he has ducats for his wife, her daughter. He also asks her to
give greetings and to take care of his horse. He dies.

There are five Kosovo songs in the first volume of the *Matica Hrvatska*
(henceforth *MH*) collection, only two of which are of immediate importance, Nos. 58 and 59. They are the longest that we have from tradition
before the twentieth century, the first having 541 and the second 522
lines. The following is a summary of No. 58.

It begins with an exchange of letters between Murat and Lazar, with
a challenge and the acceptance of that challenge; the two leaders
agree to a battle at Kosovo to decide whose will be the empire. Each
then gathers an army by writing letters. Murat's letter writing is general, but Lazar writes to Vukašin, the Doge in Venice, Jug Bogdan,
Miloš, and Vuk Branković; each letter is given in full. The army
gathers. The next scene is the Last Supper. And then Murat's army
assembles and sets out for Kosovo in order to arrive and make camp
before Lazar. When Lazar arrives, the Turks are already encamped.
Lazar seeks someone to spy out the Turkish camp and the lay of the
land for their attack. Miloš suggests Vuk Branković, who does not
take up the suggestion and then says that he will go himself, boasting
that he will kill Murat. Zemljić Stjepan goes with him. They are challenged by guards, who let them through the lines to the sultan's tent.
Miloš enters, says to the sultan "give me your hand," but the sultan
gives him his foot instead. Miloš stabs him, mounts, and flees. When
he and Stjepan are about to escape, Miloš recalls that he had said he
would put his foot on Murat's head, and so he goes back and does
so. As he flees a second time an old woman points out to the Turks
that Miloš and Stjepan are wearing armor and that their horses are
also. She tells them to put their spears on the ground in order to
strike the horses from underneath. This they do. Miloš and Stjepan
are unhorsed and Stjepan is killed. Lazar attacks, sending Vuk to the
edge of the battle, whence he flees to the mountains. He never saw
Kosovo. Miloš is sorely wounded. They bring him to the sultan's
tent. The Turks fight. Lazar too is wounded and captured, but the
others escape. The two wounded leaders lie side by side with Miloš
at their feet. Lazar curses Vuk for having enraged Miloš so that he

has lost his life and for going off to the mountains with his army, leaving Lazar himself with the forces alone in the middle. He then gives up his spirit. Murat, about to die, orders that the two emperors be buried side by side with Milos above them, because he was a hero above all others. Murat then dies, and the Turks kill Miloš. The sultan's orders were carried out.

The two *bugarštice* songs present a fair enough picture of the classical tradition. It is time now to look at the Albanian songs. I know of only three Albanian songs, i.e., in the Albanian language, of the Battle of Kosovo in addition to the one in my own collection: one collected by Elezović and published in 1923;[3] another published in Serbian prose translation by Djordjević;[4] and a third one also in Serbian translation (summary really) by the same author.[5] All of these belong to the Elezović tradition. Schmaus collected another Albanian text,[6] and said that he would give details (and one would have hoped a translation) in another place. I have not seen it. He does say that the singer, Mehmed Sejdia, sang the second part first, then the first part, and only then realized that they belonged together and in the reverse order. I collected a still unpublished text from Ali Meta in Tropojë in 1937, which also belongs in the Elezović camp. That seems to be all that we have of the Albanian (Kosovo) song tradition in the Albanian language, although I suspect that there are more texts in the archives of the Folklore Institute in Tirana.

Schmaus analyzed all these (except mine, of course) in an article in 1936.[7] In addition the Parry Collection has a few Kosovo songs in Serbo-Croatian and those most heavily indebted to Vuk, if not actually straight from him. An exception is that from the Albanian singer, Salih Ugljanin, dictating in Serbo-Croatian, recorded in November 1934. From the same singer Schmaus collected the Kosovo song which he published and analyzed comparing it with the Elezović song.[8] There is a Kosovo song in Serbo-Croatian collected from a Moslem, not necessarily Albanian, singer by Vuk Vrčević in the 1860s in the Trebinje district. It is still unpublished, but I have a microfilm of it.

These then are three unpublished Albanian texts to add to those considered by Schmaus. Do they teach us anything? For a study of my Albanian text below I am depending on an English translation of it by Professor John Kolsti of the University of Texas at Austin. I shall treat it together with the other Albanian songs in the Albanian language.

While the song that I collected from Ali Meta in Tropojë belongs clearly to the Elezović tradition, it has some elements not found in the other Albanian texts. Schmaus has studied the available Albanian texts, as I have said, comparing them with one another and also noting their relation to the Serbian tradition.[9] My text, collected in the fall of 1937, is only a year later than Schmaus's study. His study included a text that he had himself collected in Albanian. From the study (the text itself is not available) Schmaus's text differs considerably from the others he cites.

The first section of all the Albanian poems, including Ali Meta's, contains a dream of the sultan's and its interpretation. The sultan's dream in Ali Meta's song, however, is unlike that in Elezović's, where the sultan dreams of two eagles alighting on his right shoulder, all the stars falling from the sky to the earth, and the moon and the sun falling into the sea. The dream in Djordjević 1 (henceforth D1) has the sultan waging war with many states and the loss of all his commanders. Ali Meta's text (henceforth AM) is closer to this than to Elezović (henceforth E). According to AM, the sultan dreamed that he began a Battle on Kosovo with the enemy, that the men of the Sandžak (?) all died, that the High Priest of Islam, the Grand Vizier and all his sons, also died, and that the foot soldiers caused great destruction. I might comment that the dream in E is a common one, symbolic, and traditional. D1 and AM are more realistic and topical.

In E the sultan's mother interprets the dream—quite irrationally—as favorable. But the sultan summons his four main counsellors and they foretell that he will take Kosovo although he himself will perish. The sultan makes no comment. In AM the sultan summons his priest and Grand Vizier, to whom he tells his dream. The priest says he fears for the sultan's head, but the vizier makes the dream into a good omen. It is not to the sultan's advantage, he says, not to go to Kosovo; the dream is a message from God. (Again this is closer to D1.) The sultan summons his chief counsellors (like E in his respect, except that AM is shorter) to whom he tells the dream. The highest hodza opens the divine books (*božje knjige*) and says to the sultan that the time for war has come. The books are not in Albanian language versions of this song, but they are uncommon in traditional epics, and they are found in Ugljanin's text.

The next element in the songs is the gathering of the army. This is done very briefly in both E and D1. E has the sultan send a telegram to all the cities, saying that he wants all the army and pashas to assemble. They gather and appear before the sultan. D1 has: "He called the commanders and ordered them to gather the army, to prepare cannon and rifles, and to tell the soldiers they were going to war." AM is fuller and unique. The sultan informs all his people and summons them, in three weeks to "make footwear for the poor." (?) Whoever has none will be provided for by the sultan. They are to take their rifles; whoever has none will also be provided for by the sultan. They are to take groshes; whoever has none . . . , and so forth. They will assemble in three weeks in Brus. At the end of three weeks they assemble there. The sultan seeks their support.

At this point in E the sultan takes the prophet's banner, goes before the army, tells them they are going to Kosovo, counts them (70,000) and then says that if any have regrets, if father and mother and children are dear to them, they can go home, and the sultan will pay for their return. Forty thousand leave and thirty thousand remain. In D1 and AM the army proceeds to the sea shore before the testing, which takes place at the shore. In D1 the sultan simply says: "If anyone regrets having come, let him return home, because we must cross the sea." Nobody returns, but all shout that they have come with him of their own will to lose their heads in battle. The sultan then prays and all say "Amin!" In AM when the army has come to the sea shore, the sultan sends a messenger through the camp saying that anyone who has regrets or has been left moneyless because of the purchase of equipment, may go home, because he, i.e., the sultan, has no money with him to repay or pay them. Very few turn back.

Now in all three versions the sultan divides the sea and the army passes over dry land.

Arrived on the other side, the sultan again tests the troops. In E the sultan adds to what he had said before, "If any of you is guilty (unpure) (*aram*) and has not prayed five times a day, I do not want him with me. He is free to return. The battle will not be successful. Return before the sea closes." Eighteen thousand return, leaving the sultan with only twelve thousand. These all swear that they have not eaten anything unpure, nor have they omitted their prayers, and they want to go with him. The sultan and his army say their last farewells to one another. In D1 the sea remains opened for three days. Again the sultan says that anyone who regrets coming may return, but none does. In AM the sultan again sends a messenger through the camp with the same message as before, adding that the sea has not blocked the road. Nobody returns, and the sea rushes back. Once again AM is closer to D1 than to E.

In the second Djordjević text (henceforth D2), after the dream, the sultan orders the crier to go from town to town, along the streets, from house to house, gathering the soldiers.[10] Thus he acquired in a short time twelve thousand volunteers. Then he tested them, by telling them that anyone who did not want to die should go home. They all said they came to die, and since that was so, the sultan gave them cloth for winding sheets. In addition, he said that since they would die they should all be pure, not having done anything impure. They said that they had not. In this shortened version there is no parting of the sea.

In AM the sultan further tests the army by asking whether any had eaten anyone else's food or taken anything belonging to another. One soldier says that he had found an apple floating on the river and had taken only one bite out of it. On the sultan's orders the soldiers found the owner of the apple tree. He would forgive the crime, if he were made *sadrazem* in the army. This was granted, and the march continued.

Ali Meta's version continues to tell that when the army came to Mount Goleš, there was no water and all were thirsty. The sultan prayed and then struck a rock with his hand and water gushed forth. After a rest the armies begins to fight. They came thus to Ferizović, where a big battle was going on. Later, at Priština, they encamped, and the sultan looked out at Čičovica with seven towers. They were all locked. Then the sultan wrote a letter to Miloš demanding keys and surrender. This is where Part One ends.

In the first part of the Albanian song there is little, if anything, which is also found in the Serbian tradition. The sultan's dream seems at first to be an exception, but his dream is not like Milica's dream as found in Ugljanin's Kosovo song—and in the Serbian tradition. So far then, the traditions, i.e., the Albanian language and the Serbo-Croatian traditions, are independent of one another. In the Serbian songs there is no parting of the seas, no striking water from a rock, nor fighting at Skoplje or elsewhere on the way to Kosovo, and no testing o the army by the sultan.

The second part of the Albanian songs is, as has been noted by all, a song of Miloš. It begins when the sultan's army has arrived at Priština and the sultan sends a letter to Miloš Kopilić (E) asking for the keys to the cities and for surrender. In D1 (D2 does not go beyond the first part) the letter is sent to Lazar and Miloš, asking them to surrender. In AM it is sent to Miloš and asks for the keys, tribute for nine years, or else there will be a continuation of fighting. In E Miloš receives the letter, his wife asks what it says, he tells her, and she says, "Do not worry, the sultan cannot do anything." Miloš in anger strikes her and knocks out eight teeth. Then he mounted his horse and went to the King in Peć. He told him that the sultan was at Priština and wanted a fight. The king said it was better to surrender, because they could not fight. Miloš said that he would never surrender until he had tried him out (*proburazim*). D1 simply says that they answered that they would not give themselves into the sultan's hands, but would fight. AM is different from either E or D1. Miloš was troubled by the letter and went to the king's wife, who said she had never seen him so troubled by a letter. He told her what was in it, and added that he had not the forces to stop the sultan. The king's wife said to send him the keys and tribute. There was no shame in it, because the sultan was father of all peoples. Miloš was ready to do just that.

At this point in E the king suggests that they send thirty maidens to test the Turkish army, which they do. D1 has the battle begin on the field of Kosovo. They fought three days and three nights without ceasing. Many fell, including the Shehislam and the Sadrazem. Again the sultan wrote to Miloš to ask if he wanted to surrender. All were ready to surrender, but Miloš wanted to make one more trial, to find three maidens to test the Turkish army. In AM Avrame Begolli suggests that Miloš not hurry about sending the keys. He says that they should send thirty girls to test the Turkish army. In all texts the tests are roughly the same and the results indicate that the Turkish army is strong and ready, not corrupt. In E nobody takes the money they have, and, although they are evidently dying of hunger, nobody gives them bread. When the sultan hears that, he tells his people to give the girls bread, but not to take their money. In D1, after three days, the girls are tired and hungry and they leave the army and go to the baker, Djoka, who sells them bread. In AM they go to Vučitrn to Gjoka the Baker and offer to buy bread, but he gives it to them free.

Miloš tells the girls (E) that he will cut off their heads if they give a favorable report to the king. They should say that the Turkish army is tired and wants to die, that they had taken hold of them and had taken their money. And thus they report. In D1 the girls return to Car Lazar in Peć. Actually Lazar and Miloš go out to meet them, and they tell the

(king) and Miloš how things were. When they hear this, all still want to surrender, but Miloš want to make one more trial. This varies, of course, from
E in that a true account is given rather than deceit by Miloš. AM is closer
to ·D1 than to E. In it, when Miloš hears the girls' report, he assembles
all the men and they are all sad for three days and three nights. Then Miloš
decides on another action. Only E has the deceitful report.

The spying and testing expedition into the Turkish army is a constant
in both the "classical" and Albanian traditions. Vuk's No. IV tells of Kosančić Ivan and Toplica Milan's report to Miloš of their spying, and Miloš
tells him not to give Lazar the true report. There is no spying in Bogišić
No. 1, but *MH* No. 58 has spying suggested, and Miloš accepts the task,
which he turns into his expedition to kill the sultan. The form of the
thirty maidens (or three) seems limited to the Albanian texts so far in our
investigation.

The next episode in all texts, Albanian and "classical," is the killing of
Murat by Miloš. There are only three points of variation. The first is
whether Miloš was announced to the sultan beforehand or not; the second,
is whether the sultan offered his hand or foot, and the advice he received
as to which to do, while the third concerns Miloš's return later to the sultan's tent to put his foot on Murat's head.

Miloš is announced to the sultan in E and that officially by the guards.
In D1 and AM the situation is somewhat different. In the first Miloš suggests that they all go to the sultan and offer him their hands. He will go
last. If the sultan offers his hand, he will take it. But if he offers his foot,
Miloš will stab him with a poisoned knife. When they approach the sultan's tent, the army makes way for them. When he hears that the Serbs
are coming, Murat calls together his hodzas and commanders. AM is somewhat like this, but not quite. Miloš says that he will go to Murat. If he offers his hand he will become a convert, if he does not offer his hand he
will "plunge a dagger into his stomach." Miloš then puts armor on himself
and his horse. The news comes to the sultan that Miloš is coming. As can
be seen, our second point has already become merged with the first.

The second point was whether there was discussion about the offering
of the hand or foot. In E, when the guards announce to the sultan that
Miloš is coming, the sultan asks the Shehislam whether he should give Miloš
his hand if he seeks it. The Shehislam advises him not to give his hand but
his foot, "so that he will remain forever under your feet." The sultan then

gives orders for Miloš to be admitted. When Miloš comes in, the sultan lifts his foot, and Miloš stabs him and leaves. In D1 the sultan asks his hodzas and commanders whether he should offer the Serbs his hand or his foot since he has been told that Lazar and Miloš are coming. The hodzas say his foot, because Muslim faith does not allow Christians to kiss the sultan's hand. The sultan smiles a little at that, but says: "So be it! Miloš will stab me with a poisoned knife. See to it, that you catch him!" Miloš was the last to come in. The sultan offered his left foot. Miloš took it in his left hand, took out a poisoned knife with his right hand, and split the sultan open. He died immediately, and Miloš began to flee. In AM, when the sultan hears that Miloš is approaching, he says that he will rise to his feet and hold out his hand to him. But someone (Shehislam?) said: "Why rise to your feet?" Miloš arrived, dismounted, took off his cloak, and went in. The sultan stretched out his foot, and Miloš took out his dagger and stabbed him in the stomach. The sultan died on the spot. Milos went outside, mounted and began to fight. Note that in both D1 and AM the sultan dies immediately. As most of the time, AM agrees with D1.

The third point had to do with Miloš returning to put his foot on Murat's head. This element is not found at all in the Albanian texts.

Since Miloš's killing of Murat is not found at all, strangely enough, in the Vuk texts, we must go next to Bogišić No. 1 to observe what it does with our three points. In it the Turks announce to the sultan that Miloš is before his tent and he is admitted. Miloš says that he has left Lazar's army and come to help the sultan. The sultan says that it is their law that he kiss his knee and right foot. As he bends over to do this, he stabs the sultan. As for the third point, Miloš "returns and presses him with his foot" (1. 172). In *MH* No. 58, Milos is not announced to the sultan. He makes his way to the tent, and tells the Arabs at the door that he is seeking service with the sultan, and they open the door for him.

Miloš entered and told the sultan he wanted to talk with him and asked him to give him his hand that he might kiss it. Without a word the sultan offered his foot for Miloš to kiss his boot. Miloš seized the foot, held the other foot down with his own , and split the sultan asunder. Miloš knocked over the tent on top of the sultan and the Arabs, mounted his horse and with Zemljić Stefan cut his way out of the Turkish army. Then, however, he remembered his boast, returned through the whole army to the sultan's tent and trod on the dying potentate. This element, as we shall see, is missing in Ugljanin's text.

Our third group of Kosovo songs is from Moslem Albanian singers in the Sandžak of Novi Pazar, as represented by Salih Uglijanin. Salih's song (Parry Collection No. 650) was dictated to Nikola Vujnović on November 14, 1934 and has 800 lines. It is the longest of the Kosovo songs being studied for this paper. The following account of it is written with the foregoing analyses of the "classical" and Albanian traditions of Kosovo epics in mind.

Like the Albanian songs Salih's Kosovo version begins with a dream. Whereas in them the dream is the sultan's, in Salih's case the dream is Milica's. She arose from the dream, and in answer to Lazar's question she said she had had a bad dream. In the dream the sky had broken, the moon had fallen to earth on Kosovo, the stars had fled, including the day star and two little day stars; it was all bloody. A mist had fallen on Kosovo. Two ravens flew from Kosovo and came to Kruševac; they had flown around their tower and broken the golden apple. The dream is interpreted disastrously. That the sky was broken meant that the Turkish sultan was coming from his capital to Kosovo; that the stars had fled meant that the poor people would flee; that the day star had fallen all bloody—the day star was Milica, and she would become a young widow, and her children orphans—they were the two little day stars; that a mist had fallen on Kosovo meant that the sultan's army would meet them there; that two ravens had flown from Kosovo meant that the sultan's messengers would bring a firman to Lazar in Kruševac.

As we noted, a dream is found also in the Albanian songs, but in them it is Murat's dream and it is different from Milica's. Such dreams as Milica's are common enough in Balkan tradition. They do not necessarily "belong" anywhere, but can be used wherever they are appropriate. Actually Milica has a similar dream in Bogišić No. 1, our earliest *bugarštica* Kosovo song.

The firman which now comes from Murat to Lazar challenges Lazar either to bring keys and tribute for seven years to Kosovo or to gather an army and decide the question of who will be emperor by war. Lazar's priest advises him to summon his vojvods to gather an army and come to Kruševac. He sends out letters and his vojvods assemble with their forces at Kruševac. The leaders all come for dinner. The last to arrive is Miloš, whom Lazar greets as *"vera i nevera."* Thus the Last Supper episode, completely absent from the Albanian songs, begins among the Albanians, though in Serbo-Croatian language, in Salih's Novi Pazar version. However, the assembling of an army does follow the interpretation of the sultan's dream in E. The structure of E, i.e., a dream plus the gathering of an army, is followed, as it were, by Salih until the peculiarly Serbian Last Supper episode.[11] It is worth noting that Salih gathers Lazar's army with the same technique that he uses in other songs: letters, description of arrival, leaders being taken to the chief's tower.

The vojvods now hold council as to what answer to give Murat. Miloš hotly says he will not surrender; he will never become a "raja." Vuk Branković suggests the testing of the sultan's army by sending three hundred (it was three or thirty in the Albanian song) girls to go into the army with all kinds of wares and with Toplica Milan, dressed as a girl, at their head. If the army is good, it will not even look at the girls nor buy any of their merchandise. This incident is Albanian, but Toplica Milan is in the Serbian tradition. It is elaborated in typical Salih fashion.

When the sultan hers that the girls are coming to his camp, he gives orders for tents to be set up with portable kitchens and that the girls be treated like guests. This scene is like the greeting of wedding guests in other of Salih's songs. The "guests" are given permission to go wherever they want. After fifteen days, during which they have sold nothing, Milan asks permission to go back. The sultan orders that the treasury be opened and that Milan be given a hundred ducats and each girl thirty. So the spies return to Kruševac. Lazar looks out of the window and sees them coming. He tells the vojvods. When Miloš hears this, he asks permission to go to meet them. He meets the girls and Milan and tells them to give a deceitful report. And so it comes about. This intervention by Miloš is found also in E, although not as elaborately done.

After his episode of spying, Lazar gets his army together, and they move to the city gate. Salih gives the order of their march as he is accustomed to do in other songs. At the gate is Milica, and now an episode from the "classical" tradition is inserted again. Milica seeks someone to stay home with her. The episode is developed as in the Serbian songs.

When the army of Lazar arrives at Kosovo itself and sees the Turkish army, it is amazed and disappointed. Lazar sends a letter to Murat asking if the time has come to fight; the answer is yes. The sides are lined up, and Lazar asks who will start first. Miloš says he will, but asks Lazar not to let anyone go until he goes to the sultan's tent and kills him. When Lazar sees what happens to him then he can move the army to attack. This is somewhat like E, but there is no question of whether the sultan will offer hand or foot, or any of that element present in Salih's song; at least not quite yet.

It is announced to the sultan that one of the Serbs is coming. Murat says to admit him, but Čuprilić tells him not to give him his hand but his foot; let the Vlasi be under his feet. Miloš entered, the sultan offered his foot, Miloš took it, put his hand into his boot, pulled out a handžar, and cut the sultan open "*od ućkura do grla bijela.*" Then he went to the door, mounted his horse, and passed through the army. None could harm him.

Follows then the episode with the old woman. This is the usual story. She advises them to place their swords on the ground and cut the horse, because he is wearing armor. They separate him from his horse, beat him and bind him. He asks for the old woman to be brought near. He wants to tell her where he has hidden his treasure, so that she can tell his mother; she reminds him of her. He seized her by the nose with his teeth and hurled her half an hour away. She burst into pieces. The Turks took off his armor and beheaded Miloš. The sultan was still alive. There is nothing particularly new here. There are no reapers with scythes, no keys in Miloš's moustaches, as in E. But, as in E, the Turks kill Miloš immediately after the old woman incident. In AM the old woman suggests putting her scythe(s) in front of the horse, which they do, cutting off the horse's legs at the hooves. Otherwise AM is much the same.

In Bogišić No. 1 there is no old woman, but a voice from heaven informs the Turks that Miloš and his horse are wearing armor and will kill them all. It advises them to put their shields and swords in front of the horse. When his own leg is cut off, Miloš uses a spear as a crutch. The voice from heaven, the amputated leg, the crutch are not in Salih's version, nor any other that I can recall. Nor, as described earlier, is the calling of Miloš on Lazar for help, nor Vuk Branković's deception of Lazar when he hears the voice, a scene reminiscent of the *Song of Roland.* Although they have some few points in common, e.g. the armor and the placing of swords before the horse, points, indeed, shared by most versions, in this episode there is no influence one way or another between the tradition represented by Bogišić No. 1 and Salih's song.

An old woman is found in *MH* No. 58 (and in *MH* No. 59 also, where she is "baba Urisava"), but among the texts being considered her fate is told only in Salih and in the Albanian tradition. There is, however, a fascinating intermediate version between Bogišić No. 1 and the Albanian songs, which is found in the Ilić Collection from Slavonia (!), given in summary in the notes to *MH* Nos. 58 and 59. This section of the song is actually quoted in full, not summarized. In it an old woman, calling out from a guard house, gives the usual advice to the Turks pursuing Miloš. When Miloš hears her, he turns his horse, catches the old woman, and dashes her to the ground. From the earth where she landed springs forth water, which becomes the river Marica, which flows across the plain of Kosovo.

It seems to me most unlikely that this Slavonian version represents an original form of the episode, which penetrated south through the Sandžak to the Albanian singers. I find the opposite direction of flow, if flow there be, to be the more credible. Part of it appears to be an aetiological legend about the origin of the Marica, a local Kosovo tale, akin to other such in the Albanian tradition.

To continue with Salih's text, the sultan gives his people orders to treat the raja well, he girds his sword on Ćuprilić, who will pass it on to Pajazit. This element is, I believe, original with Ugljanin. The Turks then tell him what happened to Miloš. The story is repeated to the sultan as it was told to us, including the conversations. But to that story is added the tale of Miloš taking his head, after it was cut off, and carrying it to the river Lap, a half hour away, where a girl and her mother were washing clothes. One woman says to the other: "Here is a headless hero; run, he is carrying his head in his arms!" Miloš cursed them and they became blind, and Miloš himself fell dead to the ground. This incident is in E, but not in AM, which ends after the incident with the old woman, by telling that Sultan Mehmet (sic) was told of Murat's death, that he came to Kosovo, that he was told everything that had happened, and he built a bridge in honor of the old woman. It is still called The Old Woman's Bridge.

Murat then praised Miloš as a hero and ordered that a church be built for him and that he be buried in it. He ordered the bridge over the River Lap to be called "Babina Ćuprija." Then he ordered that he be buried in Brusa, but that monuments (*turbeta*) be placed for him on Kosovo and in Seljanika, where they are to take his "*drob.*" So was it done. The church appears also in E. It is built marvellously before the crowing of the cocks, and healing water was found in that place.

Now the battle begins on Kosovo. The Serbian army attacks. Vuk Branković goes first, but he does not wish to enter the battle. Jug Bogdan attacks and kills two pashas; then he perishes. Then general battle. Twelve vojvods perish and also Car Lazar. Visoki Stefan rose early to depart for Kosovo. His mother asked when to expect his return, and he said when the sun rises in the west. When he came to Zvečan a Bulgarian girl met him. He asked what was happening on Kosovo. She said that in the morning the Sitnica was carrying only turbans, but since noon only Christian hats. He went along the river and noted the caps of the Jugovići and of Lazar, finally that of Miloš. He came to Vučitrn and then attacked and he and his men were all killed. The Turkish army went to Zvečan, and then to Lazar's tower at Kruševac. They razed it and Milica fell to the Arabs, who led her off to Arabia. They crossed all Serbia and made raja of its people, and went to Belgrade. Visoki Stefan is Salih's version of Mušić Stefan. This is all from Serbian tradition rather than from Albanian (and the Bulgarian girl is a multiform of Kosovka devojka).

We have surveyed the "classical" Kosovo tradition, the Albanian tradition and a representative of the Sandžak tradition. It is fair to ask once again in conclusion what the relationship may be among them. It seems to me that the "classical" tradition and the Albanian tradition emerged more or less independent of one another. The first has a large mixture of church influence—this is obvious—and some relationship to early chronicles, both of which argue for a certain degree of "literary" influence from the earliest times right down to the nineteenth century. The Albanian tradition of epic songs is in part derived from aetiological legends of the Kosovo region and some religious legends known to the Moslem singers, e.g., the parting of the sea and the water from the rock. The Sandžak song of Salih is a mixture of both traditions. Salih Ugljanin and Ćor Huso[12] were in a position to know and absorb both traditions and to form a "new" song using elements from both. It is true, however, that there are some "Albanian" elements, such as the thirty girl spies and the old woman of the bridge, which are also found in the northern songs. Cultural exchanges did not move only in one direction along the trade routes and administrative interchange between the north and the south. The important thing was that they met in the Moslem populations in the intervening territories, especially those of Albanian origin in the Sandžak, thus creating a new, strong, tradition of epic song.

NOTES

1.   In 1951 I collected again in Novi Pazar and Bijelo Polje, with Miloš Velimirović, Branislav Rusić, and Mrs. Lord.

2.   Lord Collection of Albanian Songs in the Milman Parry Collection, Widener Library, Harvard University.

3.   G. Elezović, "Jedna arnautska varianta o boju na Kosovu," *Arhiv za arbanasku starinu, jezik i etnologiju,* 1 (1923): 54-67.

4.   T. Djordjević, *Naš narodni život,* Knjiga 10 (Belgrade, 1934), p. 50.

5.   T. Djordjević, "Iz arbanaskog narodnog predanja," *Prilozi proučavanju narodne poezije,* 1 (1934): 188-189.

6.   *Prilozi* 3 (1936): 74-75.

7.   "Alois Schmaus, "O kosovskoj tradiciji kod Arnauta," *Prilozi* 3 (1936): 73-90.

8.   A. Schmaus, "Kosovo u narodnoj pesmi muslimana," *Prilozi* 5 (1938): 106-21.

9.   See note 7.

10.   See note 5.

11.   For a comparison of E and Ugljanin's song see S. Skendi, *Albanian and South Slavic Oral Epic Poetry* (American Folklore Society, Philadelphia, 1954), pp. 61-67.

12.   A famous Montenegrin rhapsode.

Arshi Pipa

SERBOCROATIAN AND ALBANIAN
FRONTIER EPIC CYCLES

The frontier song is a special kind of epic song shared by South Slavs and Albanians. The former are Moslems of Bosnia, Herzegovina and Montenegro while the latter are Moslems of Kosova and Catholics living in the Albanian Dinaric Alps. The name "frontier song" is not an invention of scholars. South Slavs called these songs *krajišnice,* meaning frontier songs, and the Albanians call them *kângë kreshnikësh,* "songs of heroes," *kreshnik* (also *krashnik*) being the Albanian form of *krajišnik.* The songs are accompanied by a monochord instrument played with a bow, which is called *gusla* in Serbocroatian and *lahutë* in Albanian.

The frontier epic songs originated in Northern Bosnia, spreading southwards until they reached Albania, the limit there being roughly the basin of the Drin River. The geographic centers of the cycle, Udbina and Velika Kladuša, are found in Northern Bosnia. A borderline zone between Northern Bosnia and Croatia, the so-called *krajina (krahina* in Albanian) became a battleground between Moslems and Christians when the Turks occupied the Balkan peninsula. Bosnian frontier songs are pro-Turkish, and they exalt exploits of Moslem Bosnian heroes fighting against Christians, especially Croatians and Hungarians, then under Austrian rule. The main heroes are Mustabeg of Lika, Djerzelez (Djerdjelez) Alija, the brothers Mujo and Halil Hrnjica and Tale of Lika. Christian South Slavs, Catholic or Orthodox, have their own epic songs, which glorify heroes fighting the Turks

and Moslems in general—guerrilla songs of bandits (*hajduci*) and raids by
sea pirates (*uskoci*) having their stronghold in Senj.

The frontier songs sung in the Albanian Dinaric Alps focus on the two
brothers Mujo and Halil as well as Mujo's son, Omer—one can thus speak
of a Mujo family cycle. These songs, which can be called rhapsodies also
because pagan mythology is conspicuous in them, are neither for nor
against the Turks, although anti-Turkish accents appear occasionally. They
are shorter than their South Slavic counterpart. Other formal differences
exist. South Slav songs are unrhymed, whereas the Albanian rhapsodies
alternate rhymed and unrhymed lines. The line is trochaic decasyllabic
in both. But in the Albanian rhapsodies, the line fluctuates between the
decasyllabic and the octosyllabic, the national Albanian line.

The striking feature of the Albanian rhapsodies is that songs in praise
of Moslem heroes are sung by Catholics. Not only does this raise questions about the kind of Catholicism of these people, but it also presents
the paradox of Albanian songs exalting heroes who are Slavs. For Albanians and Slavs have not been good neighbors. In more recent times, when
nationalism has flared up in the Balkans, the relations between the two
peoples have been characterized by distrust and hostility.

Moslem Bosnian songs were not the first to be collected. In Vuk Karadžić's monumental collection, not many of them appear. The reason for
such neglect is that these songs are pro-Turkish. Moslem Bosnians identified with the Turks. Moslem Herzegovinians kept their distance. Moslem
Albanians maintained an even farther distance, as evidenced by the rebel-
lions of the Bushatli of Shkodër, that of Ali Pasha Telelena, and the pea-
sant insurrection in Southern Albania during the Tanzimat period (1847),
to mention only the most important anti-Turkish events prior to the
organized nationalistic movement of the League of Prizren (1878-1881).

The standard collection of Moslem Bosnian songs is that by Kosta
Hörmann.[1] Distinguished scholars such as Matthias Murko, Alois Schmaus,
Luka Marjanović et al., have written competently about them. A significant contribution was the publication in 1953-54 of the first two volumes
of the series *Serbocroatian Heroic Songs* by Milman Parry and Albert B.
Lord.[2] Four more volumes in that series have appeared so far. They all
contain Moslem heroic songs. The Parry and Lord collection also includes
a considerable number of Christian epic songs. The priority of publication
given to Moslem songs is explained by the more genuine nature of the

texts, unaffected or least affected by published versions (the publishing of heroic songs in South Slav countries and territories before World War I had become a sort of national contest).

The second volume of *Serbocroatian Heroic Songs* contains Bosnian songs from the Sandžak ('precinct') of Novi Pazar, a region which was under Turkish domination from the Ottoman conquest of the Balkans until the annexation of Bosnia by the Austro-Hungarian empire. Parry was eager to learn how themes, formulae and metric forms travel from one nationality to another. In Novi Pazar he found Albanians who could sing in both Serbocroatian and Albanian. He could experiment with these singers and see how translation from one language to the other functions with illiterate singers of tales.

This may be the reason why of the five Novi Pazar singers four are Albanians: Salih Ugljanin, Djemal Zogić, Sulejman Makić and Alija Fjul-janin. By far the most interesting of them is Ugljanin, an old man at the time Parry met him. Besides knowing a number of Albanian songs, some of which he sang for Parry, he had—so he said—a repertoire of one hundred Bosnian songs. A study of his texts reveals an unusual talent for combining themes and formulae and arranging them at will. Whereas other singers repeat and at best elaborate on an oral text, Ugljanin recreates it, amplifying or abbreviating according to his mood or whim. Parry was fascinated by him and kept asking him all kinds of questions, mostly through his Yugoslav interpreter, Nikola Vujnović, also a singer. Salih was a mine of information: he had traveled a good deal, fought in several wars (of which he was proud), done all sorts of jobs during his long life, and was still working in his old age "with his brain," i.e., as a counselor and a mediator. During the Greco-Turkish war of 1897, he composed a song about it while in the trenches. He was familiar with both Albanian and Montenegrin epic songs. One of his masters had been a Kolašin singer, Ćor Huso. Ugljanin's legends and myths are no less significant than his songs. One of them is about Djerdjelez Alija throwing his mace from the top of a mountain in the Sandžak. The mace flew over Kosovska-Mitro-vica and the hero marked the place where it fell by writing, in Turkish, on a boulder: "Up to here is Bosnia, farther on Kosova." Salih had seen the boulder, before it was removed by the Austrians. He hates the Austrians, the Russians, the Christians in general. His songs in "Bosnian" (Salih never says "Serbian") are in the Moslem Bosnian tradition as far as religion is concerned, i.e., pro-Turkish. Comparison of his texts with Albanian Catholic texts reveals the presence of many characteristically Albanian motives and themes. A song such as "Mujo Hrnjičić and Captain Dojčić," which is, according to Lord, unique in the Parry collection, is simply a Serbocroatian variant of an Albanian rhapsody, "The Abduction of Mujo's Wife" in the Franciscan collection of Palaj and Kurti.[3] Ugljanin's legend of Mujo's strength is basically the same as the legend in a rhapsody in the same collection. His preferred hero is not Djerdjelez, the legendary Bosnian hero, but Mujo, the Albanianized Mujo who, together with his brother Halil, is omnipresent in Ugljanin's songs, just as in the Albanian tradition. According to Salih, Mujo was born in Kolašin, whence he moved to Bosnia, his father having married the sister of a Bosnian hero. But Kolašin to Ugljanin does not mean Montenegro; it means Bosnia and even Albania, the Kolašin region having been part of the Vilayet ('governorship') of Kosova in Ugljanin's youth.

Albanologists such as Nopsca and Ippen report that the Bosnian wedge reached as far as Gusinje whose inhabitants were bilingual.[4] The Albanian frontier zone where the Albanian frontier songs developed ran all along the Turkish-Montenegrin borderline, from the Krajë district on the Shkodër Lake northwards up to the Vermosh mountain, to turn then eastwards in the direction of Gusinje and the Pejë (Peć) highland, and from there to run northwards up to the Pešter region in the western part of the Novi Pazar Sandžak. Ugljanin, nicknamed Pešterac, told Parry that his parents had settled in Ugao, coming from the Shkodër region. Ugljanin's tales about Mujo's origin, as well as his own, trace the borderline zone along which the frontier songs traveled. Albania and Bosnia are in his mind a geographical continuum, as illustrated by his myth of Djerdjelez throwing the mace. Mary Edith Durham found that North Albanian tribes have preserved memories of their emigration at some time in the past from Bosnia and Herzegovina.[5] According to Carlton Coon, that time goes back to the fifteenth and sixteenth centuries,[6] which is the period when the Bosnian frontier cycles came into existence. The Harvard anthropologist, who visited North Albania in 1929-30, found that the Bosnian phenotype is extant among Albanian highlanders. Archeological findings in the cemetery of Glasinac near Sarajevo and in that of Koman near Pukë in Northern Albania show striking similarities in skeletons and artifacts.

In the rest of this article, I shall present the results of my research on the Albanian frontier cycle, preceded by a paragraph on the status of research on this subject.

The Albanian frontier songs, usually referred to as the Mujo-Halil cycle, have been studied by Albanian as well as non-Albanian scholars. The first to undertake a systematic collection of North Albanian heroic songs was the Franciscan Father Bernardin Palaj, assisted by another Franciscan, Donat Kurti, who devoted himself to the collection of folk tales. Because of the pagan elements contained in the Mujo-Halil cycle, they thought that the rhapsodies of that cycle were very old, tracing them back to Illyrian times. This thesis was formulated in the preface of their collection *Kângë kreshnikësh e legènda* (Heroic Songs and Legends), published in 1938. The pages devoted to the Mujo-Halil cycle in Ernest Koliqi's doctorate thesis repeat the Franciscan thesis of the Illyrian substratum.[7] Eqrem Çabej abode by the same thesis in the last pages of his youthful monograph on the genesis of Albanian literature, adding some judicious observations on the heroes' names.[8] An essay by Fulvio Cordignano, an Italian Jesuit teaching at the Shkodër Jesuit College, considers various aspects of the question (origin, mythology, customs, metrics) rather from a Catholic viewpoint.[9] Maximilian Lambertz, an expert on Albanian mythology, elaborated on the Illyrian thesis in the linguistic and cultural notes following his German translation of a selection of Franciscan rhapsodies.[10] A serious attempt to compare Albanian and Bosnian frontier songs was made by Stavro Skendi in his doctoral dissertation.[11] Agnia Desnickaja found fault with Skendi's "genetic" thesis that the cycle was an "elaboration" of the Bosnian cycle in such a way as to become "a truly Albanian cycle."[12] Desnickaja's own thesis is that Albanian heroic poetry is more archaic than the Bosnian, as shown by the Albanian themes, simplicity of topics, and the large use of mythology. According to her, Mujo originated in the Albanian tradition.[13] Qemal Haxhihasani maintains that the Turkish (meaning Bosnian) influence represents an external and superficial layer affixed to the content and form of the Albanian cycle, which developed in a zone close to the coast line. He points out the specific traits of the Albanian cycle: educational function, presence of nature, the hero as shepherd, and absence of the idea of foreign conquest.[14]

With the exception of Cordignano who relied on his own collection, all the other scholars based their theories on the sole Franciscan collection.

Apart from the fact that the texts in this collection have often been edited, something the authors themselves note in their preface, the collection is highly selective, made with the preconceived idea of showing that which is characteristically and genuinely Albanian. The rhapsodies come from singers most of whom live in a rather impervious zone, the Nikaj region, which has been less affected by Bosnian influence. They are the very best the Albanian genius has produced, superior in poetic power even to Gjergj Fishta's *Lahuta e Malcís* (The Mountain Lute), an epic considered by North Albanians as their representative monument. In the Cordignano collection the selective criteria are less apparent, also because the collection concentrates on only one singer, the famous Gjergj Pllumbi. Comparison between these two collections shows that rhapsodies with the same motive and themes have often a different treatment: the heroic, one could say Homeric, ring of the texts in the Franciscan collection is tuned down in Pllumbi's texts, where the heroic borders at times on the mock-heroic.

Both these collections contain rhapsodies sung only by Albanian Catholics. But the Albanian frontier songs are also sung by Albanian Moslems. Already in 1934, Schmaus advanced the thesis that the Albanian epic song of the Kosovska-Mitrovica surroundings, called *kraina,* is a continuation of the Moslem Montenegrin *krajišnica.*[15] In 1952, a collection of Kosovar heroic and frontier songs appeared.[16] The songs, not surprisingly, have a strong Islamic ring while, surprisingly enough, Mujo in them is less conspicuous than in the Catholic rhapsodies. The artistic value of the collection is slight. But that is not a reason to disregard it. A picture of the Albanian frontier cycle that ignores the Moslem component results mutilated and distorted.

In 1937, Lord traveled to Northern Albania searching for heroic songs. The result of his search was a collection of 115 epic songs, half of which are frontier songs. The singers are both Catholic and Moslem, with a slight prevalence of the latter. The Moslem songs come for the districts of Gusinje, Pejë, Bityç, Bicaj, Pukë, i.e., from Kosovar districts and contiguous North Albanian ones. Heroes and themes are not quite the same as those in the Catholic rhapsodies. The role of Halil is often taken by Ali Bajraktari. "Ali Bajraktari and Begije Devojka," sung by Ukshin Ismaili (from the Bityç district) takes place in far-away lands and deals with sea monsters. The song numbers 617 lines. The themes of the song and its length place it in the Bosnian-Albanian tradition, as represented by Ugljanin.

This is also the case with the gifted singer Ali Brahimi from Vûthaj (Gusinje). His "Ali Bajraktari" has 1,041 lines, his "Sirotin Alija" 2,163 lines. In "Ali Bajraktari and the Queen of England," sung by Ali Meta from Isniq (Pejë), a main theme is the capture of a foreign city, a theme alien to Catholic rhapsodies, but recurrent in Bosnian songs. In Ali Meta's text, just as in Bosnian songs, Mujo is fighting for the Sultan, at the orders of the Vizier Çuprili, a Bosnian hero in Bosnian songs (the Köprülü were an Albanian family). Meta's "Ali Bajraktari and Captain Rustem" numbers 900 lines, in regular decasyllabics, which is not the case for most of the Albanian rhapsodies showing metric irregularities. In the Moslem songs in the Lord collection, slavophobia is stronger than in Catholic rhapsodies, compounded as it is with Islamic fervor.

A *first conclusion* is that only collections such as the Lord collection, which includes both Catholic and Moslem songs, are truly representative of the Albanian frontier cycle, whereas the others are only partially so.

My *second conclusion* is that the Novi Pazar songs sung by Albanian singers, as found in the Parry and Lord volumes, are closely related to Kosovar songs. The Novi Pazar songs link together the Kosovar songs with the Bosnian frontier cycles.

A *third conclusion,* derived from the first two, is that the Albanian frontier cycle is tripartite as well as bilingual. We are faced with a frontier cycle that manifests itself in three components in two languages: Moslem Bosnian-Albanian in Serbocroatian, Moslem Kosovar in Albanian, and Catholic Albanian in Albanian. The first component is mostly a Slavic cultural phenomenon, considering the language in which it is expressed. But language alone does not exhaust culture, which is defined by an ensemble of other ethnic features such as religion, laws and customs, ways of living, historical traditions and folklore in general. Differences are bound to occur when the same epic material travels from a nationality to another, from one religion to another. The differences found in the Catholic Albanian component and in the Moslem Kosovar component are conspicuous. But we should not lose sight of the affinities, too.

Let us consider, as an example, the concept of *besë* (pledged word) in the Moslem Bosnian-Albanian component. The Albanian *besë* appears as "Turkish *besu*" in the texts of Makić and Fjuljanin. I quote from the latter: "Znaš ti tvrdu besu u turćina./Što je reko, porekao nije" (You know the inflexible *besë* of the Turk./ What he said, he never will take back") (The Captivity of Četić Osman Bey, *SJP:* 151-52). Here "Turk" means Moslem; in the first line, *"besë"* has a religious coloring. But the second line defines the concept exactly as do the Albanians, be they Moslems or Christians, i.e., by abiding to the pledged word. Except for the name of the heroes and various elements related to material culture, Fjuljanin's song praising Četić Osman Bey's faithfulness differs in no way from an Albanian rhapsody in the Franciscan collection, "Ali Bajraktari [or] Besa." The ethical substance is the same. The texts of Ugljanin and the other Albanian singers in Serbocroatian contain several Bosnian cultural features besides toponomy and onomastics: feudalism, polygamy, sensuality, the Sultan cult. Except for the latter, the other elements are usually absent from Kosovar songs while being totally alien to Catholic songs. They represent a layer of Turkish civilization superimposed on the older social structure as mirrored in the customary North Albanian code of ethics, the Code of Lekë Dukagjini. Traditional Albanian virtues such as *besë*, honor, *burrni* (manliness and magnanimity combined) hospitality, family solidarity, respect of women and elders, but also traditional vices such as abduction of women, the implacable vendetta, preying on the neighbor, the fierce instinct of domination—all these ethical elements are found to a greater or lesser degree in the texts of Ugljanin and the other Bosnian-Albanian singers. Strangely enough, a scholar such as Cordignano could not find traces of the customary code in the texts he collected. The best part of Skendi's study shows that a main difference between the Bosnian and the Albanian frontier songs is ethical in the sense just explained. The major difference, however, the overwhelming role of pagan mythology in the latter, escaped him. Desnickaja is right when she notes that Skendi's study is based on affinities rather than differences. Whereas the Moslem Bosnian songs are feudal heroic, the Albanian rhapsodies are pagan heroic with overlaid and inlaid Bosnian elements in its essentially Albanian structure *(fourth conclusion).*

At times even these alien elements are missing. The most beautiful rhapsody in the Franciscan collection, "Gjergj Elez Alija," is a legendary epic-lyrical song, without the slightest trace of Bosnian influence. This is true not only for the rhapsody's theme, the rather characteristically Albanian love between brother and sister, but also for the name of the hero. Gjergj is an Albanian name, the Slavic form being Djuradj (Djuro)—the national Albanian hero is called Gjergj Kastrioti. Elez and Ali are Moslem names, common to both Bosnians and Albanians. But Gjergj Elez Alija is a tripartite name, a usual way of naming people among North Albanian tribes. The custom of the tripartite name does not exist among South Slavs.

In another Franciscan rhapsody, "Mujo's Wedding," the Zânë, the Albanian oread, petrifies people by blowing breath into them. Mujo subdues the Zânas by capturing the three ibexes in which the Zâna's strength lies. The ibex functions here as a totem. The verb for petrifying is *ngrafisë*, an obsolete word that has long disappeared from Albanian speech. The close of the rhapsody sounds very much like a charm—and magic songs are the oldest songs. The rhapsody is about Mujo's marriage to the king's daughter. The wedding escort is composed of three hundred paranymphs, dressed in golden arrays, bound for Jutbinë (Udbina). These are the Bosnian incrustations on the primitive pagan myth. Not even these incrustations (except for the Jutbinë toponym) appear in another rhapsody, "Mujo's Strength." There the hero acquires superhuman strength by suckling the breast of a Zânë. The story of Mujo and the Zânë is also told about the Serbian hero Marko Kraljević and the Bosnian hero Djerzelez Alija. The song about Djerzelez and the Vila, the Slavic counterpart of the Zânë, is found in a Herzegovinian song.[17] In a legend told by Ugljanin, Djerdjelez is said to be a native of Nevesinje in Herzegovina.[18] An Albanian settlement, Burmazi (from Alb. *burrmadhi* 'big man'), located in the district of Stolac, is not far from Nevesinje.[19] Considerations such as these must have led Desnickaja to state that Mujo comes from an Albanian tradition. The legend of Mujo and the Zânë is then of Albanian origin? One thing is certain: the Vila does not petrify as the Zânë does. And petrification in the Albanian rhapsodies is organically related to her dwelling-place, the rocks of the *bjeshkë*, the Albanian Dinaric Alps. The ubiquitous *bjeshkë* in the rhapsodies is a mythological topos, in keeping with the mythology of the characters. Mythology is not what characterizes Bosnian epic songs.

Çabej, probably influenced by De Rada, conceived of Albanian rhapsodies as relics of an Illyrian poem shattered to pieces by the Slavic invasion. The pieces were then elaborated in various South Slavic cycles, from which the Albanians took them: a case of cultural *reconquista*.[20] Haxhihasani referred the cycle to the medieval period in which the Balkan nations began to take shape, emerging from the Byzantine matrix.[21]

Desnickaja rejected the thesis of the Bosnian priority of the cycle, maintaining that Bosnians, Herzegovinians and Albanians developed it at about the same time while fighting together as Turkish soldiers in the Lika borderline region.[22] Her hypothesis is fascinating. But how can it be proven? And how many Albanians were Moslems at the end of the fifteenth century or the beginning of the next, when the songs were born? Schmaus suggested that the Albanians adopted the Bosnian songs when Montenegrins, fighting against the pashas of Shkodër and those of Herzegovina, developed their own frontier cycle.[23] This begins to make sense, based as it is on historical evidence while also being philologically sound in abiding by the semantic field of the technical term *krajišnica = kângë kreshnikësh,* by which the cycle is designated.

This is not to say that some Albanian frontier songs did not exist before the beginning of the nineteenth century. Songs as well as legends and myths do not recognize political borders, they travel from a country to another without having to ask for a passport. Yet a special kind of song becomes a national institution not only by way of mere imitation. Historical conditions must exist that are conducive to its formation. For frontier songs to arise, a frontier situation must exist. It remains to explain that situation.

When Montenegro, instigated by Russia, began causing problems for Turkey, those who bore the brunt of the Montenegrin offensive were mostly Bosnian and Albanians along the border zone. These people, peasants and shepherds, were threatened with losing their lands and their lives. A rhapsody in the Franciscan collection, "Basho Jona," illustrates what happened: an old man solicits Mujo's assistance, offering him money, to punish a Slav who has invaded his pasture lands. The example suggests that the cultural problem under consideration must be envisaged in an economic-political context.

The Kosovars were devoted to the Sultan, whom they called "(our) Father King," almost as the Bosnian Moslems. Religion and politics to the Kosovars were more important than language.[24] Since they were all Ghegs and overwhelmingly Moslems, they were not pressed to identify as an ethnic group by language, as was the case with the Albanians in the homeland who were divided by regional and confessional differences. The adoption by them of the Bosnian songs was facilitated by their language attitude. A Bosnian-Kosovar alliance against Christian Montenegrins was

cultivated by the Turkish administration, with the Turkish language serv-
ing as a *trait d'union* between "Bosnian" and Albanian (Turkish words
abound in both Bosnian and Albanian songs, including the Catholic
rhapsodies). In such cultural-political climate, the Moslem Bosnian frontier cycle was transplanted onto Albanian soil. The transplanter was the
bilingual singer. He was not always an Albanian. Matthias Murko mentions
as bilingual Reso Hadžic from Herzegovina.[25] A tradition of Albanian
singers in Serbocroatian existed before Ugljanin became the central figure
in it. He told Parry that he learned a song, "Halil Hrnjičić Rescues the
Daughter of the Vizier of Travnik," from the Albanian Hamza Alibasić
from Suhi Do in Pešter some fifty years before the song's dictation
(1934),[26] when the singer was an old man. Ugljanin also told Schmaus
that a man in his family, Pam-Zuku, could sing Bosnian songs, accompany-
ing them with the *lahutë*.[27] And Rexhep Zeneli from Trestenik (Pejë
district) told Lord that he had listened to Ćor Huso sing in both "Bosnian"
and Albanian, and that he had learned a song, "Halil Captures Captain
Ivan" from him.[28]

While this information allows us to infer that a tradition of Albanian
singers in Serbocroatian existed in the second half of the nineteenth century, not even this much can be said about the North Catholic Albanian
rhapsodies. The various Austro-Hungarian intellectuals and scholars who
visited Northern Albania in the first decade of the twentieth century are
silent about the existence of frontier songs and heroic songs in general.[29]
When, in 1863, Hahn went up the Drin River on a boat, departing from
the Shkodër surroundings, he was accompanied by a Catholic priest,
Engjëll Bardhi (Angelo Bianco) from Bardhaj in Gash (Kosova). The priest
told him a tale about Marko Kraljević, but none about Mujo.[30] It is hardly
conceivable that Hahn, the father of Albanology and an eager collector of
everything concerning Albania (while in Mat, he traveled to a village only
to meet an old man who knew, he was told, a song on Scanderbeg) showed
no interest in North Albanian heroic songs.

Edith Durham devoted to Albania and Albanian culture most of her
life. In her first book on the Balkans, she tells how she met the Gusinjan
Gjoka Vučović in Andrijevica, a Montenegrin village on the Turkish border.
"'Art thou Christian or Mohamedan?' he was asked when his 'visitors'
form' was being filled. He looked up lazily from the bench where he was
a-sprawl, and 'By God, I know not,' was all the reply he vouchsafed."[31]

In the evening there was singing around a bonfire.

> They [the Montenegrins] sang of Kosovo and of the Servo-Bulgarian
> war and of the border fights of the neighborhood. The song ended
> often in a yell of triumph. . . . Djoka, the man from Gusinje, took
> his turn and varied the subject of song by singing the sorrows of a
> Turkish woman whose husband the Montenegrins had killed. He sang
> in a clear high voice, and manipulated the gusle more skillfully than
> any other man I have heard . . . . The Montenegrins retorted with a
> similar song in wich the conditions were reversed.[32]

In her next book, Miss Durham writes pages on the Nikaj tribe, where
she was obliged to stay longer than she had planned because of the swollen
leg of her Albanian guide. She describes their customs and ways of life,
dwelling on a shooting party during a religious holiday. She does not mention heroic songs heard by her in this district from which originate the
most beautiful rhapsodies in the Franciscan collection.[33] In her scholarly
book, the result of her lasting research on the Balkans, she mentions and
even quotes Montenegrin and Serbian heroic songs.[34] But there is nothing
about Albanian heroic songs.

Argumentum a silentio can be misleading. Another eminent Albanologist, Lambertz, who visited Albania in the next decade, included in his
collection of Albanian folk tales one on Djerdjelez Alija, another on the
brothers Mujo and Halil as well as a frontier song on the wounded Mujo,
a variant of which appears in the Franciscan collection.[35] And in the preface to his own collection of North Albanian epic songs, Prennushi states
that he did not include songs on the brothers Mujo and Halil because he
considered them translations from Serbocroatian.[36] Was the silence on
frontier songs by Austro-Hungarian authors and perhaps even by Miss
Durham herself motivated by political considerations? The *Drang nach
Osten* policy of the Habsburg Empire favored the creation of an Albanian
state barring the Serbs from reaching the Adriatic Sea. The Albanian frontier songs, no doubt, existed. The question is how old they are.

One of the arguments advanced by Lambertz to prove the antiquity of
the Franciscan rhapsodies is that weapons there are mostly primitive:
sword (but no shield), lance, mace, arrow (but no bow). Primitive weaponry appears in folk tales, too, wherefrom they could have been borrowed.

The presence of primitive weaponry only proves the existence of a tradition. Because one writes a poem on Achilles' shield, that does not mean that the writer is living in heroic times.

The decisive argument is of linguistic pertinence. The language of the Albanian frontier songs contains only exceptionally an obsolete word, or a magic formula, or a worn-out hardly intelligible expression, valid criteria ascertaining the antiquity of a text. And as to the metrics of the Albanian frontier songs, its decasyllacbic line is very often an octosyllabic filled with paddings to meet the norm.[37] The phenomenon strongly suggests that the Albanian bard has not yet mastered the *deseterac* and his ear is not yet accustomed to that alien line. The verse must therefore be of recent origin. How recent exactly?

In 1878, Bosnia-Herzegovina was occupied by the Austro-Hungarian Empire. The modification of the Balkan map after the decisions of the Congress of Berlin made Pešter a borderline zone, suitable for the development of frontier songs. One of the Novi Pazar bilingual singers, Djemal Zogić, originating from Rugovë, told Parry that Albanian (frontier) songs were still being sung in that region. Rugovë is located in the Pejë highland which borders on the Plavë and Gucî districts, whose inhabitants were bilingual, as already seen. The Bosnian Albanian and the Kosovar frontier songs must have developed in a bilingual zone along the modified Turkish-Montenegrin borderline, with Pešter and Gusinje at is extremities, at a time when these districts were part of the Vilayet of Kosova (*fifth conclusion*). When Bosnia-Herzegovina went to the Austro-Hungarian Empire, the Novi Pazar Sandžak was included in the Vilayet of Kosova, together with the Sandžak's western part constituted into a separate sandzak, that of Plevlje. In the thus reduced Novi Pazar Sandžak, 65 percent of the population was Albanian.[38] Ugljanin told Parry that in his youth he sang only Albanian songs; only later he learned how to sing in "Bosnian." This must have been in the days when Bosnian songs were being "translated" into Albanian. Ugljanin sang them mostly in Serbocroatian. The Gusinjan Ali Brahimi, belonging to the next generation, sang them in Albanian.

Now it was precisely Gusinje who started the fight against Montenegro when the Congress of Berlin assigned the town to that principality. The most popular leader of the League of Prizren was Ali Pasha Gucîa, judging from the many epic songs on him. In his *Mountain Lute,* Fishta has him eradicate an oak tree to demonstrate his strength. Similar tests of strength are attributed to Mujo in the rhapsodies in the Franciscan collection, where the very name Mujo means powerful to the highlanders. And since Gusinje borders on Shalë in Dukagjin, whose dialects its shares, one is led to conclude that the transplantation of Bosnian songs onto North Albanian soil was mediated—though not exclusively—by Gusinjan bards (*six conclusion*). But once those songs were appropriated by Albanian Catholic highlanders, they had to undergo a radical transformation under the action of a different language and religion, oral poetry and its metrics, mythology and customary law. The outcome was a new type of frontier song, something between legendary epic and hajduk songs, an original recreation of the North Albanian highland genius.

We can now answer the question of the temporal rise of these rhapsodies. They are quite recent, they coincide with the rise of Albanian nationalism inaugurated with the League of Prizren; they are the expression of the naive nationalism of the North Albanian highlanders (*seventh conclusion*). While it is quite possible that some frontier songs have been sung in North Albania and Kosova before that date, the bulk of them, i.e., those collected by the Franciscans as well as by Cordignano, are no older than the two last decades of the nineteenth century.

Arisen at a time when Russia was enlarging Montenegro at the expense of North Albanian territories while Turkey could rely only on the Albanians to maintain what was left from the Ottoman dominion of the Balkans, the Catholic highlanders originated frontier songs in which the enemy is Slav and the heroes are Turks. The difference of religion did not bother them much, their Christianity having always been epidermic. Their brothers in the Dukagjin Plateau had converted *en masse* to Islam. And they themselves had no qualms to give in marriage their daughters to the bordering Moslem tribes, who "paid well."[39] Durham writes:

> Nikaj believes itself pre-eminently Christian. But nearly every member of the tribe drops his baptismal name and calls himself by a Turkish name—Seid, Suliman, Hussein, etc., though they hate the Turks. . . . Shala, like Nikaj, is very found of Turkish names.[40]

The anti-Serb policy of the Austro-Hungarian Empire must have been a strong factor for exacerbating the highlanders' slavophobia. The Empire exercised the right of *Kultus-Protektorat* over the Catholics of Albania, and the Albanian Franciscan fathers who officiated to the Catholic tribes were both very nationalistic and austrophiles. It was a Kosovar Franciscan, Shtjefën Gjeçov, who inspired younger members of his order to collect the North Albanian folklore. Bernardin Palaj, who devoted himself to collecting heroic songs, was a poet as well as a priest. A study of his poetic production, compared with his manuscript collection of rhapsodies would be most important to determine how far he has altered the songs he collected. More reliable as to textuality are the collections of Cordignano, and Lord. A study of the frontier songs must begin with them.

The fact that Lord could not publish his Albanian collection makes excusable Albanian and foreign scholars who have ignored it. But they should have paid more attention, one thinks, to available collections, such as the Kosovar collection (1952) and the Parry-Lord volumes with the Novi Pazar songs (1953-54). Consideration of these two works alone change the existing picture of the Albanian frontier songs and epic songs in general. That picture is a partial one. It excludes not only the Kosovar and the Novi Pazar collections, but also the Cordignano collection.

From what has been said, it would follow that study of the Albanian frontier cycle must be considered systematically, on the basis of all existing collections, as well as comparatively, with reference to South Slavic collections. The study should begin with a philological investigation of the texts collected, in order to ascertain their textuality, something taken for granted so far, and it should proceed with a critical examination of each collection in chronological order. The examination should bear on formal elements (language and metrics) as well as motives and themes, in close relation with the socio-political situation. Aesthetic reflections will come last.

This is hardly something to be achieved by an individual; it requires contributions by specialists in various fields. An Institute of Folklore is the competent body to undertake the job. Such an institute exists in Tirana and another is taking shape in Prishtinë. Let us hope that a change of climate in both capitals will create propitious conditions for a truly scientific study of the Albanian frontier songs, immune from nationalism and sectarianism and in the spirit of democratic internationalism.

* * * * *

NOTES

1. Kosta Hörmann, *Pjesme Muhamedanaca u Bosni i Hercegovini,* 1-2, 2nd ed., Sarajevo, 1933 (1st ed., 1888-89).

2. *Serbocroatian Heroic Songs.* Collected by Milman Parry, edited by Albert B. Lord. Vol. 1, Novi Pazar: English Translations. Harvard University Press and Serbian Academy of Sciences: Cambridge and Belgrade, 1954. *Srpskohrvatske Junačke Pjesme.* Skupio M. Parry, uredio A. B. Lord. Vol. 2, Novi Pazar: Srpskohrvatski tekstovi. Srpska akademija nauka i Harvard University Press, Beograd i Kembridž, 1953. Abbreviated as *SHS* and *SJP* respectively. A review article on these two volumes is Arshi Pipa, "Rapsodi albanesi in Serbocroato," (*Atti del IX Congresso Internazionale di Studi Albanesi:* Palermo, 1982), pp. 371-408.

3. Bernardin Palaj and Donat Kurti, *Kângë kreshnikësh e legenda.* Tirana, 1938.

4. Franz Nopcsa, *Aus Šala und Klementi* (Zur Kunde der Balkanhalbinsel. Reisen und Beobachtungen 11. Sarajevo: Kajon, 1910), p. 76. Theodor A. Ippen, *Die Gebirge des nordwestlichen Albaniens* (Abhandlungen der K. K. Geographischen Gesellschaft in Wien, vol. 2, No. 1, 1908), p. 4.

5. Mary Edith Durham, *Some Tribal Origins and Customs and Laws in the Balkans* (Allen and Unwin: London, 1928), pp. 18-34.

6. Carleton Coon, *The Mountains of Giants* (Papers of the Peabody Museum of American Anthropology and Ethnology. Harvard University, 1950), pp. 44-45.

7. Ernest Koliqi, *Epica popolare albanese.* Gruppo Universitario Fascista: Padova, 1937.

8. Eqrem Çabej, "Per gjenezën e literaturës shqipe," *Hylli i Dritës,* 1938, pp. 647-61, and 1939, pp. 8-15, 84-93, 149-80.

9. Fulvio Cordignano, *La poesia epica di confine nell'Albania del Nord.* Venezia, 1943.

10. Maximilian Lambertz, *Die Volksepik der Albaner.* VEB Max Niemeyer: Leipzig, 1958.

11. Stavro Skendi, *South-Slavic and Albanian Oral Epic Poetry.* American Folklore Society: Philadelphia, 1954.

12. Ibid., p. 202.

13. Agnija Desnickaja, "Mbi lidhjet boshnjako-shqiptare në lëmin e poezisë spike," *Gjurmime albanologjike. Folklor dhe etnologji,* 1977, p. 58.

14.   Qemal Haxhihasani, "Recherches sur le cycle des *kreshnik*," Studia albanica (1964) 1:215-21; "Questions d'étude comparée de l'epopée héroique," *Studia albanica* (1966) 2:215-25.

15.   Alois Schmaus, "Volksepik in der Umgebung von Kosovska-Mitrovica (Ibarski Kolašin, Kosovo, Drenica)" in *Zeitschrift für slavische Philologie* 11 (1934): 432-39—now in *Gesammelte slavistische und balkanologische Abhandlungen* 1 (Trofenik: Munich, 1971), p. 74.

16.   *Kangë popullore të Kosovë-Metohis 1. Legjenda dhe kangë kreshnikë.* Ed. V. Dančetović. Mustafa Bakija: Prishtinë, 1952.

17.   V. Vrčević, *Hercegovacke narodne pjesme.* Cited by Lord in *SHS*, p. 366.

18.   *SHS*, p. 398.

19.   Nikola Vujnović, Parry's interpreter, is from Burmazi.

20.   "Per gjenezën" (see n. 8).

21.   "Recherches" (see n. 14).

22.   "Mbi lidhjet" (see n. 13).

23.   A. Schmaus, "Die balkanische Volksepik," *Zeitschrift für Balkanologie,* 1962; now in *Gesammelte* 2 (see n. 15), p. 42.

24.   A certain lack of sensitivity to the problem of language was manifested in later times. In 1968, the Kosovars, who are Gheg-speaking, adopted the basically Tosk literary Albanian before Tirana itself decided to make it official in Albania. They did this for mere political reasons, with the naivete characterizing young state formations whose rash decisions, motivated by immediate political gains, my turn out to be detrimental to lasting national interests.

25.   Cited by Lord in *SHS*, p. 416.

26.   *SHS*, p. 398.

27.   A. Schmaus, "Beleške iz Sandžaka I," in *Prilozi proučavanju narodne poezije* 5 (1958), p. 276.

28.   Lord Collection of Albanian Songs in the Milman Parry Collection, Widener Library, Harvard University.

29.   The reference is to the following authors and works: Karl Steinmetz, *Eine Reise durch die Hochländergaue Oberalbaniens. Zur Kunde der Balkanhalbinsel. Reisen und Beobachtungen 1.* Hartlebens: Vienna, 1904; *Ein Vorstoss in die nordalbanischen Alpen. Zur KB.RB 3.* Hartlebens: Vienna, 1905; *Von der Adria zu dem schwarzem Drin. Zur KB. RB 6.* Kajon: Sarajevo, 1908. Theodor A. Ippen, *Skutari und die nord-*

albanische Küstenebene. Zur KB.RB 5. Kajon: Sarajevo, 1905; *Die Gebirge des nordwestlichen Albaniens.* Abhandlungen der K. K. Geographische Gesellschaft, vol. 7, Vienna, 1907; Erich Liebert, *Aus der nordalbanischen Hochgebirge.* Zur KB.RB 10. Kajon: Sarajevo, 1909.

30.   Georg von Hahn, *Reise durch die Gebiete des Drin und Wardar. (Denkschriften der K. Akademie der Wissenschaften. Phil.-Hist. Classe.* vol. 15, Vienna, 1867), p. 69.

31.   M. E. Durham, *Through the Lands of the Serb* (Arnold: London, 1904), p. 293.

32.   Ibid., pp. 297-98.

33.   M. E. Durham, *High Albania.* Arnold: London, 1909.

34.   M. E. Durham, *Some Tribal* (see note 5), pp. 133-35, 257, 168.

35.   M. Lambertz, *Albanische Märchen (und andere Texte zur albanischen Volkskunde).* Akademie der Wissenschaften in Wien. Linguistische Abteilung: Vienna, 1922.

36.   Vinçenc Prennushi, *Kangë popullore gegnishte.* Sarajevo, 1911.

37.   See Arshi Pipa, *Albanien Folk Verse: Structure and Genre.* Albanische Forschungen 19. Trofenik: Munich, 1978. Chapter, "The Rhapsodic Line."

38.   Peter Bartl, *Die albanische Muslime zur Zeit der nationalen Unabhängigkeitsbewegung* (1878-1912). Harrassowitz: Wiesbaden, 1968, p. 63.

39.   Durham, *High Albania* (see n. 33), p. 210.

40.   Ibid., pp. 208 and 215.

Hartmut Albert

KOSOVA 1979, ALBANIA 1980.
OBSERVATIONS, EXPERIENCES, CONVERSATIONS

The following account is not the result of observations and inquiries systematically designed according to sociological principles with its goal the comparative study of two related cultural spheres, which nevertheless are developing differently in many ways. Instead the comparative aspect was added later by the author because the possibility of a contrastive study of visits following each other so quickly came as a surprise and could scarcely have been anticipated. Another reason is that such an analysis was not the primary goal of the two visits. The trips were motivated above all by philological studies, i.e., work on a lexicographic project encompassing all the Balkan languages. This work required empirical research on the latest linguistic developments in Albanian and collection of lexicographic materials not available in Heidelberg.[1]

The description which follows is limited to impressions gathered in the empirical manner described above; it does not incorporate information from other sources. The author has consciously accepted the somewhat fragmentary nature imposed on the study by this methodology: not all of the thematic complexes dicussed in connection with Kosova have parallels in Albania and vice versa.

Residence and Personal Contacts. A journey to Kosova seemed the quickest, most promising, indeed, the only accessible way to achieve the goal stated above. A scholar from the University of Prishtinë helped to engage an elementary school teacher from Pejë, who was free at that time, as a private tutor and instructor. Throughout the visit, which lasted several weeks, the author lived with the teacher's family and participated fully in the domestic life and outside contacts of the host family. In the course of the visit there were contacts especially with the following groups of people: the family's relatives from a rural milieu, scholars and journalists in Prishtinë, a Catholic priest and members of his parish, and tradesmen and merchants in Pejë.

The four-week visit to Albania at the invitation of the Academy of Sciences was organized differently, but it too was exceptionally personal in character. (As far as we know, this was the first visit of this type since the war by a scholar from the Federal Republic of Germany.) The author used the visit primarily for the study of Albanian lexicography.[2] First, the visa for a single visit brought the necessary mobility. Then, the hospitality, whenever it was explicitly sought; the willingness to engage in conversation; and the access to material and study space at the National Library and at the Institute for Language and Literature at Tirana were exemplary. Naturally, there was no possibility of direct participation in a family setting as in Kosova. In many respects, however, residence in the Hotel Dajti, rich in traditions and apparently the preferred meeting place especially of the Albanian academic and artistic elite, offered compensation for the less intimate setting because all sorts of informal contacts could be arranged at the hotel.

A linguist and historian of the younger generation were always available as companions, conversation partners, instructors, and mediators for further contacts. People were available for detailed and, in part, very intensive discussions (detailed and intensive because they took place in small groups and scarcely had an official character). The author held such discussions with the President of the Academy, leading linguists and historians, the junior members of these two disciplines, teachers and instructors, guides in museums, directors of vacation resorts for workers, public service staff in libraries, factory workers, sales personnel in book stores, athletes and spectators at soccer stadiums, drives on car trips through the country, etc.

There were also opportunities for serious discussion with scholars, businessmen, etc., from other countries, especially from Kosova (historians, teachers, physical education students).

Naturally, here the author's insight into domestic life, the structure of families or the role models between various family members, was not what it had been in Kosova. In Albania impressions of family life were gathered indirectly through conversations about families or piecemeal through observations of families in public settings.

The Pre-Visit Image of Kosova and Albania of A "Non-Albanologist" from the Federal Republic of Germany. In light of the impressions and information synthesized later, the author finds it tempting to venture a brief look back at his own level of information and the outline of his impressionistic image before he decided to visit Kosova. The results can be described metaphorically as "nebulous" and "dark."

The role of "Albanians in Yugoslavia" had barely entered into the author's Yugoslavian observations, presumably because he approached them from the discipline of Slavic Studies. Despite previous journeys through Kosova and areas bordering on Albania in Montenegro and Macedonia, since this area was for the most part closed, Albanian settlements had never become obvious. To name just one example: Peć remained a place symbolic of South Slavic history; the alternative form of the name, Pejë, was not taken into consideration.

The author's image of the Albanian homeland was admittedly just as nebulous. True, fleeting speculations had emerged during previous visits to Lake Ohrid while the author looked from St. Naum across to the "inaccessible" shore. These suppositions amounted to little more than an image of a predominently rural, patriarchal, conservative society, unfamiliar in its Oriental tendencies and with pronounced martial characteristics. Certainly the image reflects childhood readings of Karl May's works.

In contrast, the Kosova region was associated with initiatives toward a modern industrial society much more often than was the Albanian homeland.

A random sampling of academic acquaintances from various disciplines in the Federal Republic of Germany indicates that the author's knowledge of the two areas prior to his visits can be viewed as typical. This poll allows one to draw the conclusion that information about Kosova and Albania is all but non-existent here—except among scholarly specialists and a small group of Marxists favoring the Albanian political system.

Surprisingly, when the author questioned Yugoslavian scholars, friends of his, in the Croatian area in 1981, the results revealed a level of awareness not significantly better. Indeed, the topic of Kosova and Albania seemed to be alarmingly taboo here. As soon as these names were mentioned, voices were lowered and the topic was changed as quickly as possible.

Society's Perception of Itself. Thoughts on the "Relatives" in the Other Country. The global impression which follows will be preceded by a statement made by an Albanian colleague during a conversation with the author. The gist of the quotation is almost diametrically opposed to the author's impressionistic view depicted above: "Kosova," the speaker said, "that is Albania thirty years ago"! Such pronouncements can be understood only to a limited degree as expressions of euphoric pride in one's own technical progress, even if this aspect cannot be completely overlooked. Evidence for this thesis includes the significance of the Permanent Exhibit on Albanian Industrial Production and Technology at Tirana, pride in certain manufacturing centers, success in exporting oil and electricity, etc. The Albanian speaker both knew the basic outline of the economic problems in Kosova and was just as aware of the current technological deficiencies in his own land.

To a greater extent, the proud tone in this Albanian's quotation stems essentially from his appreciation of the social system and collective political and social awareness which developed in Albania after the Second World War. This system, in comparison to that of Kosova's society, was perceived as progressive. From it the Albanians in their native land derive a self-confidence, which is apparently associated with modernity. This is reinforced by irritating remarks regarding a particular genre of literature which presents the Albanians primarily as wild and warlike even though the depiction refers to a much earlier historical period. In reference to Karl May one speaker said, "He describes us like the Indians!" A further source of the progressive self-esteem of this Albanian contact was apparently the successful implementation of a national state of far-reaching sovereignty and development of a unified sense of national feeling. The reform movement for the standardization of the Albanian written language and the enlightenment campaign carried on in connection with it are not to be underrated in this context. This factor was particularly evident in conversations with Professor A. Kostallari. The spontaneous reaction of an official to the question whether he was a Gheg or a Toskë serves to underline the significance of the thought about national unity. The question was posed naively for purely philological purposes. Apparently the linguistic perspective of the question never occurred to the speaker when he answered in a friendly but determined manner: *Unë jam shqiptar!* And with that he dismissed this topic.

Such a serious basic stance, of course, does not rule out feelings of local patriotism. These came to light among speakers from various cities in the country. For one it was pride in the cultural tradition of his hometown Korçë; for another, the Shkodran, it was an appreciation of his fellow citizens' talent for comedy or of the soccer team. Without the least bit of reservation the locals joked about certains speakers of dialects.

The progressive self-esteem of Albanian society, in so far as it is represented in the author's contacts, is based on the perception that the Albanians have achieved a basically rational social order, in which elements hostile to progress, such as existed in Albania's past, have been eliminated. Such elements limiting progress are still present to a great degree in Kosova, such as a high birth rate, patriarchal family structure, influences of the various religious communities, especially the clergy; factors militating against national unity and self-realization include the lack of a strategy to enact social equality and a national foreign determination.

Turning to the conversations with contacts in Kosova in an effort to formulate an initial overall impression, it is not possible to sift out a similar compact social awareness with an analogous, well-defined goal. Latent uncertainty about the role of a national group in the Yugoslav alliance and about the potential for self-realization in it appears to be the principal factor inhibiting Kosova, but at the same time uncertainty about the role which the Albanian homeland can play in this "national" self-realization is a contributing factor. A student at Pejë, who had just taken his exams, but who saw no chance of finding a position in Kosova polemicized in a conversation against the "capitalistic system in Western Europe controlled by the U.S.A." and praised the Albanian system. But, when he expressed his intention to work in the Federal Republic of Germany, I asked him "Why don't you go to Albania?" His somewhat uncertain answer was, "They won't take us."

The thesis which Reuter suggested for discussion on the possibility of a "Piedmont Idea" for the Albanian nation cannot be confirmed among the Kosovan Albanians—at any rate not through the personal experience of the author.[3] If among the Albanians of the native land the slogan "pas çlirimit"—always repeated even in the literature—is used for the great historical ceasura (that is, after the liberation from the German occupation), then the counterpart to it in Kosova would probably be the much more modest *"nakon Rankovića,"* which often occurred in the conversations. This usage reflects a very modest expectation of national self-realization, and expectation tied to a certain resignation.

Images of Cities and Streets. Public Life. A Sense for the Present and a Change in Traditions. To the extent that they can be compared in their significance, public function, and their position in the consciousness of the population at any given time, the largest cities, in particular, in Kosova and Albania have experienced a very different development. Here, as there, people have their preferences. Pejë was the most popular residential city in Kosova for the people with whom the author spoke. Many scholars employed in the comparatively more sober Prishtinë would prefer to live in Pejë, even if this meant a long distance to work. And, as for Kosovo-Mitrovica with its frightful smog-index, one may work there as an engineer, but live elsewhere—if one can afford to.

In the same way the Albanians in their native land have their "inner" preferences. Korçë has probably remained the secret capital even to this day. Of the Albanian cities I became familiar with it exuded the most intensive atmosphere as a residential city. An Albanian colleague told me, "When one wanted to travel in the 'wide world' in earlier days, one went to Korçë."

Social goals and apparent minute planning, even in the area of population growth in individual cities, sketch upon the face of Albanian cities more and more individual features. Here one can not conceive of an uncontrolled expansion of the central cities such as can be noted on the Balkan peninsula and in Yugoslavia—to a lesser extent in Kosova on account of its poorer economy. For example, people I talked with knew exactly the projected figures for population growth in Vlorë, once construction would begin on a new international harbor; or for Shkodër, which, after Tirana, is expected to become Albania's second city with a population over 100,000. It will expand as a commercial transfer center once it becomes part of the European rail network and as an industrial city when it increases mining. People I talked with were also aware of obstacles to be overcome, for example, expansion and renovation of the canal system in Shkodër. The cities in Albania now seem to be much more orderly thanks to this precise planning. There neither hectic construction frenzy nor gigantic, vast projects are visible. The only modern residences with more than five stories which I can recall are the hotels in the largest cities of the country.

The most striking, most salient difference in the appearance of cities in Albania and Kosova is probably based on two other characteristics: on the one hand a drastic reduction of sacred buildings, especially mosques; on the other hand, a phenomenon which could be expressed as "the loss of oriental character." The *çarshia* (market), the traditional residential and work center, and the bazaar are losing their function. A scene like that in Pejë, where on many a day almost the whole city is transformed into one huge marketplace with so many people crowded together that drivers in their cars just have to give up, belongs to the Albania's past. Small marketplaces can still be found. Traditional bazaars are being scaled down and updated. In Krujë, for example, the bazaar has preserved the character of a little boutique city. Through the transformation the original charm of these centers of communication has naturally been lost to a great extent; yet the people with whom I spoke scarcely understood this. People were amazed at my curiosity about and pleasure in the bazaar in Korçë, which is still operating in part though it will be renovated.

Among other things the reason behind this loss in the function of the bazaars is the drastic reduction of the private sector. (It is legal to culti-vate only a small area surrounding one's own home or to raise animals for one's own need. Any slight excess can be sold at the market only at the binding prices determined by the state.)

As these changes take place, the function of the market is now being taken over by small to medium-sized stores (not by department stores). These are well supplied with food and clothing goods. (In this respect there is no need to avoid comparison with the countries of Comecon.)

The "de-orientalization" of the cities has its parallels in Albania in the noticeably negative attitude towards all Turkish (Ottoman) influ-ences. This phenomenon is latently noticeable in Kosova too, but it does not appear nearly as often in actual practice. An example of this trend in Albania is the tendency to emphasize eradicating Turkisms as part of the language reform and the effort to "recapture the purity of the Albanian language." But there also appears to be a certain prejudice against using the Turkish language in scholarly contexts. A well-known Albanian historian explained—with what the author perceived to be a certain measure of stubborn pride—he had learned all the important languages, but he had an interpreter for Turkish. A young historian from Kosova revealed a similar inner dislike.[4]

The impression outlined above is reinforced as mosques cease to be part of the character of the Albanian cities. In the "Atheistic Museum" at Shkodër a graphic shows 150 such structures just for the area surrounding this one city during the period before the war. In contrast the author cannot recall even ten mosques, which he had seen during his travels throughout the country. The earlier sacred buildings have been marginalized, for example, the mosque below the citadel of Shkodër or in the center of Berat. They no longer are integrated in the character of the city as in Prizren or Pejë.

In general Albania deals with its tradition very differently than Kosova does. Things of artistic value or folkloristic significance and expressions of ethnic or national identity are assigned to the domain of museums or receive intensive scholarly study. This tendency can be seen in relation to church structures (during the author's visit two Austrian scholars of Byzantine culture recorded one such building in photographs), the collection of icons in the museum at Korçë, the establishment of Gjirokastër as a "museum city," and the way national costumes are treated. These are disappearing more and more from daily life, limited to the realm of folkloristic occasions and studied as objects of research in cultural history. (According to information from Professor A. Buda, the Academy is preparing an atlas of national costumes.) In Albania I saw a large group of people wearing the national costume only once: they were part of a funeral procession not far from Krujë.

In Kosova the traditional image may have been destroyed by the West European influence partially dominating the lifestyle, the presence of western goods and luxuries, and the relatively stronger individual commerce. Yet despite this noticeable change, obvious traditional elements determine the code of behavior and social values to a greater extent and they are more explicitly present. The difference is especially blatant in the religious tradition, which Albania does not wish to preserve. By way of documentation, in Albania a religious structure in Shkodër was transformed into a sports arena, while in Prishtinë a secular building (I think it is the university library) has the shape of a mosque's cupola—perhaps just for architectonic or stylistic reasons.

In conversations with Albanians an extreme national, central thought was present in connection with the question of cultural traditions and also played a dominant role in scholarly thought. Among speakers in Kosova this same type of thought seemed vigorous, but not pronounced to the same extent. Certainly, pride in things Albanian was evident in the museum of the Prizren League, but other cultural places of interest such as the Patriarchate of Pejë, or the Cloister of Deçan were quite naturally visited, as if out of pride for a great regional historical tradition, not reserved only for Serbs. My companions of Albanian nationality took part in my conversations with Serbian monks without reservation or polemics. On such occasions they naturally stressed the contributions of Albanian artists to the buildings and arrangements. Incidentally, I also learned that Miloš Obilic, the hero of the Battle of Kosova, was an Albanian.

Even in the external appearance of the people, the movement away from tradition seems to have been more uniformly carried out in Albania than in Kosova. National costumes, or even the typical headdress appear to be an exotic exception in the large cities (in the north they can be seen more often than in Tirana or in the south). Since smooth-shaven faces prevail, "respect for the beard" has lost its natural foundation. Although the author had reduced his full beard to one like Lenin's prior to his trip, even this beard sometimes grew great attention. For example a little boy cried so loudly that he forced his mother to follow me around a street corner so that he could admire my beard a little longer.

Judging only by the external picture of the people, an observer who happened to be in Tirana during the evening promenades, which are just as popular here as in Kosova, would more easily believe he was in a southern Italian city than in a typical Balkan one. The style of clothing is relatively modest, plain, lacking in fashionable accessories even for women. The length of skirts is determined by a rather strict norm, but of late a little latitude has been allowed.

In contrast the extremes are much more distinct in Kosova, emphasized especially by the student youth in Prishtinë. Their models for dress can be found in Belgrade or Zagreb.

Attitudes toward Morality. Moral Behavior. Social Categories and Social Commitment. Social Control. A young man in Kosova, trained at a post-secondary technical institute, said in all seriousness, "The special characteristic of us Albanians is our elevated morality." The sense of morality was in no way paired with a religious conviction—the man called himself an atheist; instead it is related to respect for strong moral norms and requirements, rooted in the laws of the patriarchal system. With great satisfaction this man described to me a recent case, which he knew about through good friends: A man was said to have shot his own sister because she had committed adultery. The normative system depicted here was still quite noticeable in the urban milieu of Kosova. In the secluded rural area, especially in the border zone between Montenegro and Albania, this tradition seemed to continue without interruption, according to my observations (see below).

In Albania too a feeling for certian norms which have been handed down still seems to be very deeply rooted. This was particularly striking in the conduct of couples in public. On the whole, however, the traditional normative sensitivity seems to be largely connected with newer social goals, and slowly they are partially replacing it. Evidently a conspicuous collective discipline has developed from these goals. I first noticed this behavioral code in connection with an incident that was not very significant in itself, namely, in the conduct of the spectators at a soccer match. Expressions of enthusiasm for the home team took the form of quick shouts and clapping, but never a continuous roar, or such, as can be heard in our stadiums, in Zagreb, Belgrade, or also in Prishtinë.

This sense of discipline, which has been called for and evidently implemented, takes on a more significant function in other areas where it draws upon the traditional norms. Thus in Albania the institution of marriage has preserved its value even though it no longer has a religious foundation. For example, during a visit to a kindergarten in Korçë a teacher told me about the child-rearing and certification proceedings to which the mother of an illigitimate child is subjected before she is allowed to keep her child —of course illigitimate births do take place. In essence she must be judged entitled to raise a child.

Naturally there were minor violations of this sense of discipline. School children at a theatrical performance in Tirana provided one example, which I found fully understanding and amusing, while my Albanian colleague seemed unnecessarily embarrassed by it. The play, which I think was called "Lenin and the Children," was simply on too high a level for the age group fo the children at the performance, both in the demands it made on the audience and the complexity of its dialogs. The children preferred to play catch in the dark theater auditorium, and their teachers were unable to quiet them down. Lenin, who could not overcome the noise made by the children, finally had to acquiesce.

Social controls and the contents of communal training processes are visible everywhere in the political commercial art, which replaces the advertisements for consumer goods found in Yugoslavia and, naturally, also in Kosova. When individuals, particularly young people, deviate from the norm showing a lack of enthusiasm for work, a lack of political commitment, stylish clothing in imitation of western dress, their offenses are made known through display cases—and names are listed. Blatant comparisons of the accomplishments and faults of work collectives are posted in public. Several slogans on the political posters seem to have been very carefully chosen to achieve a psychological effect. They link the sense of discipline with a particular social goal. For example, the slogan under a corresponding picture read: "In one hand a weapon, in the other a hoe." I spontaneoulsy recalled Gesemann's thoughts on "Heroic Laziness."[5] If this had been present in the mind of the slogan writer, then it was quite subtly alluded to in the poster. The pre-eminence of the soldier is guaranteed by the order in which the tools are listed (weapon and hoe). I also thought at once of the quotation of Njegoš: "Lions became farmers!"[6]

The annual mobilization of school children and students, male and female, for work details and their military service is supposed to support this process. (In contrast to Kosova a specifically requested element of emancipation is evidently expressed through a young woman's military service in Albania.) The mood in the student work groups, for instance, those extending the railroad in the direction of Shkodër or building terraces for fruit plantations in the coastal region north of Sarandë, reminded me of the revolutionary mood in Yugoslavia, as it was during the initial phases of construction of the Adriatic railroad. When I asked Professor A. Buda whether it was sensible economically to have students working on such technologically complex projects, he answered my objection by referring to the very valuable training. The young people studying in Kosova have viewed such social expectations as anachronisms for a long time. The difference between young students from Kosova and Albania—in deportment, appearance, and attitude—struck me very much after a direct comparison when a ping-pong team from the University of Prishtinë competed in Shkodër and Tirana. The Kosovars actually seemed high-strung and individualistic in comparison to their colleagues from Albania.

The obligatory zeal for work, on the one hand, combined with the principle of relatively equal distribution of the small but adequate collective production, produces a certain positive psychological effect, as can be seen in the common pride in the terrace and irrigation projects in the south, carried on through collective work.

Among the youth studying in Kosova I could sense a certain vacuum, perhaps even resignation. The problem of insufficient career opportunities and impending unemployment came up repeatedly in the conversations. The high level of solidarity within families seemed to mitigate the problem somewhat, without providing an alternative (an example will follow). The desire to get work in the Federal Republic of Germany functioned as a primary safety-valve.

The people with whom I spoke regarded the expansion of the economy in Kosova primarily as a process dependent upon the Yugoslavian member republics. They felt excluded from assuming responsibility and showing initiative. This sentiment sometimes erupted in a rather illogical way, for instance, in complaints about the poor quality of the streets: "The Macedonians built these, and they purposely made them so bad," etc.

Family Structures. Family Life. An Urban Family in Kosova Undergoing Change. The host family, with whom the author stayed during his visit in Kosova, lived at the edge of Pejë's central city in an expanding district where one-family houses prevailed. The family had evidently inherited a strong Islamic tradition (the grandfather was a *hodja*). It's social standing prior to the father's death would have to be characterized as upper middle class (the father was an independent merchant). In the meantime one of the four sons who still lived in the house (a truck mechanic) has become the sole supporter of an eight-person household. The family includes the mother, a daughter who attends a college-preparatory high school, a son who is a student, my tutor, a school-aged son, the daughter-in-law; and her young child. Another son, about 35 years old and no longer living with the family, has four children of his own. This family seems typical—with the exception of some academic

families with fewer children. The exceptionally high birth rate in Kosova
is reflected in the sketch of this family. This impression was strengthened
by the large number of children playing on the streets. This too constrasts
very much with the picture in Albania.

The family's property consists of about 500 square meters of land—
quite typical for this area of the city. The land is surrounded by a high
wall with a defensive quality about it (reinforced by the strong dog in the
yard). On the property there are two one-story houses of about equal
size. One is reserved mainly for the men and for receiving guests (in this
case the separation of the sexes is no longer taken too seriously); the
other serves primarily as the living and work area for the women. The
married and the school aged son also lives here. The land and the rooms
are neat and well kept up, but there were no modern sanitary facilities
such as a toilet, bathtub, or shower. A covered watering stand outside
was used for washing.

The area for the women was naturally taboo for me. Nor did I ever
enter the kitchen.

The inner structure of the family was undergoing a fundamental change,
at a rate that continued to quicken. This change affected other urban
families which I had met, but not those in the country. In particular the
lattitude allowed to women in public was expanding quickly. I heard that
ten years earlier the women hardly ever left their domestic realm. In the
meantime the daughter of this family, who attended high school, could
scarcely be distinguished from girls her age in Belgrade either in her clothing or in her confidence in the appearance she made. She spoke freely
about her school life and plans for the future, expressing her own opinions, and she spoke with me alone. Apparently she was allowed more freedom than her married sister-in-law, who appeared in "male" company only
in the presence of her husband and mother-in-law.

The mother in this family is a strict and active adherent of the Islamic
religion. She enjoys absolute authority in her domestic domain. But for
the most part the eldest son (my tutor) was responsible for maintaining
norms within the family and representing the family to others. My tutor
called himself an atheist—evidently a fashionable acknowledgement for
one part of the younger generation in Kosova, since I encountered many
self-declared atheists. Through this gesture my tutor wished at the same
time to express his sympathy for Albania. In spite of his conviction,

however, he strictly controlled the enforcement of norms in the family, even though these norms originated in the Islamic tradition.

As as guest of the family I fit into their family customs and daily routines reasonably well. Therefore, I too was under the care of my tutor, who was not about to make any concessions on the basis of my central European cultural heritage, much of which struck him as strange and incomprehensible. I should add that in this role he was no longer taken very seriously by his younger brothers and sisters. I reached this conclusion as a result of some indirect ironic comments; there was no overt lack of respect shown to him.

I was expected to adapt to certain formalities, such as removing my shoes while in the house or the ritual of washing my hands (which my tutor evidently did not expect me to do automatically). I also had to display proper table manners: eating primarily with my fingers, squating on the floor at a low table (*sofra*) with my legs crossed, using the overhang of the table cloth as a napkin. In the surroundings of my host family I internalized these rituals very quickly. In the very different atmosphere of a rented apartment in Prishtinë, a setting suggesting Middle Europe, I quite naturally forgot to remove my shoes while visiting a colleague. My host appeared not to have noticed and even seemed surprised when I later apologized. Expectations evidently change very quickly here as the milieu changes.

My instructor and teacher supervised my conduct toward his mother and sister-in-law very decisively. I was strictly forbidden to photograph them. He also informed me just as explicitly that I was not to look at his sister-in-law, a prohibition that was de facto impossible to observe.

The attempt, outlined here, to preserve the system of norms intact as far as possible even in an urban area seems rather anachronistic and not very promising. Life outside the family is changing and women evidently want to participate more in public life.

The Relatives in the Mountains. Heroic Life Style within Reach. The patriarchal family structure seemed to be fully intact among the teacher's relatives in the border area near Albania and Montenegro, in the rural environment of mountain shepherds.

The physical setting featured an imposing homestead, constructed entirely of wood, and situated away from the road on a high meadow pasture, and accessible only by a long foot path. Here too as in Pejë there were two separate buildings for men and women. The two worlds do not mix here. I saw the female family members only at a great distance—with the exception of the housewife who took care of us. The women had to suppress their curiosity.

The living room for the men, in which I was received, was almost completely covered by several layers of beautiful carpets made by the women of the house. An unbelievably comfortable atmosphere arose in the low room with the smoke of cigarettes the men rolled themselves, and some *raki,* sweets and rose water which the women made. At the same time a short, severe storm raged outside, shooting lightening through the electrical outlets. This was about the way I had pictured the "heroic milieu" to myself. The clothing—particularly for the men—is generally of a modern cut, but the traditional headdress is absolutely part of the outfit, just as the loaded pistol in the belt worn by the head of the household. "Around here all men wear these as protection against the bears," he assured me with a laugh and immediately invited me to target practice.

But the "heroes" revealed themselves above all in their tales. All men in the family, from the oldest man to the youngest son, had their heroic tales, which were told with pleasure. If I had come here some time earlier, I would have experienced four male generations together and would have met the most famous member of the family. But the father of my host, who had dominated a forty-person extended family, had died a few years earlier. Now he was present only in the tale of his son. The grandfather begins the round of tales with his account of the war and his experience as a prisoner of war in East Prussia. He proudly recites the two words of German he has remembered. The Montenegrins are the victims in his heroic comparisons: "They never fought as we did, they just say so in order to get their pensions . . ."! The tale of his grandson, the current head of the family is also adventurous enough. As a young man he wandered across the Albanian border with his herd, was detained there a long time, then was allowed to return. He met his wife over there and brought her back with him. Even the youngest male offspring of the family, the fourteen years old son of my host had his heroic tale. He had set out with a friend of the same age from a neighboring house. Four days and nights the two lived in the woods and ate berries. All the men from the surrounding villages took part in the search. When the children were found safe, they told of cows without horns which they had seen. From the tracks they found, the men identified these animals as bears. The center of the narrative session, however, was the story of the late head of the extended family. During his lifetime he had ridden to Pejë in a few days to shop for his large family and for visiting shepherds who often stayed with the family. At that time the road from Pejë to Titograd had not been completed. Formerly, one always had to watch out for robbers. As we returned to Pejë, my teacher showed me the spot where his uncle supposedly hid his money when robbers threatened.

During our meal between the tales the patriarchal order in the household was evident once again. Only the men (including the fourteen year old son) gathered around the *sofra*. Our host's wife approached only to serve our food and clear the table. Then she waited silently at the door with water and a hand towel until we wanted to wash our hands. As was the case with my hostess in Pejë, all food was prepared according to recipes handed down in the family. Here in the mountains, however, the food tasted even more delicious thanks to the fresh dairy products made by the family.

To contrast the milieu described here with that in Albania, a visit to the Albanian Alps would have been necessary. I did not have the opportunity for that. When I related my impressions from Yugoslavia to Albanians I spoke with, they believed the life style I had described would no longer be found in Albania because the material conditions had changed as had the educational system.

Rational Thought. National Consciousness. Attitude towards Religion. What do the observations outlined above tell us about the difference in conditions in Albania and Kosova? The observations themselves in no way imply a socio-political evaluation, rather they merely strive to reproduce the social atmosphere observed more or less by chance on various occasions. For the author the difference between the two was the impression that in Albania a euphoria of reason was spreading through the land, a new mood of enlightenment, incited and fostered very intensively by cultural political programs and received rather well. It follows the priniciple of national unity and identity. In Kosova there was little trace of such a collective emphasis. Scholarly activities with an analogous goal—at least those I learned of—seemed to have an individualistic, isolated character.

This high regard for reason may seem naive to the West European observer. The expression must be considered in relation to the particular
development needs and conditions in Albania. This principle of reason
finds expression in "views" about the necessity of subordinating the individual to the needs of society, for example in relation to the birth rate
(people in general agreed that two to three children were enough) or
religion. The author neither began nor provoked the discussion about
this topic. The theme arose spontaneously while the author visited the
"Atheistic Museum" in Shkodër or the museum in Korçë which is located
in a former Orthodox church. The matter was already settled in the rea-
soning of people I spoke with or in the didactic conception of the museum
in Shkodër. Without exception all religious communities formerly represented in Albania had inhibited social progress, national unity, and the
implementation of national interests. (The accomplishments of individual
clergy were recognized, however.) After entering the "Atheistic Museum,"
one does not immediately see Marx's slogan about the "Opiate of Religion," but instead a statement of the national hero, Skanderbeg. In it he
expresses his disgust that the Pope failed to support him in his battle
against the Ottomans. A common saying that I often encountered in
Kosova too was that religion had never meant much to the Albanians;
their religion is the Albanian national idea.

I asked a historian whether he saw a movement toward the union of
national idea and religion at any time in the course of Albanian history.
(As an example I mentioned the Serbian Church in the Ottoman Empire.)
He emphatically denied this possibility. Rather he countered my question by expounding on the history of his own family (he came from an
Orthodox family). This account also documented a part of Albania's
cultural history. As a boy an ancestor of my informant, probably his
great grandfather, entered the service of an Italian doctor, who traveled
through Albania during the summer months and practiced there. The boy
was taken to Italy and returned with such a wealth of medical knowledge
that he was able to practice medicine himself in the Albanian area. In so
doing he had laid the foundation for a middle-class family life. The family
was placed in a position to immediately give the children a better education. The family felt obliged to observe nationalistic sentiments and chose
the schools accordingly (first a French high school in Thessalonica, then
Bitola). Greek influence was avoided, and that set the stage for a collision

with the Greek clergy. The family was excommunicated. According to my informant that disturbed his grandmother very much.

The life of a Catholic Albanian priest, whom I met in Kosova, serves as somewhat of a counterbalance to this story. (He is the head of an obviously very active parish with 1800 members.) This story does not present contradictory evidence in relation to the union of national idea and religion, but it does reflect the individual commitment of one clergyman in the setting of the Albanian nation. The priest compiles the history of his parish and its surroundings. Here in the middle of the nineteenth century people in the Albanian area of the Ottoman Empire first dared to declare their Catholic faith in public. This led to a sorrowful mass migration to Anatolia. To finance his search for historical source material in Istanbul, Vienna, and Rome, the priest took a job as a guest worker in a chemical factory in the Federal Republic of Germany.[7]

The series of individual observations, conversations, episodes connected with the two visits could be substantially increased: about learned matters, cultural life, the organization of museums and their didactic conception, the educational structure, multi-lingualism, etc. Because of limited space only a few observations could be discussed here—those which seemed paradigmatic for the main points of a rather tentative contrastive comparison.

Naturally there can be no all-encompassing answer to the statement of an Albanian colleague quoted above (Kosova is Albania thirty years ago). For various aspects of the study the decision shall be left to the reader's judgement, which will certainly depend on his or her perspective at any given time.

* * * * *

NOTES

1. J. Schropfer (editor-in-chief), editors H. Albert and A. Honig. *Wörterbuch der vergleichenden Bezeichnungslehre, Region Mittle-, Ost- und Südosteuropa.* Heidelberg 1979 ff.

2. For this compare the author's contributions in *Semantische Hefte* Vol. IV. Heidelberg, 1981: "Beobachtungen zur neueren albanischen Lexikographie" and the review of the new *Wörterbuch der heutigen albanischen Sprache.* Tirana 1980.

3. Jens Reuter. *Die Albaner in Jugoslawien*. Munich 1982, p. 115.

4. This speaker bitterly emphasized over and over that the Turks would not surrender the bones of the Frashëri Brothers which were preserved in Istanbul.

5. G. Gesemann. *Heroische Lebensform*. Berlin 1943, p. 99ff.

6. "*Postadoše lafi ratarima.*" P. P. Njegoš. *Gorski vijenac*. Quoted from the edition published at Sarajevo 1979, p. 56.

7. The author was able to furnish one source from an archive in the GDR and together with a colleague from Heidelberg helped decipher sources in the German language. The work apparently has not yet been published. It was completed in 1981.

PART II

THE ECONOMIC AND POLITICAL SITUATION

Peter Prifti

KOSOVA'S ECONOMY:
PROBLEMS AND PROSPECTS*

A popular saying in Yugoslavia these days is: "If the other regions in Yugoslavia walk, then Kosova must run." It is a pointed comment on Kosova's economy. The trouble is that Kosova's economy is not running. It is not even walking. More often than not, it is plodding or even crawling.

But before we examine that situation, let us look briefly at Kosova's background, in terms of its geography, economic history and other basic data that have a bearing on its economy.

Background Sketch

Kosova occupies a more or less central position in the Balkan peninsula. As presently delimited in the Federation of Yugoslavia, it occupies an area of 10,887 km², or 4.25 percent of the total area of Yugoslavia. It is known officially as the Autonomous Socialist Province of Kosova, and is one of the two provinces in the Republic of Serbia, the other being the province

* In preparing this paper, I benefited greatly from the assistance—in the form of advice, research materials, and other aid—of the following persons: Arshi Pipa, Zef Shllaku, Sami Repishti, Leonard Newmark, Zen Hajrizaj, John Sinishta, Sejdi Bitiçi, and Zef Nekaj. I express my gratitude and thanks to all of them.

125

of Vojvodina. The topography of the province comprises lowlands and valleys, highlands and mountains, and is generally above sea level; the plain area is an average of 440m above sea level. The rivers that drain the terrain of the province empty into all three of the seas surrounding the Balkan peninsula: the Adriatic Sea to the West, the Aegean Sea to the south, and the Black Sea to the east.

Kosova has an abundance of flora and fauna, including wild chestnut, oak and beech; lynx, brown bears, deer, wild boars and rabbits. It is particularly rich in mineral wealth. The province has 50 percent of all known nickel deposits in Yugoslavia, 48 percent of the lead and zinc, 47 percent of the magnesium, 36 percent of the lignite, and 32.4 percent of the kaolin deposits. It is also rich in quartz, asbestos, limestone, marble, chrome, bauxite, and cement materials.

Historically, the beginnings of Kosova's economy date back to the pre-Christian era of the Illyrians, the "earliest inhabitants of this region, who worked in metals to make tools, arms and ornaments."[1] The manufacture of arms, in particular, reached a high stage of development in recent centuries. The silver-gilted revolvers made in Gjakovë (Djadkovica) and Pejë (Pec), and the finely-crafted rifles of Prizren found markets throughout Europe. Handicrafts, livestock, agriculture, trade—these were the chief branches of Kosova's economy in the past.

Feudal economic relations persisted in Kosova down to our own century; that is to say, until the end of Ottoman rule in the region in the second decade of the century. Yet, even later, when it became a part of monarchial Yugoslavia, Kosova remained one of the most undeveloped areas in the country. According to Fehmi Pushkolli, a Kosovan scholar, the "Greater Serbia bourgeoisie treated Kosova as a colony, to be exploited to the utmost for its wealth and for its labor power."[2] Hence, agriculture of a largely primitive variety, was, until recently, the chief branch of the economy, employing approximately 85 percent of the active population of the province. Even though Kosova, as already mentioned, is very rich in mineral resources, the mining industry developed slowly. The greater part of the mines was in the hand of foreign capital: English, French and German. The most prominent mines, including that of Trepça —the biggest and best known—were the property of Selection Trust Ltd., of London. Of the entire capital invested in Kosova between the two world wars, 72.8 percent belonged to foreign states.

We see that, apart from the backwardness inherited from Ottoman rule, Kosova suffered from a double exploitation, domestic colonialism coupled with foreign colonialism. It was a heavy handicap with which to begin efforts at modernization. This legacy became a pattern whose effects have persisted in some form or degree down to the present.

Population

In terms of its population, Kosova has stood apart from the rest of Yugoslavia for a number of reasons. It is the most densely populated area in the country, having (in 1975) 133 inhabitants per km^2, as against 84 for Yugoslavia as a whole. It has the highest natural growth rate in Yugoslavia, and indeed in Europe: (in 1979) 26.1 per 1,000 population, as against 14.5 for Macedonia, 4.1 for Croatia, 7.6 for Slovenia, and 8.6 for the Yugoslav national average.[3] With more than half of the Kosovans under the age of twenty, Kosova has the youngest population in the Federation of Yugoslavia. It has also the largest ethnic group among the numerous groups that make up the federation, the Albanians.

These figures add up to a "demographic explosion" of a dominant ethnic group, with significant implications for the region's economy and that of Yugoslavia as well. In itself, a high natality is not necessarily a burden for a region or a country. If its economy is stable, well organized and progressive, a high birth rate can be absorbed and used productively. It can be an asset. That is not the case with Kosova, however. There, galloping fertility has been a growing strain on the economy, creating problems, or worsening them, in such areas as housing, food, employment, and a variety of social services. It has had the effect of depressing Kosova's standard of living across the board.

Population thus emerges as one of the major problems in the economy of the province.

The most recent national census, taken in 1981, showed Kosova with a population of 1,584,558, an increase of 27 percent (341,000) since 1971. The table on the following page shows the national composition of the population over the last two decades.

As the table shows, the Albanian population (and that of the Moslems) has been growing steadily, while that of the Serbs, the Montenegrins, and the Turks has diminished since 1961. It gained over 6 percentage points

TABLE 1

National Composition of the Population of Kosova According to
the Census of 1961, 1971, 1981
(rounded to nearest thousand)

Population	1961	%	1971	%	1981	%
TOTAL	964,000	100	1,244,000	100	1,585,000	100
Albanians	647,000	67.1	916,000	73.7	1,227,000	77.5
Serbs	227,000	23.5	228,000	18.3	210,000	13.2
Montenegrins	38,000	3.9	32,000	2.5	27,000	1.7
Turks	26,000	2.7	12,000	1.0	13,000	0.8
Moslems	8,000	0.8	26,000	2.1	59,000	3.7
Other	19,000	2.0	29,000	2.4	49,000	3.1

Source: *Rilindja* (Rebirth), Albanian-language daily, Prishtina, March 4,
1982, p. 7.

from 1961 to 1971, and nearly 6 additional points in the last decade. There
are, in addition, many more Albanians in the other republics of Yugoslavia and the Autonomous Province of Vojvodina. The total number of
Albanian ethnics in the country in 1981 stood at 1,732,000.[4] For their
distribution in the country, see Appendix B.

The number of Serbs in Kosova decreased by 18,172 between 1971
and 1981, and that of the Montenegrins by 4,680. This fact has economic
implications of some consequence for the province. One, because the
migrating Slavs represent the highest percentage, in proportion to their
numbers, of professionals and specialists in Kosova's population. Their
exodus means a drain of expertise in industry, technology, science and
the professions. Two, the property of the departing Serbs has become an
acute ethnic issue for the reason, it appears, that they "dread the transfer
of any property . . . to Albanians."[5] The issue became particularly aggravated following the demonstrations in the province in the Spring of 1981,
with the result that what seemed at first glance a question of economics
took on strong political coloration. It became a burning emotional issue
in the Yugoslav press, which claimed, in disregard of the official statistics,

that some 57,000 Serbs and Montenegrins left the province in the last decade.[6]

It is not my purpose here to comment on the political dimension of the issue, but rather to clarify, if possible, the economic element in that issue. Was the exodus due to Albanian pressure, as the Serbian press generally charged, or primarily on account of economic reasons? According to *Rilindja* (Rebirth), daily organ of the Communist League of Prishtina, capital of Kosova, the major causes of migration have been economic. The paper cited the problem of widespread unemployment in the province as the leading factor for the departure of the Serbs and Montenegrins. Other factors cited were the housing problem, and unfavorable educational conditions in Kosova. Many of those who moved out, the report said, did so in order to further their professional training or instruction elsewhere in Yugoslavia.[7] In general, it appears that those who migrated from the province took that step on the one hand to escape the hardships of life in the province, and on the other hand to take advantage of opportunities for a better and more prosperous life in other parts of Yugoslavia.[8] Furthermore, it is not only Slavs who have been moving out of Kosova. From 1971 to 1981, a total of 44,808 Albanians left the province as well, chiefly for economic reasons.[9]

Inter-ethnic mistrust and tensions, generated by unfavorable economic conditions, emerges as another problem besetting Kosova at present.

Comparative Date*

Kosova has been, and continues to be, the poorest and least developed area in the Federated Socialist Republic of Yugoslavia. It is a reality borne out by statistics in all areas of economic activity in the province: level of development, productivity, urban-rural ratio of the population, income and wages, education, employment, and living standards. A look at Table 2 shows the level of economic development in Kosova, compared with other regions of Yugoslavia.

---

* Statistical data on Kosova need to be read with caution. They vary, sometimes appreciably, from one source to another. This is true, in my experience, of data in Yugoslav sources, as well as in outside sources.

TABLE 2

Level of Economic Development in the Republics
and the Provinces (1979)
(in percentages)

Region	Share of Total Population	Share of Total Social Product	Reproductive Capacity per Cap.
ALL YUGOSLAVIA	100.0	100.0	100.0
Bosnia-Hercegovina	19.9	12.2	66.5
Montenegro	2.8	1.9	76.1
Croatia	19.6	26.1	130.2
Macedonia	9.1	5.7	64.5
Slovenia	8.0	16.5	222.5
Serbia (inner)[n]	23.7	24.1	86.9
Kosova	7.8	2.1	13.8
Vojvodina	8.7	10.8	116.2

Note: "inner" signifies "Serbia without the provinces."
Source: Jens Reuter, *Die Albaner in Jugoslawien,* München, 1982, p. 60.

In 1979 Kosova accounted for 7.8 percent of Yugoslavia's population
(22 million in 1979), yet its share of the total social product of the country was considerably below its proportion of the population—only 2.1
percent. Slovenia, with only a slightly higher population percentage,
namely 8.0 percent, accounted for 16.5 percent of the country's social
product, or about eight times that of Kosova. In terms of reproductive
capacity per capita, Kosova again had the lowest percentage, 13.8 percent as against 222.5 percent for Slovenia, a figure sixteen times above
that of Kosova. The region's lag in development is revealed also by statistics on the social product (GNP) per capita, as the table on the following
page makes clear.

The table shows that all the underdeveloped regions in Yugoslavia:
Kosova, Macedonia, Montenegro, and Bosnia-Hercegovina, registered a
drop in the social product per capita from 1969 to 1979; while the developed regions: Croatia, Slovenia, inner Serbia, and Vojvodina registered

TABLE 3

Social Product in Yugoslavia Per Capita (1969, 1979)
(at 1972 prices)

Region	Amount in Dinars		In Percentages	
	1969	1979	1969	1979
ALL YUGOSLAVIA	10,210	16,758	100	100
Bosnia-Hercegovina	7,030	10,924	69	65
Montenegro	7,735	11,586	76	69
Croatia	12,408	21,276	122	127
Macedonia	7,014	11,202	69	67
Slovenia	19,055	34,050	187	203
Serbia (inner)	9,998	16,625	98	99
Kosova	3,472	4,648	34	28
Vojvodina	11,467	19,324	112	115

Source: Jens Reuter, *Die Albaner in Jugoslawien*, München, 1982, p. 59.

increases for the same period. The striking fact here is the wide gap not only between Kosova and the developed regions—28 percent in 1979 compared with 203 percent for Slovenia—but between Kosova and the other underdeveloped regions. Kosova stood 37 points behind Bosnia-Hercegovina (with 65 points) the region with the next lowest per capita social product.

Other economic indicators support these findings. Kosova has the highest illiteracy rate in Yugoslavia for persons over ten years of age: 31.5 percent, as against the national average of 15.1 percent, and a mere 1.2 percent for Slovenia.[10] In 1979, the per capita income in Kosova was $795 (U.S. dollars), compared with $2,635 for the Yugoslav national average, and $5,315 for Slovenia, a difference of seven times. Monthly industrial wages in 1980 averaged $180 per capita in Kosova, while the Yugoslav average was $235, and the figure for Slovenia was $280, or 55 percent higher than in Kosova. With an annual inflation rate of 40 percent, Kosova held an unenviable first place in Europe, according to a recent study.[11] In the field of employment, the picture was equally dreary. In 1979, only 107 Kosovans per 1,000 in the active population were employed, compared with 253 for the Yugoslav average, and 427 for Slovenia, the highest in the federation. And while one in every five Serbs and Montenegrins in the province was employed in 1980, only one in every eleven Albanians held a job.[12]

These statistics translate finally into a low standard of living for Kosova. Figures for 1978 show that only 4.8 houses per 1,000 population were built in Kosova, which as noted earlier is the most crowded region in Yugoslavia, while the number in Slovenia was 7.7. The proportion of houses with plumbing facilities (i.e., water supply and sewerage) was less than fifty percent (43.6) in Kosova, and practically a hundred percent (99.6) in Slovenia. The proportions for houses with a bathroom were about the same: 41.1 percent for Kosova; 97.9 percent for Slovenia.[13] Although Kosova, as we have seen accounts for about eight percent of the total population of Yugoslavia, it had but 2.4 percent of the automobiles in the country, and 2.5 percent of the radios and television sets.[14] The urban-rural ratio of the population further illustrates the backward character of the province. As late as 1978, 42.9 percent of the population was engaged in agriculture, while 57.1 percent was urbanized. These figures were far away from the 13.5 percent rural and 86.5 percent urban population figures for Slovenia in the same year.

The evidence is conclusive that Kosova is in a very backward state. Whether one looks at industry, agriculture, foreign trade, investments, or social services, one encounters complex and stubborn problems. They are of such magnitude that at times they seem to defy solutions, at least in the short run. The picture is obviously discouraging.

Evidence of Progress

Relative to other regions in Yugoslavia, especially the developed ones, Kosova is backward. Indeed, it has even regressed in recent years. Relative to its own past, however, it has moved forward. In absolute terms, it has made progress since the end of World War Two.

At the end of the war, the province was shattered, debilitated by the legacy of its past and by the effects of the war. Seventy percent of what little industry there was in the province has been destroyed during the war.

Since 1944, the province has confronted its general backwardness, and attained some degree of success. It has laid the basis for industrial development, and created a professional and technical body of workers.

Compared with 1947, the social product in 1979 was 6.5 times larger.[15] By 1981, industrial production had increased 18 times, and industry had become the leading branch of the economy.[16] Production in agriculture had tripled. The rural-urban ratio of the population had changed significantly since the war, dropping from about 85 percent (rural) in 1944 to 42.9 percent in 1978. There was development in the infrastructure of the region, including the expansion of construction and communication systems. At the end of the war, Kosova did not have a single km of asphalted road. By 1970, about 25 percent of the road system had been modernized, and all the large towns of the province were connected by railroad. The total railroad mileage by that year was 300 km, an increase of 129 km since the war. Air service was added to the transportation system in 1965, with the inauguration of the Prishtinë-Belgrade airline.[17] The number of employed in the public sector of the economy grew about five times since the war, reaching a total of nearly 180,000 by 1981.

The Brioni Plenum in 1966, which brought down Aleksandar Ranković, the Albano-phobe Minister of the Interior, gave a further impetus to progress in Kosova, especially in education, culture, and social services in general. The illiteracy rate among the Albanians, which at the end of the war stood at 90 percent, had dropped to 36 percent by 1971.[18] By 1975, the University of Prishtinë (founded in 1969), had more students than had all of Yugoslavia before the war.[19] At present, 96 percent of the children in the province reportedly receive an elementary education.[20] There have been advances in the training of medical personnel and in health care for the population. Whereas in 1952 there was one doctor per 8,527 inhabitants, in 1978 the ratio was one per 2,009. Similarly, life expectancy, which in the immediate postwar period was 45 years, had risen to 68 years by 1980. Over a period of three decades since the war, cultural life developed in a variety of ways. The number of cultural institutions, such as libraries, museums, theaters and cinemas has grown steadily. By 1980, Kosova had a modern radio-television station, and a vigorous publishing industry, which printed scores of books annually in the Albanian and Serbo-Croatian languages, plus over two dozen newspapers and magazines.

The record shows that when viewed against the background of its condition in the immediate postwar years, Kosova has made progress. Endowed with vast natural resources, and with an increasingly sophisticated labor force, Kosova has the potential for growth and a decent standard of living for its people. The question is how to harness that potential so as to achieve and sustain a level of development that would keep pace with the rest of the country.

A Closer Look at the Problems

Investments:

A doctoral thesis in 1978 by a Kosovan scholar on investments in Kosova concluded that the investment policy of the province for a quarter of a century (1947-1973) had been "misguided." Further, that this policy had resulted in an "unsuitable" or lop-sided structure for the economy of the region, which made it "practically impossible to synchronize the development of the province."[21]

The complaint of Musa Limani has been echoed loudly in Kosova's press in recent years. The imbalance, it is claimed, came about principally because the emphasis on investments was put on basic industry, meaning the extractive or "raw materials" industry, to the relative neglect of other branches of the economy. Furthermore, there was an insufficiency of investment funds. Investments during this period benefited not so much Kosova, as the major recipients of the raw materials, namely the other regions of Yugoslavia. This was true also of the electric power produced in Kosova, of which at least two-thirds flowed to other republics, leaving the province "notably behind" the republics in per capita use of electricity. Another example of what might be called the "semi-colonial status" of Kosova, insofar as returns on investments was concerned, relates to its lead industry. The "Trepça" complex delivered lead to other republics at a price well below that of the world market, with annual losses of 300 million dinars.[22]

Compared with other regions of Yugoslavia, Kosova's investment pace began to slow down in the early 1970s. During the 1971-75 period, investments fell short of the plan by 26.4 percentage points, and dropped still more (53.8 percentage points) in the following 5 Year Plan (1976-80).

Unable to generate capital on its own, Kosova relied heavily on outside sources for investment funds, mainly on the Federal Development Fund.

Unlike the other undeveloped republics, which used federal funds as supplementary credits, for Kosova such funds served as the "basic source" of credits. For example, during the ten-year period from 1966 to 1975, federal funds comprised 64.4 percent of the province's total investments.[23] Two other seemingly chronic problems that have hampered the efficacy of investments have been inordinate delays in the completion of projects, and huge cost overruns. A survey in 1978 revealed that projects under construction were on the average 14 months behind schedule. A number of major projects, such as the "Ibër-Lepenci" water system, and the Gllogovc Nickel-Iron complex were several years behind schedule. Delays coupled with inflation created paralyzing cost overruns. During the last 5 Year Plan (1976-80), fully one-third (33.5%) of investment funds were spent to cover cost overruns, reducing thus the investment capacity of the current 5 Year Plan, inasmuch as it had to absorb the investment lag of preceding plans.[24]

Furthermore, in spite of the comparatively low wage scales in Kosova, there was a reluctance on the part of the developed regions in Yugoslavia to invest in the province. One reason for this was a lack of trust on the part of prospective investors in the discipline and work habits of Kosova workers.[25] The fact also that Kosova had a weak technological infrastructure and was comparatively short of engineers and technicians, apparently discouraged many outside firms from investing in the region.

The results of the plan for 1981 revealed the extent of the malady in the sphere of investments. Investment activity in the province was 35.7 percent lower than in 1980, a most discouraging start for the 1981-85 plan.

Industry:

Even apart from Lenin's motto that communism is "soviet power plus electricity," it made sense for Kosova, in view of its rich natural resources, to strive for modernization by placing the accent on the development of industry. The basis therefore of development in Kosova has been the exploitation of its natural wealth, above all its raw mineral wealth. Since the mid-1940s, more than sixty new industries have been built in the province. By 1965, industry overtook agriculture as the leading contributor to the social product. The progress of industry is shown in the table on the following page (Table 4).

TABLE 4

Structure of the Social Product in Kosova for Selected Years
(1947, 1957, 1970)
(in percentages)

Branch	1947	1957	1970
TOTAL ECONOMY	100.0	100.0	100.0
Industry & Mining	17.4	25.1	38.3
Agriculture & Forestry	64.0	60.1	33.6
Other	18.6	14.8	28.1

Source: J. Reuter, *Die Albaner in Jugoslawien,* München, 1982, p. 56.

By 1970 industry has taken a commanding lead in the structure of the social product, accounting for 38.3 percent of the total social product, compared with 33.6 percent for agriculture. Among the many projects initiated, expanded or completed since the war, several stand out for their size, complexity and importance. The largest of these is the "Trepça" mining-metallurgical-chemical complex in the Mitrovica district, which utilizes the most modern technology, and employs nearly 21,000. The Trepça conglomerate has plants not only in Kosova, but in inner Serbia, Montenegro, and Vojvodina as well. Unlike former times when it produced only raw materials, today the Trepça industries are engaged increasingly in processing operations and the production of finished goods. The mid-1970s saw the completion of the "Kosova" mining-energy-chemical combine, consisting primarily of the construction of five thermal power plants, known as Kosova I, II, III, IV, and V. The plants had a total capacity of 790 megawatts, and an annual output of five billion kwh. Another major project is the Nickel-Iron plant in the Gllogovc district, whose completion was expected this year. The plant is seen as vital to Kosova's economy, because of the foreign currency it is expected to earn from the sales of its products abroad, a matter of great importance for the region's export-import trade.

The watershed year in the development of Kosova's industry was 1957. From 1944 to 1957 industry, and indeed the entire economy of the province was stagnant. The main reason for this condition was a Federal policy which discriminated against Kosova in the distribution of investment funds. At that time, such funds were given gratis to the undeveloped regions. Kosova however was excluded.

After 1957, Kosova became a recipient of investment funds from the Federal budget, and it was only then that the region began to industrialize. Unlike the first period, however, funds granted after 1957 had to be repaid with interest, within a given period of time. This policy had the effect of burdening Kosova with heavy obligations, on account of high interest annuities it had to meet.[26] As a consequence the province was severely handicapped in its efforts to accumulate working capital and develop its economy.

The effort to generate capital suffered also from the lopsided character of industry, for the reason that it was heavily oriented toward the "basic branches of industry," such as metallurgy, chemicals, and energy. These capital-intensive industries required, on the one hand, large investments of funds, and on the other hand created relatively few job openings. The capital-intensive basic industries accounted for 61.4 percent of the total industrial production, while the labor-intensive manufacturing industries accounted for only 38.6 percent of the total.

Ironically, Kosova's industry—in part because it is a young industry—is 80 percent automated, more modern even than that of Slovenia. But precisely for this reason, it has not provided many job opportunities.

In brief, the development of industry in the province has been hampered by a number of problems, including a discriminatory Federal credit policy, inadequate investment funds, an inability to generate capital, and industrial development policies that contributed to, rather than alleviate the problem of unemployment. As recently as July 1982, the Provincial Assembly of Kosova noted that key construction projects, including projects in the Trepça conglomerate and the Gllogovc Nickel-Iron complex, faced acute problems. The Assembly complained about the slow pace of construction, huge cost overruns, and shortages of funds that threatened to upset production targets of the plan.[27]

The cumulative effect of these problems surfaced earlier in the results of the last 5 Year Plan (1976-80). Industrial production, which was supposed to grow at an annual rate of 11.8 percent, actually grew by only 5 percent.[28]

Agriculture:

A report on a meeting of the Kosova Assembly in November 1981 said that agriculture presented "a serious problem" in the development of the economy. It noted that the difficulties in that sector "continue to worsen, as the needs of the population increase, while productivity remains low."[29] As with industry, Kosova's agriculture at the beginning of the 1980s was in deep trouble.

Like industry, agriculture was in a stagnant state until 1957. After 1957 a part of the agricultural economy was socialized, but the greater part of the land has remained in private hands, as the following table shows.

TABLE 5

**Social vs. Private Land Acreage in Serbia and the Provinces
1975
(in percentages)**

Region	Socially-Owned Land	Privately-Owned Land
Serbia (inner)	5.7	94.3
Kosova	11.6	88.4
Vojvodina	37.3	62.7

Source: *Facts About the SR of Serbia,* Belgrade, 1977, p. 37.

It was the same with livestock. As of 1975, 70 percent of the livestock was privately owned, and 30 percent was in the social sector. Compared with the private sector, the social sector has proved superior in terms of productivity. For example, in 1970 from one ha. of land, the social sector realized 5,600 dinars worth of produce, while the private sector realized only 2,100 dinars. The chief reason for this apparently is the higher level of technology employed in the social sector.

Yet the edge enjoyed by the social sector has not rescued Kosova's agriculture from its morass. Among the many problems hampering its progress is that of fragmentation of arable land, owing to the splitting up of large families, a common practice in the province. It is a phenomenon that creates difficulties both for agriculture and industry. The table below shows the structure of private farms, in terms of their size, in Kosova.

TABLE 6

Structure of Private Farms in Serbia and the Provinces (1969)
(in percentages)

Size of Farms	Serbia (inner)	Vojvodina	Kosova
up to 2 ha.	24.2	28.3	33.9
2-3 ha.	15.6	13.6	23.5
3-5 ha.	26.4	21.9	24.8
5-8 ha.	21.5	21.7	13.1
8-10 ha.	6.8	12.3	2.3
over 10 ha.	5.5	2.2	2.4

Source: M. Maletić, *Kosovo nekad i danas* (Kosova Formerly and Today), Borba Publishing House, Belgrade, 1973, p. 531.

While in Serbia and Vojvodina farms up to 3 ha. accounted for 39.8 and 41.9 percent, respectively, of the total farm area, the figure for Kosova was a high 57.4 percent. Owing to the small size of the plots, such farm economies preclude the use of modern agricultural machinery. The result is low yields, which in turn means meager accumulation of capital. Indeed, the process of dividing arable land into ever smaller plots leads inevitably to the point where they become so awkward to operate, and so unproductive, that they are abandoned. Such a backward practice weakens not only agriculture, but industry as well, insofar as industry depends on agriculture for primary materials like sugar beet, sunflower, tobacco, meat, wool, and dairy products.

Livestock breeding and the dairy industry are in disarray. A plan to establish "mini farms" aimed at the development of livestock bogged down, in spite of a grant of one million (U.S.) dollars in credit by the International Bank for Development and Reconstruction. Begun in the last 5 Year Plan (1976-80), the plan called for the creation of 1546 mini farms, but by mid-summer of 1982 only 760 units had been completed. It was much the same with a plan of "Agrokosova" to increase milk production during the current 5 Year Plan (1981-85). Agrokosova is a ten-year-old complex of farm organizations, employing 15,500 people in 18 of the 22 districts in the province. The plan envisioned the establishment of five milk producing farms, each having 500 heads of cows. Yet, a year and a half into the plan, work had not started on even one farm.[30]

These problems translated into shortages in a variety of food items. A meeting of the LC of Kosova in June 1982, noted that "for some time there has existed a shortage of agricultural produce," and that "Kosova at present is facing a food problem."[31] In fact, as of December 1981, the province fulfilled only 60 percent of its food needs. Wheat production has decreased steadily since 1976. In recent years production of this key cereal amounted to about 221,000 tons annually—103,000 tons short of the tonnage needed. The low productivity in grain cereals in Kosova is shown in the table on the following page.

As the data indicate, in 1975 Kosova's yield in wheat production (24.4 m^3 per ha.) was slightly ahead of inner Serbia, but considerably behind Vojvodina (40.6 m^3). In corn production, Kosova's yield in 1975 (22.8 m^3 per ha.) was notably behind both Serbia (34.1 m^3) and Vojvodina (with 57.6 m^3). (Nonetheless, compared with 1939, Kosova had doubled its productivity in wheat, and tripled it in corn by 1975.) This pointed to the need for the "intensive" development of agriculture in the region; that is, the increase in productivity per given ha. of arable land.

Faced with low grain yields and increasing food needs of a rapidly growing population, Kosova has been obliged to turn to other regions in Yugoslavia, or to foreign markets, to secure the food grains it lacks. But the importation of food means spending badly needed foreing currency, a situation that aggravates the balance of payments position of the province, and contributes further to its economic instability.

Migration of rural inhabitants to urban areas is also a problem of some urgency, since the countryside needs labor power for the development of agriculture. Yet, the rural population has not decreased in absolute numbers. In fact, it is greater at present than it was in 1948, in consequence of the overall growth of the population in the province over the past three decades.

The results of the last 5 Year Plan confirmed the plight of agriculture in Kosova. The biggest failures of the plan occurred in the agricultural sector of the economy. The rate of growth in agriculture was only 0.6

TABLE 7

Wheat and Corn Yields in Serbia, Vojvodina and Kosova
(1939, 1975)

		1939		1975	
Crop	Region	ha. sown (in 1,000s)	Yield per ha. (in m^3)	ha. sown (in 1,000s)	Yield per ha. (in m^3)
Wheat	Serbia (inner)	595	12.7	504	22.7
	Vojvodina	675	15.2	389	40.6
	Kosova	91	12.6	106	24.4
Corn	Serbia (inner)	801	12.9	687	34.1
	Vojvodina	689	22.7	623	57.6
	Kosova	109	7.4	100	22.8

Source: Adapted from data in *Facts About the SR of Serbia,* Belgrade 1977, p. 37.

percent per annum, as against 4.5 to 5 percent projected in the plan. The food industry plan also failed, registering only a 5 percent increase, as against the 12.1 percent foreseen by the plan.[32] The gloomy food picture was corroborated by the American tourist to Kosova (mentioned earlier), who reported seeing bread lines, and that people in villages were eating corn bread again, as in prewar Kosova or the years immediately following the war.

Employment:

In the Spring of 1982, a Swedish reporter in Prishtinë quoted an Albanian student as saying: "I am the only one in our family who has had the chance to study at the university. But what will I become? What are my prospects? Will I find a job?" He did not think so. At any rate, not in Prishtinë.[33] According to one observer on the scene, unemployment in

Prishtinë and several other major centers was widespread in the Summer of 1982.[34]

The bleak employment picture in Prishtinë reflected the critical job problem in the province. Of Kosova's total population of over 1.5 million in 1981, only 178,000 were employed, while a total of 67,000 were registered as unemployed. The following table provides data for employed and unemployed, according to nationality.

TABLE 8

Nationality Structure of Employed and Unemployed in Kosova
(1980)
(in percentages)

Nationality	Share of Total Population	Share of Total Employed	Share of Total Unemployed
Albanians	77.5	64.9	76.1
Serbs	13.2	25.6	17.0
Montenegrins	1.7	4.2	2.0
Turks	0.8	1.3	0.7
Moslems	3.7	1.5	1.8
Other	3.1	1.3	2.4

Source: J. Reuter, *Die Albaner in Jugoslawien,* München, 1982, p. 63.

A glance at the data shows that the number of employed among the Albanians (64.9%) was 12.6 percentage points lower than their share of the population (77.5%), while the number of Serbs with jobs (25.6%) was 12.4 points higher than their share of the population (13.2%); in other words, nearly double. The Serbs' share of the unemployed, on the other hand, was proportionately higher than that of the Albanians. An updated report with absolute figures concerning the unemployed in Kosova is given on the following page (Table 9).

The actual number of the unemployed however, is much higher than 67,000, when account is taken of the unregistered unemployed, who constitute a majority. Western observers have reported that in 1980 there were an estimated 250,000 unemployed in Kosova.[35] Kosova has the highest

TABLE 9

Unemployment in Kosova in 1979, 1980, 1981
(in absolute figures and percentages)

Nationality	1979		1980		1981 (as of June)	
Albanians	48,590	(76.0)	52,926	(76.1)	52,170	(77.6)
Serbs	11,216	(17.6)	11,812	(17.0)	10,202	(15.1)
Montenegrins	1,491	(2.4)	1,405	(2.0)	1,267	(1.8)
Turks	412	(0.7)	464	(0.7)	447	(0.7)
Moslems	691	(1.2)	1,228	(1.8)	872	(1.4)
Rums	982	(1.6)	1,361	(1.9)	1,301	(2.0)
Other	610	(0.5)	390	(0.5)	890	(1.3)
TOTAL	63,992	(100.0)	69,576	(100.0)	67,148	(100.0)

Source: *Rilindja* (Rebirth), Prishtina, March 6, 1982, p. 6.

unemployment rate in Yugoslavia, with only one in ten employed, compared with one in five for the whole country.

The competition for job openings is fierce. As of mid-1982, there were 33 applicants per job in the region.[36] This figure is about three times above the national average. The situation is especially critical in the cities, where the large number of unemployed, particularly among the youth, put additional strains on the already burdened social services. Social inequalities created by the "free market" character of Yugoslavia's economic system, are bitterly resented. A primary cause of this condition is the immense growth of the administrative sector in the province. A study indicated that "one in every four employed Kosovars is a well-paid civil servant who enjoys the privileges of good housing, cars and easier access to leisure facilities."[37] The study added that such symbols of material well-being are "resented by lesser-paid workers and unemployed graduates." Another source of tension is the "disparity of incomes" between the comparatively productive urban areas, and the less efficient, tradition-bound rural areas.

The Federal Government has made efforts to create new jobs through allocations of development funds and the establishment of new industries. But such efforts have failed to alter appreciably the employment situation.

The pressures for employment have induced many Kosovans to seek jobs in other regions of Yugoslavia or abroad in Western Europe. Estimates of migrant workers varied, but they ran into the tens of thousands, as many as 80,000 according to a recent report.[38] Albanians in other parts of Yugoslavia, however, have difficulty getting jobs, in part because of the language barrier, in part because of their somewhat low level of technical and professional preparation, or because of ethnic prejudices they encounter. Most often, those employed were doing menial work for low pay.

In 1979, a total of 65,000 Kosovans were reported to be in West Europe.[39] Wages earned by workers abroad were helpful in increasing Kosova's foreign currency reserves, and reducing Yugoslavia's foreign trade deficit. But when they return home, the workers add to the existing pressures in the labor market.

The problem of employment affected deeply every sector of Kosova's economy, and was perhaps the most telling symptom of its many weaknesses.

Education:

The demonstration that flared up in Kosova in the Spring of 1981 began at the University of Prishtinë. The causes, at least initially, were economic in nature. Students complained over bad food, crowded dormitory conditions, and inadequate allowances in the face of galloping inflation (about 40 percent, the highest in Europe). At the time, the university had an enrollment of 36,000 full-time students, and an additional 18,000 in extension study programs. It is the third largest, in size, in Yugoslavia. Yet, the university "was built to accommodate only a third of its actual student body."[40] As a result, students were obliged sometimes to sleep two to a bed.

The doors of the educational system were thrown wide open, in part as a stopgap to the solution of the unemployment problem. It was better to keep the youth in the classroom—so reasoned the authorities—than to have them roam the streets. Consequently, Kosova has the highest ratio of students in the country: 274.7 per 1,000 inhabitants, compared with 194.9 for the Yugoslav national average, and 165.7 for Slovenia, the most advanced republic in the Federation. One out of every three inhabitants in the province is enrolled in some kind of educational program. The total number of pupils and students swelled to 470,000.[41] The following table shows the student enrollment for 1980-81.

TABLE 10

Number of Students[n] in Kosova According to Nationality
(1980-81 academic year)

Nationality	Total	Enrollment	Regular	Students	Corresp.	Students
TOTAL	42,700	(100%)	28,227	(100%)	14,473	(100%)
Albanians	30,724	(71.95)	21,358	(75.66)	9,366	(64.71)
Serbs	7,107	(16.64)	3,829	(13.56)	3,278	(22.64)
Montenegrins	1,766	(4.13)	998	(3.53)	768	(5.30)
Turks	300	(0.07)	215	(0.76)	91	(0.62)
Moslems	1,974	(4.62)	1,328	(4.70)	646	(4.46)
Other	600	(0.21)	288	(1.01)	312	(2.14)
Foreigners	223	(0.52)	211	(0.74)	12	(0.82)

Note: In Kosova "student" normally connotes a person who studies in college or in an advanced institution of learning.

Source: *Rilindja* (Rebirth), Prishtina, March 6, 1982, p. 5.

In spite of the high involvement of the population in education, illiteracy continues to be a problem in the province. More than a third (36%) of the Albanian population was illiterate at the beginning of the 1970s. Efforts to eradicate illiteracy are hampered by the patriarchal tradition—still influential in the region—which discourages girls from attending school.

The inflated educational system poured annually into the labor market several tens of thousands of graduates who, under existing conditions, only aggravated the unemployment problem. Moreover, too many of the graduates have a liberal arts or humanities background, and cannot be absorbed by an economy which needs instead more graduates with technical, scientific and mathematical backgrounds. For data on course enrollment of new students in the 1982-83 academic year, see Appendix D.

Foreign Trade:

Reports on the region's foreign trade in recent years have been almost uniformly depressing. Imports have exceeded exports by substantial margins, creating serious trade deficits, and reducing steadily foreign currency reserves. It appeared that unless exporting enterprises increased their exports substantially, they would soon not be able to import anything, because of the lack of foreign currency.

The imbalance in foreign trade can be attributed partly to unstable economic conditions in the world, partly to the troubled economy of Yugoslavia, but also to the quality of the merchandise in Kosova that is destined for export, which more often than not lacks appeal to foreign buyers.

Trade in 1981 with both East and West Europe fell short of the plan. However, trade between Yugoslavia and Albania expanded rapidly in recent years. It increased nearly five times between 1978 and 1981, rising from $28 million (U.S.) to $135 million. Kosova expected to profit from this exchange. A plan was under discussion in 1980 to import electricity from the Fierza hydroelectric power station in northern Albania, to a point near Prizren in Kosova.[42] It is not clear how far the plan advanced.

In its efforts to improve its balance of payments position, Kosova looks also to tourism as a source of income. In 1985 it expects to attract some 280,000 tourists: 230,000 of them from other parts of Yugoslavia, and 50,000 from abroad. But even if this goal is achieved, tourist income is not going to do much to improve the difficult financial position of the province.

Summary and Analysis of Problems

At present, even a partial listing of Kosova's economic problems reads like a litany of woes: inflation, unemployment, shortages of food and other commodities, housing crisis, illiteracy, high birth rate, a weak infrastructure, poverty. Added to these are problems of deficit spending, foreign trade deficits, a rising foreign debt, an overloading economy with taxes and tariffs. Still other problems are the so-called subjective weaknesses of the economy which include among others: work inefficiency, growing sick leaves, frequent work stoppages, and waste of funds and material.

Yet, the most critical problem of the economy is Kosova's lag in development with regard to other regions of Yugoslavia. What makes this lag particularly disturbing is that the gap between Kosova and the republics has been continually growing rather than narrowing. In 1947, Yugoslavia as a whole had a level of development that was twice as high as that of Kosova and the undeveloped republics of Macedonia, Montenegro and Bosnia-Hercegovina. In 1980, the gap in development between Yugoslavia and Kosova was in the ratio of 4:1.[43] What is still worse, the province has fallen behind even the undeveloped republics. Already by the mid-1970s, Kosova was in the same relationship to the undeveloped republics as those regions and Kosova were with respect to all-Yugoslavia in 1947. By 1980, the gap between Kosova and the undeveloped republics had grown to two and a half times.[44] The problem was succinctly stated by Mahmut Bakalli, former chairman of the LC of Kosova, in December 1980. Speaking about the results of the 1976-80 economic plan for Kosova, he said:

> The aim of reducing the gap in the degree of development of Kosova has not been achieved . . . . On the contrary, a further widening of this gap has taken place . . . . Instead of a rate of development 60 percent above that for the country, as had been planned, the rate of development of Kosova was 46.9 percent below the average for the country . . . . The tendency to the widening of this gap has continued . . . from 1947 to the present day.[45]

How did this situation come about? The reasons are many, but cannot all be dealt with here, since they include not only economic, but political, ethnic, cultural, linguistic and other reasons. Nevertheless, the major responsibility for the condition that developed must be laid, it appears, at the door of the Federal Government. The Federation discriminated against Kosova in its policy of economic development for the country. It is a charge that has been made repeatedly by Kosovan scholars and economists. According to Milija Kovačević, perhaps the leading economist in Kosova, for fifteen years following the war, Kosova was not included in the category of undeveloped regions, and as such was denied financial grants from the Federation (unconditional, at the time), and help from technicians and specialists that were dispatched to regions qualifying for Federal aid. When Kosova was included in the group of undeveloped areas, toward the

1960s, it received aid in the form of credits that had to be paid back with interest.[46] This policy of the Federation so burdened the economy of Kosova that it has never been able to recover from its effects.

The province is also reaping the consequences of the so-called "unsuitable structure" of its economy that has prevailed through three decades. The reference is to an economic policy that was mainly geared to production of raw materials, which were processed in the Republics, and which made Kosova dependent on the Republics for finished goods— a "condition that is not conducive to economic growth."[47] The stress on mining and energy resulted in relative neglect of agriculture, and because it was a capital-intensive policy, it had an adverse effect on the employment situation as well.

The human resources or personnel problems affecting the economy of the province include a lack of qualified cadres, made worse by the "exodus of experts" in the Serb and Montenegrin segments of the population; a mobile population of urban workers originating from the villages who have not yet adjusted themselves to the new life in the cities, and who have left in their wake a dislocated countryside; and the emergence of an "academic proletariat" made up of newly-graduated students, intellectuals and professionals with rising expectations, but with no jobs in which to employ their skills and knowledge. The plight of the idle intelligentsia is due in part to the fact that the majority of college students were enrolled in liberal arts curricula, and the developing economy of Kosova has relatively little need of them at present.

The problem of investments has been a chief concern in Kosova ever since the Federal Government began to allocate developmental funds in the mid-1960s. The leadership and the press in the province have complained loudly and insistently that investment funds, in the form of Federal aid, have been erratic and insufficient to meet the pressing needs of the province. The complaint seems valid. But there is evidence also of mismanagement of funds, such as investing in the wrong projects, in the wrong locations, or yet again spending vast sums of money on projects of prestige. Two examples are the radio-TV palace and the glass-and-marble university library in Prishtinë. The province has also suffered from an inability to attract foreign investors. But the suggestion that this is due to the difficulties of exploiting the natural resources of the region on account of the mountainous terrain, does not seem persuasive.[48] Albania, for example, which is even more mountainous, apparently has had no difficulty in exploiting its natural resources.

An obvious problem in Kosova, as in the rest of Yugoslavia, is the pervasive bureaucracy, which has rightly been called a "non-productive privileged class,"[49] causing a drain on the finances of the province and arousing strong resentments among the jobless and the poor. Like the birth rate, the growth rate of the bureaucracy in Kosova since 1968 has been greater than that of the economy. As a result, "one in four among the working population works in the administration and the 'infrastructure', as against one in seven in Slovenia."[50] Kosova can ill afford such an inflated and extravagant administration.

In April of 1980, the *New York Times* wrote that the "Albanians in Yugoslavia are the dispossessed of Yugoslavia, the lowest paid menial workers, looked down upon . . . ."[51] The comment underlines the profound economic and social inequalities between Kosova and the other parts of Yugoslavia. It is a situation that has led Albanians in Kosova to charge that they are victims of "economic exploitation" by the Serbs and Montenegrins.[52] This complaint is not far from the charge of "colonialism" hurled against the prewar Serbian bourgeoisie. The gloomy economic prospects bred an atmosphere of anxiety and even hopelessness among many in Kosova. The pent-up resentments and frustrations exploded, as we know, in the violent demonstrations of March and April 1981.[53]

How did the leadership in Belgrade respond to the demonstrations, from an economic point of view? The leaders had the objectivity to grant that economic factors were a cause of the rioting. Unfortunately, their analysis of the problems of Kosova's economy was in general defective: polemical rather than dispassionate, superficial rather than rigorous.

They mistook effects for causes, and instead of assuming at least partial responsibility for the fiasco of Kosova's economy, they put the blame on the local leadership of the province. In a Plenum in November 1981, devoted to Kosova, the LCY Central Committee admitted that not enough was done to develop Kosova, but the reason for this was not a Federal policy of neglect and discrimination against the province, but rather the war-ravaged economy of Yugoslavia and the "consequences of the Cominform blockade" against Yugoslavia.[54] The obvious retort to that, of course, is: Why did not the effects of the war and the Cominform blockade prevent the Federal Government also from giving economic aid and support to the other undeveloped regions of Yugoslavia?

Current Five-Year Plan (1981-85)

Before discussing the prospects of Kosova's economy, it seems useful to consider the main features of the 1981-85 economic plan of the province. The plan gives data on production goals and investments, as well as some notions about the thinking of the planners for curing the ills of Kosova's economy. The following table shows the production targets of the current 5 Year Plan.

TABLE 11

Production Targets of Kosova's 1981-85 Plan

Branch of Economy	Percent of Total Production (1980)	Percent of Total Production (1985)	Average Annual Increase (in %)
Total Economy	100.0	100.0	7.2
Social Sector	80.3	83.8	7.9
Private Sector	19.7	17.2	4.4
Industry & Mining	36.2	38.3	8.5
Agriculture	18.6	17.4	5.7
Forestry	0.7	0.5	2.2
Water Economy	0.4	0.4	7.9
Construction	13.5	13.4	7.3
Communications	5.0	4.9	6.5
Trade	18.9	18.5	6.8
Tourism	1.8	1.8	6.7
Handicrafts	2.9	2.8	6.1
Communal Activity	0.6	0.6	8.7
Other	1.5	1.4	5.5

Source: *Gazeta e Delegatëve* (Journal of Delegates), biweekly organ of the Kosova Assembly, VII, 143 (November 3, 1981), p. 6.

The plan puts emphasis on the development of industry, which is expected to account for 38.3 percent of the total production in 1985, followed by trade (18.5%), agriculture (17.4%), and construction (13.4%).

Also, the role of the social sector will increase from 80.3 percent to 82.8 percent at the expense of the private sector, which will decrease 2.5 percent (from 19.7% to 17.2%). The dominant role of industry becomes particularly evident when we look at the distribution of investments for the current plan, as the following table shows.

TABLE 12

Distribution of Investments in Kosova's 1981-85 Plan

Branch of Economy	Percent of Total
TOTAL ECONOMY	100.0
Industry	63.7
Agriculture	6.7
Forestry	1.0
Water Economy	5.4
Construction	3.6
Communications	9.3
Trade	3.5
Tourism	2.8
Handicrafts	1.8
Communal Activity	2.1
Finance	0.1

Source: *Gazeta e Delegatëve* (Journal of Delegates), Prishtina, VII, 143 (November 3, 1981), p. 7.

Nearly two-thirds of the total investment funds will be allocated to industry. The drafters of the plan see industry as the primary vehicle for the development of the province, and for narrowing the gap between the province and the rest of Yugoslavia.

The new plan is said to have a "new structure," which favors the development of the processing industries, above all metal processing, as well as agriculture, small business, and the service industries. The shift to these "labor intensive" branches of the economy is expected to generate more income and capital, and thereby strengthen the feeble financial position of the province; more jobs, which should alleviate the dire unemployment situation; and more food to relieve current food shortages and, more importantly, move the province toward becoming self-sufficient in food production.

But the concept of giving prominence to the processing industries has been talked about for a decade. It was intended to be a primary goal of the 1971-75 economic plan.[55] The transition however did not occur, either during that plan, or during the plan that succeeded it.

For the current plan to succeed, and make a start toward closing the yawning gap between the province and the developed regions of the country, Kosova has to develop at a rate 60 percent above the Yugoslav national average. A most ambitious goal, indeed, but almost certainly unrealistic. The idea moreover is not new. The same goal had been set for the preceding 5-Year Plan, but the plan, as has already been pointed out, not only failed to meet its objectives, but actually ended up with Kosova sliding back and widening the gap between itself and the rest of the country.

Ninety percent of the funds to finance the plan will come from sources outside Kosova, mostly from the Federal Development Fund. Because of its special legal status (since December 1980), as the province with a "pronounced order of underdevelopment," Kosova is due to receive higher amounts of money from the Federation, and favored with better credit terms, than the other underdeveloped regions. The province is expected to receive 140 billion dinars (about $3,250,000,000 U.S.) during the current 5-Year Plan.[56] Furthermore, to ease the pressure on its budget, Kosova is freed from payment of 80 percent of its financial obligations to the Federal Budget for the duration of the plan. The unpaid share will be assumed by the six republics and the province of Vojvodina.

The financial aid allocated to Kosova is substantial, but its actual investment value for the 1981-85 plan will be curtailed. Its efficacy will be considerably reduced by the fact that vast amounts of money are tied up in projects under construction that are carryovers from previous 5-Year Plans. As a result, 43 billion dinars from the Federal Fund will be diverted to finance the completion of such delinquent projects.[57]

The plan envisages a close collaboration between Kosova and the other regions of Yugoslavia, through joint economic ventures between industries in Kosova and enterprises in the six republics and Vojvodina. Accordingly, each of the republics and Vojvodina have undertaken to build at least one project in Kosova during the current 5-Year Plan. The idea is based on the premise that in order for Kosova's developmental plan to succeed, its economy needs to be "integrated" with the economies of the other regions in Yugoslavia. This, too, is not a new idea. It was a part of the package of the 1976-80 Plan. But it did not get off the ground, as none of the republics and Vojvodina fulfilled its commitment to construct a project in Kosova.[58]

The reality is that the rich republics are reluctant to finance the development of the poor republics and the province of Kosova. And on the other hand, the poor republics resent the special treatment accorded Kosova by the Federal Government in terms of aid, because of its "special status."[59] Furthermore, the policy of inter-regional economic integration runs counter to the trend toward autarchy that has been gathering momentum in Yugoslavia over the past decade. Inter-regional trade in the country has been steadily decreasing, dropping 10 percent since 1970. In the case of Kosova, trade with the other republics fell from 34.1 percent in 1970 to 24.5 percent in 1978. It will be no mean accomplishment to reverse this trend.

Progress reports on the unfolding of the Plan for the year 1981 and the first half of 1982 were far from encouraging. Of the funds allocated to implement accords reached with the republics and Vojvodina, less than fifty percent was utilized by the end of 1981. Far from achieving the 60 percent figure in overall productivity, necessary to narrow the developmental gap, Kosova's social product increased only 5.5 percent in 1981.[60] A June 1982 meeting of the provincial LC noted that "the basic aims for this year are not being realized."[61] Press reports complained about decreasing rates in industrial productivity and imports, diminishing wages, rising prices and higher unemployment figures. The only positive development seemed to be an increase in exports of 23 percent over the same period (January-May) in 1980.

Prospects of the Economy

If one were to consider the inherent resources of Kosova alone, one could conclude that the province has a bright economic future. On the face of it, it seems that the province has all the preconditions for a "take-off" in economic development. It has abundant energy resources, including fossil fuels and water resources. It has a variety of organic and inorganic raw materials, in sufficient quantity to meet domestic needs and to export. It has a sufficiently fertile land to produce enough food to feed its population. And it has the potential in human resources to meet labor needs and to create a technical intelligentsia to answer to the sophisticated demands of modern society. But a closer look at Kosova shows, as we have seen, an economy in disrepair and out of focus.

Kosova's natural resources have been, and continue to be, the basis of its development. And the fundamental goals of development remain what they have been for decades: to raise the province's dismal standard of living, and close the disquieting gap between itself and the rest of Yugoslavia.

The demonstrations in the province in the Spring of 1981 crystallized the whole range of problems that have destabilized Kosova's economy. In assessing the demonstrations, voices in the Yugoslav leadership concluded that the much heralded "self-management system," which is the foundation of the country's economic system, had stagnated in Kosova. There were complaints that "the system of self-management existed only on paper and that there was no real dialogue between the government and the people."[62] Since then, press reports in Kosova have noted tendencies to "turn back to centralism," that is, to let Belgrade do the economic planning, etc. for the country; but such tendencies have so far been successfully resisted.[63]

In its plenum on Kosova in November 1981, the LCY leadership stated that the elimination of economic inequality between Kosova and the other regions in Yugoslavia is a long-term project. Nevertheless, the plenum expressed optimism regarding the prospects of the region's economy, urged the strengthening of self-management relations in the province, encouraged the integration of Kosova's economy with the economies of the republics and Vojvodina, and pledged to continue the Federal policy of giving aid to Kosova, including "special incentives" to stimulate its development.

The plenum reaffirmed the Federal Government's policy that greater infusions of money into Kosova's economy will enable the province to "turn the corner" and proceed toward economic recovery and eventual prosperity. But is money the key factor to recovery? Over the years

Kosova has been the receipient of considerable funds from the Federal Development Fund and other external sources; yet its per capita social product today, compared with the Yugoslav national average, is lower than ever—only 28.8 percent. As one observer has noted, the "policy of leveling out economic inequalities has been a complete failure, as far as Kosovo is concerned."[64] From this perspective, the 1981 riots amounted to a "repudiation of more than ten years of intense effort to accelerate development" in Kosova.[65]

The suspicion is raised that the failure to eradicate economic and social inequalities in Kosova is linked to the nature of Yugoslavia's economy. The "market socialism" of the country has increased, rather than leveled out, regional differences. A critic has suggested, not without reason, that Yugoslavia's system "not only tolerates but appears to breed" conditions of inequality in which "the rich seem to become richer and the poor poorer."[66]

Another factor that deserves attention is Kosova's relation to the Republic of Serbia, into which it is presently incorporated as an "autonomous province." Since the founding of the Yugoslav Federation at the end of the war, Kosova has been subordinated to Serbia. Yet, Serbia has not been able to bring Kosova out of its backward state. From an economic point of view, Kosova's special relationship to Serbia, that is, its subordinate status in the Serbian Republic, has not worked, inasmuch as the province remains in a critical state of underdevelopment. There is evidence that the people of Kosova are not content with this relationship. According to a recent report, ". . . the population of the region has hopes of better accounting for its needs, if it becomes more independent of Serbia."[67] This view was expressed also at the London Seminar on Kosova in May of this year. According to one participant at the Seminar, "Once the Kosovars feel that they are their own masters, they should be able to improve their economy."[68]

The consensus of scholars, journalists, and travelers to Kosova is that the economic prospects of the region are grim. It would be surprising if the province does not slide further back by 1985. The stagnation that has gripped the economy, and the resulting malaise that afflicts the Kosovan population, particularly the volatile youth, is cause for concern. It is reminiscent of the condition of the province in the early postwar period.

Back in 1979, Milija Kovačević, President of the Council of Finances in Kosova, observed that while Kosova has 7 percent of Yugoslavia's population, its social product accounted for only about 2 percent of the total social product of Yugoslavia. He warned that this discrepancy has not only economic, but social and political implications as well.[69] That same year, another Kosovan leader, Musa Limani, warned that ". . .the new generations in the underdeveloped regions, equipped now with a higher education and greater sensitivity to social relations, will not accept to remain all their life in an inferior economic and social position."[70] Their warnings proved to be prophetic, as events in Kosova showed two years later.

Conclusions

Before bringing this study to an end, it seems proper to make some brief comments about the tie between economics and politics in Kosova. Since the Spring events of last year, this has been a recurrent theme in the Kosovan press, and has been commented upon widely by the foreign press as well.

The press of the province, and the Yugoslav media in general, view economic equality as a precondition to national equality, and economic stabilization in Kosova as a "precondition to political stability."[71] Kosovan authorities admitted that the 1981 disturbances "occasioned extraordinary budget expenditures," and that economic difficulties at present "sometimes become ideological problems as well."[72] A meeting of the Political Aktiv of the Provincial LC in October 1981, concluded that "economic stabilization is a fundamental ideological and political task."[73] Another party meeting, held in June 1982, urged party members to take steps to halt "negative tendencies in the economy which could jeopardize efforts to achieve general stability in the Province . . . ."[74]

Belgrade's attempts to put the blame for the disturbances on local Albanian "irridentists" or on the Albanian Government, have not had, in general, a favorable reception. The French review, *L'Express,* and *Le Monde,* are but two of the organs that have printed sympathetic or favorable articles concerning Albanian grievances with regard to the question of Kosova.[75] Other Western sources concur that the Federal Government has so far failed to take the necessary steps to deal with the special case of underdevelopment presented by Kosova.

An unfortunate consequence of the riots, relative to the economy of Kosova, is the Serbian backlash against Kosovan Albanians. Reports from

Belgrade have noted that Serb nationals resent the financial support being given by the Federation to Kosova. They speak of such aid as "a reward" for the rioters, and urge instead a cut-off even of the forms of aid that Kosova has been receiving heretofore from the government.[76] More serious than these verbal attacks, have been the economic reprisals on the part of governmental authorities against the rioters. According to a Western observer:

> Those identified as having been involved in any way with the events of last spring [i.e., 1981], have in most instances been dismissed from their schools, colleges and workplaces. Since in Kosova . . . wage earners often support large families, the sentences and the dismissals have often caused enormous hardship. What is more, any help to families left unsupported is rigorously discouraged.[77]

Apart from the dangerous political consequences such a policy could have, it is plain that it does not contribute to the stability and advancement of Kosova's stricken economy.

In summing up, attention might be drawn to the following: One is that the socialist leadership of Yugoslavia, despite the supra-nationalism of its Communist ideology, was unable to overcome the ethnic prejudices against the Albanians harbored by its predecessor, the prewar Greater Serbia bourgeoisie. In the light of that "built-in" prejudice, it is not surprising that the Federal Government neglected the development of Kosova for over a decade following the war. The current Serbian backlash regarding economic aid to the province, and economic reprisals against the rioters, is but a continuation of that deep-seated prejudice. It is hardly necessary to say that a basic change of attitude in Belgrade is needed before a basic and positive change in Kosova's economic and general welfare can take place.

Inasmuch as Kosova has not been able to solve its economic problems through nearly four decades under the tutelage of the Republic of Serbia, the logical alternative, it seems, is to let the Kosovans assume full responsibility for the management of their economic life, as is the case with the Macedonians, the Montenegrins and other peoples of Yugoslavia. They ought to be given the chance—or rather allowed to exercise the right—to run their economic affairs as seems advisable to them, in fruitful cooperation with the other republics.

There is no guarantee, of course, that left to themselves, and acting as masters of their own economy and their own house, the Kosovans will create a stable and prosperous economy. But they can hardly do worse. And in any case, Kosova, like grown-up people, ought to have the right to make its own mistakes, and find its own solutions to problems. I expect that Kosovans would do better if they were to manage their own economy, according to their perceptions and their particular needs and interests.

I believe the entire Yugoslav economy and society would benefit as a result. It is an experiment worth trying, for the need for a change of momentum, if not of direction, in Kosova's economy is great enough.

APPENDIX A

Population of Kosova According to Communes (1981)

Commune	Total	Albanians	Serbs	Montenegrins	Other[n]
KOSOVA	1,584,558	1,227,424	209,792	26,875	120,467
Deçani	40,661	39,195	247	914	305
Dragashi	34,894	18,582	88	20	16,204
Ferizaji	113,935	90,645	18,642	317	4,331
Gjakova	92,091	87,448	1,936	1,953	754
Gjilani	84,196	59,802	19,339	176	4,879
Gllogovci	40,522	40,443	35	5	39
Istogu	50,011	35,806	7,728	1,875	4,602
Kaçaniku	31,075	30,393	310	15	357
Kamenica	48,216	32,352	14,759	62	1,043
Klina	54,449	45,418	6,878	971	2,172
Leposaviqi	16,941	853	15,035	81	972
Lipjani	60,094	43,110	10,297	355	6,332
Mitrovica	105,097	66,618	25,867	1,972	10,640
Peja	111,067	79,793	8,037	9,810	13,427
Podujeva	75,320	72,089	2,226	603	402
Prishtina	211,156	140,907	44,227	6,276	19,746
Prizreni	134,689	93,902	11,671	517	28,599
Rahoveci	61,048	56,208	4,039	212	589
Sërbica	46,907	45,467	1,116	136	188
Suhareka	59,406	55,663	3,581	30	132
Vitia	47,112	35,234	7,576	169	4,133
Vuçitërna	65,671	57,496	6,158	406	1,611

Note: Includes Turks, Moslems, and others.

Source: Adapted from a table in *Rilindja,* May 14,1 981, p. 8.

APPENDIX B

Distribution of Albanian Ethnics in Yugoslavia
1981
(rounded to nearest thousand)

Region	Number
Kosova	1,227,000
Macedonia	378,000
Serbia (inner)	72,000
Montenegro	37,000
Croatia	6,000
Bosnia-Hercegovina	4,000
Vojvodina	4,000
Slovenia	2,000
TOTAL	1,732,000

Source: *NIN,* weekly Belgrade periodical, February 28, 1982.

APPENDIX C

Employment in the Republics and Provinces
1969, 1979
(per 1,000 inhabitants)

Region	1969	1979
ALL-YUGOSLAVIA	183	253
Bosnia-Hercegovina	135	191
Montenegro	144	205
Croatia	212	298
Macedonia	154	220
Slovenia	308	427
Serbia (inner)	180	257
Kosova	81	107
Vojvodina	205	273

Source: Jens Reuter, *Die Albaner in Jugoslawien,* Südost-Institut, Oldenbourg Verlag, München, 1982, p. 61.

APPENDIX D

Distribution of New Students According to Departments
at the University of Prishtinë
(1982-83 academic year)

Department	Full-Time	Part-Time
Engineering	1,533	
Mathematics and Natural Sciences	900	320
Mining and Metals	705	
Medicine	500	
Philosophy	940	500
Law	545	450
Agriculture	400	150
Economics	300+	
TOTAL	5,823	1,420

Source: *Politika,* Government daily, Belgrade, May 19, 1982.

NOTES

1. Tahir Abdyli, *Zhvillimi i industrisë në Kosovë* (The Development of Industry in Kosova), Rilindja Publishing House, Prishtinë, 1978, p. 15.

2. Fehmi Pushkolli, *Lëvizja revolucionare e sindikatave dhe Lidhja e Sindikatave të Kosovës, 1919-1975* (The Revolutionary Movement of Trade Unions and the League of Trade Unions in Kosova, 1919-1975), Prishtinë, 1977, p. 12. In a harsh indictment of the prewar Serbia, another Kosovan scholar notes that the Serbian bourgeoisie "was not interested in the progress [of Kosova], for the reason that this land was inhabited by Albanians, and Albanians, it was thought, should be displaced, terrorized and physically eliminated." T. Abdyli, op. cit., p. 27. See in this connection, Dr. V. Čubrilović, "The Expulsion of the Arnauts [i.e. Albanians]," memorandum to the royal government in Belgrade, March 7, 1937.

3. *Statistical Pocket Book of Yugoslavia, 1980,* Belgrade, 1980, p. 38.

4. Official Yugoslav figures for the Albanian population in Yugoslavia are consistently contradicted by Albanian exiles from Yugoslavia. They claim there are over 2.5 million Albanians in the country.

5. Pedro Ramet, "Problems of Albanian Nationalism in Yugoslavia," *Orbis,* Vol. 25, No. 2 (Summer, 1981), p. 376.

6. Michael Dobbs, "Why Ethnic Unrest in Serbia Has the Yugoslavs Worried," *Albanian Catholic Bulletin,* Vol. 3, Nos. 1-2 (1982), pp. 80-81.

7. *Rilindja,* March 6, 1982, pp. 4-5.

8. This appraisal is supported also by the observation in the Summer of 1982 of a visitor to Kosova from America—an engineer by profession—who is known personally to the writer.

9. Sami Repishti, "Albanians in Yugoslavia: the Struggle for National Affirmation," *Albanian Catholic Bulletin* 3 (1982):1-2, p. 64; "The Truth About 'The Migration of Serbs and Montenegrins' from Kosova," memorandum of The Albanian Kosovar Youth in the Free World, New York, May 1982.

10. Catherine Verla, "Après les émeutes du Kosovo: une question nationale explosive," *Inprecor,* Paris, June 1981, p. 10. The figures are from the 1971 census.

11. Patrick Moore, "The Kosovo Events in Perspective," *RFE* (Radio Free Europe) *Research* (Yugoslavia), 28 April 1981, p. 2.

12. Jens Reuter, *Die Albaner in Jugoslawien,* Südost-Institut, Oldenbourg Verlag, München, 1982, p. 63.

13. W. B. Bland, *The Albanians in Yugoslavia,* The Albanian Society, Ilford, Essex, England, June 1981, p. 8.

14. Patrick F. R. Artisien and R. A. Howells, "Yugoslavia, Albania and the Kosovo Riots," *The World Today,* November 1981, p. 420.

15. Albert Dushi, "Socialist Autonomous Province of Kosovo," *Socialist Thought and Practice,* Belgrade, May 1981, p. 64.

16. Sinan Hasani, interview, "What Happened in Kosovo?" *Socialist Thought and Practice,* August 1981, p. 16.

17. Mihailo Maletić (ed.), *Kosovo nekad i danas/Kosova dikur e sot* (Kosova Formerly and Today), Borba Publishing House, Belgrade, 1973, p. 540.

18. P. Ramet, op. cit., p. 372.

19. F. Pushkolli, op. cit., p. 151.

20. LCY-CC Plenum, November 17, 1981, "Political Stabilization and Socio-Economic Development in the Socialist Autonomous Province of Kosovo," *Socialist Thought and Practice,* December 1981, p. 114.

21. *Rilindja,* March 14, 1978, p. 9.

22. J. Reuter, op. cit., p. 68.

23. *Rilindja,* March 14, 1978, p. 9.

24. Ibid., August 26, 1981, p. 7.

25. J. Reuter, op. cit., p. 68.

26. T. Abdyli, op. cit., p. 75.

27. *Gazeta e Delegatëve* (Journal of the Delegates), biweekly organ of the Kosova Assembly, Prishtinë, No. 162, August 4, 1982, p. 2.

28. *Rilindja,* December 27, 1980, p. 7.

29. *Gazeta e Delegatëve,* November 3, 1981, p. 3.

30. Agricultural land accounted for a little over one-third (36%) of the total area of Kosova. The province is rich in water resources, but as yet they have been only partially exploited for land irrigation, electric power, and other needs. At present, the prospects for the development of agriculture depends heavily upon the completion and operation of two large water reclamation projects: the "Ibër" and the "Radoniq," which will add considerably to the total area of irrigated land in the province. *Rilindja,* April 14, 1982.

31. *Rilindja,* June 22, 1982, p. 6.

32. Ibid., September 16, 1981, p. 7.

33. "World Press on Events in Kosova," *Zëri i Popullit* (Voice of the People), Albanian Party of Labor daily, April 20, 1982, p. 4.

34. Personal source.

35.   Reuter, op. cit., p. 62.

36.   Memorandum of The Albanian Kosovar Youth in The Free World, New York, September 21, 1982, p. 2.

37.   Artisien and Howells, op. cit., p. 422.

38.   Michele Lee, "Yugoslavia's Albanian Crisis—Wrong Turn in Kosovo," *Labour Focus on Eastern Europe,* Vol. 5, Nos. 1-2, Spring, 1982.

39.   *Rilindja,* March 30, 1981, p. 15.

40.   C. Verla, op. cit., p. 13.

41.   J. Reuter, op. cit., p. 61.

42.   *Rilindja,* May 22, 1980, p. 7.

43.   One big source of loss of funds was the increase in personal incomes of workers that was not matched by an increase in productivity and revenues in the enterprises where they worked. In short, losses due to unearned income. *Rilindja,* September 24, 1981, p. 7; June 22, 1982, p. 4.

44.   T. Abdyli, op. cit., p. 79; J. Reuter, op. cit., p. 57.

45.   *Rilindja,* December 5, 1980, p. 6.

46.   Ibid., July 30, 1979, p. 5.

47.   Paraphrase of remark by Michael Kaser, at the "London Seminar on Kosova," held on May 19, 1982, *Dielli* (The Sun), Boston, June 16, 1982, p. 3.

48.   Remark by C. Verla, a generally most astute observer, in her article, cited above, p. 10.

49.   P. Moore, op. cit., p. 9. A reflection of this condition is the substantial difference in income of workers, some of them (hotel and tourist personnel) earning less than 4,000 dinars a month (about $93), while others (technical and finance personnel) earning over 50,000 dinars per month (about $1,160). Calculation based on the January 1982 rate of exchange of 43 dinars = $1. *Rilindja,* November 2, 1981, p. 7.

50.   C. Verla, op. cit., p. 13.

51.   J. Darton, "Tito's Yugoslavia," *The New York Times Magazine,* April 13, 1980, p. 84.

52.   Artisien and Howells, op. cit., p. 423.

53.   In the wake of the riots, sources in the West noted the appeal Albania has for a portion of the Albanians in Kosova. They speculated that Kosovars are attracted by Albania because in some ways Albanians in Albania "are better off" than those in Kosova. Nationalism is a motive, but in addition, Kosovars are influenced by the order and discipline that

prevails in Albanian society, by the claim of Albania that it has solved the problem of unemployment, and even more by the egalitarianism that characterizes the social order of Albania.

54. LCY-CC Plenum, November 1981, op. cit., p. 113.

55. M. Maletić, op. cit., p. 549.

56. *Rilindja,* April 30, May 1-2, 1981, p. 8. The calculation is based on the exchange rate of 43 dinars = $1 U.S.

57. Ibid., September 10, 1981, p. 7.

58. Ibid., September 19, 1981, p. 7.

59. C. Verla, op. cit., p. 10; J. Reuter, op. cit., p. 64.

60. *Rilindja,* July 11, 1982, p. 5.

61. Ibid., June 23, 1982, p. 9.

62. Anton Logoreci, "Riots and Trials in Kosova," *Index on Censorship,* London, April 1982, p. 40.

63. *Rilindja,* October 27, 1981, p. 7.

64. P. Ramet, op. cit., p. 387.

65. Ibid., p. 383.

66. P. Moore, op. cit., p. 12.

67. C. Verla, op. cit., p. 14.

68. "London Seminar on Kosova," *Dielli* (The Sun), Boston, June 16, 1982, p. 1.

69. *Rilindja,* August 4, 1979, p. 5.

70. Ibid., August 26, 1979, p. 8.

71. Ibid., June 22, 1981, p. 7; November 2, 1981, p. 7; J. Reuter, op. cit., p. 58.

72. *Rilindja,* January 26, 1982, p. 6; June 22, 1982, p. 6.

73. Ibid., October 27, 1981, p. 7.

74. *Rilindja,* June 23, 1982, p. 9.

75. L'Express, April 9, 1982; A. Ducellier, "Les Albanais et le Kosovo," *Le Monde,* June 2, 1982.

76. *Rilindja,* January 26, 1982, p. 5.

77. Michele Lee, op. cit.

Adi Schnytzer

THE ECONOMIC SITUATION IN ALBANIA AND KOSOVA: NOTES ON A COMPARISON

Introduction

In his address to the Eighth Congress of the Party of Labour of Albania, First Secretary Hoxha made clear his feeling that Kosova is a backward province of Yugoslavia, kept so by the merciless oppression of its population and exploitation of its natural resources by the wealthier Yugoslav republics. Such sentiments are, in themselves, perhaps not surprising. Rather, it is their public pronouncement that represents a distinctly sensitive elevation in the level of antagonistic rhetoric between Tirana and Belgrade.

Given the relative underdevelopment of both Albania and Kosovo prior to World War II, one might suspect an independent Albania to have taken considerably greater strides on the path to economic development than its "oppressed" neighbor. This paper sets out to test this hypothesis, special attention being focused on the period 1976-80, the five-year plan period immediately preceding the "difficulties" of Spring 1981.

Economic Systemic Context

It is best to begin with a summary of the nature of the two economic systems involved in our comparison. Albania is a centrally-planned economy, directed by its leadership in accordance with the purest milk of Stalinist doctrine. The system thus implied has the following characteristics:[1]

(a)   There is social ownership of the means of production. In the Albanian case, this means that industrial enterprises and state farms are state-owned, agricultural cooperatives are group-owned, and higher-type agricultural co-operatives are owned jointly by the state and the resident group.[2]

(b)   There must be no significant economic decision-making located within the primary producing units of the economy. Thus, plans are formulated within the policy, planning and administrative hierarchy on the basis of goals set by the Party leadership. The precise location of decision-making within the Albanian hierarchy underwent a dramatic shift during the period under consideration.

Since the mid-1960s, the Albanian government had experimented with various devolutions from central ministries to the local organ of state power, the Executive Committee of the People's Council. These measures, combined with a number of ideological campaigns, were designed to elicit greater goal-congruence between the leadership and workers and to complement pressure from above on enterprise management for better economic performance with pressure from below in the form of party-managed "worker control." Like all systems of organization, this one had its weaknesses. However, the lavish quantity of aid provided by China enabled such rapid rates of growth of output to be achieved that the leadership perceived no need for dramatic systemic changes.

Around 1975[3] the flow of foreign aid ceased and by 1978 Albania and China had severed all relations. Under these circumstances, the Albanian leadership felt that continued high rates of economic growth could be achieved only if economic decision-making were recentralized with ministries and the traditional order of one-man management restored at enterprise level. The economic implications of the 1978 systemic change are considered below.

(c)   Needless to say, information flows in the Albanian economy are essentially vertical, with price playing only a minor role as an allocator of resources.

(d)   The Albanian liturgy provides that material and moral incentives be utilized in motivating economic agents to perform their assigned tasks. In practice this has meant an egalitarianism more pronounced than elsewhere in Eastern Europe, with regular small increases in real income for workers and peasants and occasional wage-cuts for management.

Kosova is an Autonomous Region of the Yugoslav Republic of Serbia. It is thus a geographical part of the Yugoslav economic system.[4] The system has the following basic characteristics:

(a)   For the most part there is social ownership of the means of production, although a small-scale private enterprise in the service sector is permitted and most agriculture is in private hands.

(b)   The distribution of economic decision-making within the Yugoslav economy has been well summarized by Tyson:[5]

> Since the major economic reforms of the early and mid-sixties the Yugoslav economy has functioned as an imperfect market system, based on the principles of social ownership of the means of production and workers' self-management in enterprise decision-making. Within this system the role of the government at the federal, republican and communal levels has been mainly limited to selective ad hoc interventions in monetary policy, investment policy, price policy and foreign trade policy. Such interventions have been designed to change the parameters which influence the actions and decisions of enterprises and households on the market rather than to directly change the actions and decisions themselves. As distinguished from indirect interventions of this type, direct controls over economic activity have been concentrated in three main areas: government financing of investment projects and priority sectors, an important part of which reflects continued efforts to achieve regional development goals; government regulation of economic activity in the private sectors and government regulation of the use of foreign exchange.

(c)   Information flows in this economic system are thus essentially horizontal, price playing an important role as an allocator of resources. It should be noted, however, that given the relatively backward nature of the Kosova economy, distortions in both factor and product markets are liable to render the use of market forces less efficient than in the more developed regions of Yugoslavia.

(d) Motivation of economic agents is based mainly on the profit motive, although the ever-growing field of self-management microeconomics[6] has shown that, relative to the perfectly competitive capitalist firm, the "Illyrian" firm tends to reduce output and engage in less investment. In Priština this problem has been considerable.[7] Thus, for the first nine months of 1981, industrial production was 11 percent below the planned target while real incomes rose by up to 54 percent. At the same time losses had trebled in comparison with the same period in 1980 and funds for accumulation had been dramatically reduced.

On the basis of the above discussion, several points may be made:

(i) In terms of political freedom, *a priori* consideration of economic system structure would suggest that the Albanians of Kosova have considerable advantages over their western neighbors. However, given traditional ethnic animosities and the monolithic position of the Yugoslav League of Communists, comparisons around political performance criteria are difficult to make with any degree of confidence.

(ii) The Albanian system is well suited to the rapid mobilization of resources in pursuit of specific economic goals. On the other hand, underdevelopment notwithstanding, the allocation of resources is likely to be more efficient in Kosova than in Albania if efficiency is measured *for the Yugoslav economy as a whole.* Given the relatively high level of migration of labor and capital between Kosova and other parts of Yugoslavia, it is difficult to assess the likely implications of system structure for efficiency in Kosova alone.

(iii) Almost regardless of the performance criteria chosen, the comparison of economic development in Albania and Kosova is complicated by the fact that the former is a sovereign state whereas the latter is part of a larger nation and fully integrated into the Yugoslav market. In particular, this implies that whereas the Albanian authorities are free to choose appropriate policy measures in the face of any given economic situation, the Kosova economy will inevitably be effected—perhaps adversely— by policies introduced in Belgrade to solve economic problems of consequence which have emerged elsewhere in Yugoslavia. Adverse implications for Kosova are rendered more likely by the immense difference in economic development between it and other parts of Yugoslavia. Suffice it to note that in 1977, if the level of global social product per capita is taken as 100 for Yugoslavia, the respective figures for Kosova and Slovenia—the richest republic—were 30 and 200![8] It is most unlikely under such circumstances that macroeconomic policy could impact with equal efficiency on all parts of the economy.

Development Strategies

The Albanian development strategy has remained remarkably consistent over the past 35 years, temporary modifications being predicated on major upheavals in foreign relations such as 1961 split with Moscow and the recent crisis with the Chinese government. In line with Stalinist requirements it displays the following features:

(a)   The rate of growth of output in heavy industry should always exceed rates of growth in other sectors of the economy. Likewise, industry must grow more rapidly than agriculture and the growth of productivity must outstrip wages. Centralized direction of the economy is seen as the most effective way to achieve these goals. On the development of heavy industry for the 1976-80 period, the former Prime Minister Mehmet Shehu[9] wrote of:

> . . .the rapid development of industrial production, the extension and improvement of the structure of production by giving greater priority to the industry producing means of production, utilizing the natural resources and wealth of the country in a more complex manner, to create a broader and sounder base in meeting the needs of the economy for raw materials, electric power, spare parts, chemical fertilizers and other indispensible products of broad scale use.

Heavy industrialization has been one aspect of the Stalinist development strategy to which the Albanian leadership has clung particularly tenaciously. Thus, even in the wake of a Soviet blockade after 1961, domestic resources were redirected to ensure that even if all else failed—as it did—the plan for global industrial production would nearly be met. Again, in the early 1970s, when difficulties with China suggested that a more balanced line of development might be in order, a number of high ranking officials were purged and subsequently accused of sabotaging mining and oil projects.[10]

(b)   On the other hand, clearly the rapid growth of industry has not been sufficient to enable the Albanian economy to become a major exporter of manufactured products as yet. Thus, when faced with the loss of Chinese aid, difficulties in sustaining further rapid industrialization were certain unless there were marked improvements in the agricultural sector of the economy. Enver Hoxha showed his awareness of this point in his address to the Seventh Party Congress:[11]

> . . . the construction of socialism requires advanced and modern agriculture. Agriculture is the basis of the economy, which to a large extent, determines and conditions the fulfillment of tasks in other branches, the raising of the general wellbeing of the people, and the strengthening of the defence potential of the country.

A progressive redistribution of income for the urban to the rural sector of the economy has formed a major policy initiative in the past decade. Because prices and wages are centrally determined in the Albanian economy, the leadership has found it relatively easy to implement this policy.

(c)   In the Albanian context, Stalin's "Socialism in one country" has been replaced by "relying on one's own resources." Although this slogan has long been part of the Albanian literature, the presence of large amounts of aid from first the Soviet Union and then China, gave it a somewhat hollow ring. Albanian sources rationalized the aid as an example of "proletarian internationalism" and, therefore, a good thing! However, since 1978, Albania has been—in terms of its own rhetoric—the world's only Marxist-Leninist state and it has steadfastly refused to yield to any temptations to borrow from the West.

(d)   The Albanian interpretation of Stalin's fundamental law of socialism has always been more literal than its author's own. The law may be put as follows:[12]

> . . . the securing of the maximum satisfaction of the constantly rising material and cultural requirements of the whole of society through the continuous expansion and perfection of socialist production on the basis of higher techniques.

On the consumption side, the Albanian leadership has always taken this law to imply that per capita consumption must rise annually if this is at all possible. Prior to 1976 this objective had been met in most years.[13]

(e)   In summary, we may quote again from Hoxha's 1976 report,[14] where he provides a most succint statement of both the aims and means of his development strategy:

> To go on at rapid rates with the socialist construction of the country for the transformation of socialist Albania into an industry and agriculture, according to the principle of self-reliance, for the further allround strengthening of the economic independence of the country; to further improve the socialist relations of production and the superstructure; to strengthen the dictatorship of the proletariat and enhance the defence potential of the homeland; to raise the material and cultural level of the working masses higher by carrying further the narrowing of distinctions between town and countryside. This is to be achieved on the basis of the consistent waging of the class struggle and the mobilization of all forces and energies of the people under the leadership of the party.

Turning now to a consideration of the Kosova development strategy it must be said that Kosova per se probably does not have one. This is because, as has already been stated, Kosova is an integral part of the Yugoslav economy. It is thus necessary to consider the extent to which the Belgrade leadership has a strategy for the development of the country's backward regions. According to Tyson and Eichler,[15] the following are the important features of the strategy:

(a)   The basic element in Yugoslav national policy is the transfer of investment funds from the more developed regions to the less developed ones. Notwithstanding high rates of "domestic" saving in the poor regions, the transferred investment funds have been insufficient to narrow the gap between Kosova and richer parts of the country. This policy has probably failed because it has not been attended by appropriate micromeasures:[16]

> The effectiveness of regional development policies focusing on the provision of investment funds at concessionary terms has been hampered by failure to encourage the optimal allocation of these funds among competing projects. For a variety of reasons, including the strategy of complimentarity in Yugoslav regional development

planning, whereby the less developed regions have been assigned the role of supplying to more developed regions with raw materials and semi-finished products, investment funds have been concentrated in large, capital-intensive projects that have high capital-output and capital-labor ratios. A bias towards capital intensity has also been encouraged by the subsidized rates at which investible resources are made available and by the need to devote a substantial share of investible resources to capital-intensive infrastructural projects.

(b)   About 50 percent of Yugoslavia's coal reserves and 30 percent of its total power potential lies in Kosova. During the 1976-80 plan period, this sector was accorded preferential treatment in respect of credit and foreign exchange. It was hoped that this might set Kosova on the road to industrialization by encouraging a pooling of resources between local suppliers and manufacturing enterprises elsewhere in Yugoslavia:

> Under the new planning system . . . enterprises using energy and raw material inputs are expected to negotiate self-management agreements with their suppliers for the joint financing of investment projects to expand their capacity, and such agreements could serve to increase capital flows to the less developed regions.[17]

Tyson and Eichler are sceptical about the likely effectiveness of this strategy. In particular, they suggest that the attraction of capital to Kosova —and other poor regions—is not, of itself, a sufficient regional development strategy. They argue that "unemployment and underemployment problems that underlie regional income disparities" cannot be overcome unless "its distribution among competing projects is based on estimates of the opportunity costs of capital and labor that reflect the relative abundance of labor."

The strategy may however also be criticized from a Marxist viewpoint. Thus, great stress is laid on *equality* in agreements between enterprises in different regions.[18] Not only are development projects to be based on income sharing in proportion to the value of factor inputs, but also it is deemed essential that projects be acceptable to both sides. Since we are concerned here with the distribution of income between different regions of a market economy, there is no reason to suppose that outcomes will be any different than is argued by Marxists to be the case *either* within a capitalist economy *or* in international trade. As the Yugoslav economist Milentije Popović put it:[19]

> Under the conditions of a capitalist economy then not only is labor exploited by capital. In addition to this basic form of exploitation an extra profit is extracted from backward production branches for the benefit of more advanced branches . . . . [In foreign trade this is also the case] . . . . So those countries in which the organic composition of capital exceeds the world average at the time . . . draws an extra profit at the expense of those were the composition is lower.

Whilst it may be reasonable to argue that the combination of worker's self-management with social ownership of the means of production has eliminated exploitation—as defined by Marx—in the Yugoslav economy, it is difficult to see how these institutions mitigate the possibility of unequal exchange between enterprises of rich and poor regions. (It should be noted that the gross income per capita in less developed regions is only about 63 percent of the Yugoslav average).[20]

On the basis of the above discussion several points may be made:

(i) Whereas the Albanian economic system is well adapted to the pursuit of growth objectives and the Albanian leadership's quest for high rates of growth has been almost pathological, the Yugoslav government has opted for a "road to socialism" which has almost guaranteed the continual exacerbation of regional economic disparities.

(ii) On the other hand, it may be somewhat unfair to criticize the Yugoslav authorities for failing to adopt a regional policy which would equalize incomes when the measures necessary to achieve such a goal would strike at the root of Yugoslav socialism. After all, there are a few, if any, instances of market economies in which *enormous* regional disparities in income have been alleviated.

(iii) As with economy system, so with development strategy, it is clear that Albania has the upper hand in being a soveriegn state able to determine—to a large degree—its own future.

Economic Performance 1976-80

Albanian expectations for the 1976-80 period were set out by Prime Minister Shehu in his report to the Seventh Congress in 1976. A summary of plan targets and results is set out below:

TABLE 1

Global Indicators	Planned Increase 1980 against 1975 in percentage terms: (actual)	
Net Material Product	38-40	
Global Industrial Production	41-44	(34.5)
Global Agricultural Production	38-41	(21.4)*
Volume of Goods Transport	30-32	(30)
Volume of Investments (for the five years taken together)	35-38	(15)
Volume of Exports (for the five years taken together)	24-26	(51)
Productivity of Labor in Industry	15-17	
Productivity of Labor in Construction	12-13	
Retail Goods Turnover	22-25	(20)
Real Income per capita of Population	11-14	
Global social Product	——	(24.4)

*   For the five years taken together.

Sources: M. Shehu, op. cit., p. 39. "Direktivat e Kongresit të 8-të të PPSh për planin e 7-të pesëvjeçar (1981-1985) të zhvillimit të ekonomisë dhe të kulturës të RPSSH," *Probleme ekonomike,* No. 4, 1981. E. Hoxha, "Nga raporti mbi veprimtarinë e Komitetit Qendror të Partisë," *Probleme ekonomike,* No. 4, 1981.

TABLE 2

Industries	Planned Increase 1980 against 1975 in percentage terms. (actual)	
Oil Industry	27-29	
Coal Industry	63-65	(63)
Chromium Industry	71-73	
Copper Industry	40-42	
Iron-Nickel Industry	500-510	
Electric Power Industry	145-150	
Engineering Industry	40-42	(57.7)
Chemical Industry	140-145	
Construction Materials Industry	50-53	
Timber and Paper Industry	18-20	
Glass and Ceramics Industry	20-23	
Light Industry	22-24	
Food Processing Industry	23-25	

Sources: M. Shehu, op. cit., p. 43. "Direktivate e Kongresit të 8-të," op. cit. E. Hoxha, "Nga raporti," op. cit.

The first point to note about these results is that they are hardly comprehensive. Indeed, for no five-year plan in the past have so many outcomes remained unavailable. It seems reasonable to conclude that most sectors of the economy failed to meet their targets. Real income of both urban and rural populations was said to have risen over the period and some sectors of industry were singled out for praise—electric power, chemical fertilizer, light and food processing—although aggregate data for their performance are not given. Significantly, Peking was blamed for the failure to complete construction of certain major projects, a clear admission that the rupture with China was not without its economic costs. Immediately following the break in 1978, the Albanian press had tended to minimize the degree of Albanian dependence on Chinese credits and imports.[21] On the other hand, the author of the report on the new five-year plan—apparently given as Mehmet Shehu in printings prior to his death, but rendered anonymous in subsequent editions—goes to some lengths to show that during 1979-80 the Albanian economy performed better than it had done prior to the rupture. Thus, while global social product increased at an average annual rate of 4.2 percent during 1976-78, this rose to 4.9 percent for 1979-80. Likewise—the circumlocation is tremendous—the average annual rate of growth of global industrial production was 17 percent higher in the final two years of the period that it had been for the first three years!

What the author forgot to mention, in his clever analysis, was that Albania had stopped receiving Chinese aid by around 1975, giving the economy around four years to adjust to the dislocation. The 1978 announcement of a break was, in many respects, a mere formality.

Of the results in the above tables, several require further discussion. First, the increase of 15 percent in investment over the previous five years is very easily the worst recorded in the country's history under communist rule. On the other hand, that global social social product should have risen by 24.4 percent suggests that there must have been significant improvements in the efficiency of resource allocation. For example, over the previous five year period 1971-75, investment had risen by 50 percent, while global social production had recorded an increase of 37 percent.

Second, the dramatic increase in exports (51 percent) against a target of 24-26 indicates both the extent to which the Albanian authorities underestimated the impact of the break with China, and the relative ease with which priorities may be changed in a centrally-planned economy. There can be little doubt that the 1978 recentralization of economic decision-making power helped facilitate the shift to export-led growth.

Finally, the 20 percent increase in retail goods turnover—as against 22-25 percent planned—indicates the Albanian government's concern to avoid popular unrest in the face of economic difficulties. Given that inflation in Albania is negligible, this result reflects a continued steady increase in per capita consumption. The lessons of the Polish experience will not have been lost on so shrewd a Stalinist as Enver Hoxha.

The analysis of economic outcomes in Kosova cannot be conducted along lines similar to those adopted for Albania. First, the five-year plan in an imperfect market economy is little more than an "indicative" plan and, as such, its fulfillment or underfulfillment does not provide an accurate reflection of the success or failure of economic activity. In the rare event that outcomes match *ex-ante* targets, it is more likely due to chance than management.

Second, the critical problem facing the Kosova economy tend to be related to its location within Yugoslavia. As a consequence, analysis of outcomes in isolation—to which the Albanian case is arguably suited—are likely to throw little light on real problems.

Finally, as was noted above, the Yugoslav development strategy as it relates to Kosova is concerned with an equalization of incomes between regions of the country. It is against this yardstick that outcomes must be measured. In other words, geopolitical realities dictate that the comparison between economic development in Albania and Kosova be based on performance relative to the past in the former case and achievements relative to the rest of Yugoslavia in the latter case. To the extent that economic factors contributed to the unrest in 1981, they are unlikely to have followed a comparison of living standards in Tirana and Priština. The following data require little amplifications:

TABLE 3

Selected Indicators: Kosova and Slovenia

		Yugoslavia	Kosova	Slovenia
Population	1953	100%	4.8%	8.8%
	1978	100%	6.9%	8.2%
Active Population	1953	100%	3.4%	9.0%
	1978	100%	4.1%	9.3%
Agricultural Population	1953	100%	5.7%	5.9%
	1978	100%	9.8%	3.7%
Workers	1953	100%	2.1%	15.3%
	1978	100%	3.0%	14.0%
Investment	1953	100%	1.2%	16.0%
	1978	100%	3.1%	14.7%
Social Product per capita (index)	1953	100%	46	165
	1978	100%	30	200

Source: *American University Field Staff Report,* No. 5, 1980.

TABLE 4

Percentage Rate of Growth of Social Product (Kosova)

	1976	1977	1978	1979
Total Economy	2.1	5.1	4.2	7.2
Socalist Sector	1.9	8.1	6.4	5.3
Private Sector	2.7	−5.1	−3.3	14.3

Planned average annual rate of growth, 1976-80: 9.5 percent.
Actual average, 1976-78: 3.8 percent.
Expected average, 1976-80: 5.4 percent.
Source: *American Universities Field Staff Report*, No. 5, 1980.

From Table 4 it can be seen that at the expected average annual rate of growth of social product over the 1976-80 period of 5.4 percent, Kosova would have registered an increase of 30 percent over the five years against Albania's 24.4 percent. On the other hand, the gap between Kosova and Slovenia is widening. This is, in large part, explained by the dynamics of population growth across regions and the tendency for unemployment problems—unacknowledged, but likely to be slight in Albania—to be exacerbated in the less developed regions.

Thus, "in 1977 jobseekers per vacancy in the social sector ranged from . . . 1.4 in Slovenia . . . to . . . 32.5 in Kosova."[22] In 1979, 3 percent of the Yugoslav workforce was employed in Kosova as against 13.9 percent in Slovenia, while the percentage of persons seeking employment was 8.3 percent of the Yugoslav total in Kosova as against only 1.3 percent in Slovenia.[23] As Tyson and Eichler point out:[24]

> . . . these indicators of labour surplus understate the magnitude of the employment problem in the less developed regions because they do not fully account for the existence of underemployed workers in private agriculture, a sector which accounts for a much large portion of the active population in the less developed regions.

On the basis of the above discussion it seems reasonable to conclude, with Reuter,[25] that four factors explain Kosova's relative lack of development:

(a)   There has been relatively little investment.
(b)   What investment there has been, has been in the wrong place.
(c)   Investment has created an insufficient number of jobs.
(d)   There has been a great disproportion between economic growth and population increase.

Conclusions

The major conclusion to be drawn from this paper is methodological. At first glance, Albania and Kosova would appear ideally suited to a comparison of economic development. Both regions are populated mainly by Albanians—although the distinction between Ghegs and Tosks in Albania must be kept in mind—and levels of development were similar immediately following World War II. Further, both regions have embarked on "roads to socialism"—albeit very different roads.

Not even extreme differences in economic systems structure need pose difficulties. After all, among the variables with which a communist party can play in achieving its goals are the institutional arrangements for the allocation of resources. The trade-off between plan and market is, to a greater or lesser degree, faced by all economies.

The real difficulty in the Albanian-Kosova comparison is the question of independent statehood. The leadership of the Party of Labour of Albania has always been in a position to determine the economic goals of society, subject, to be sure, to certain foreign constraints—in particular foreign aid. The ultimate choice between policy options, however, resides with the leadership.

The case of Kosova is very different. Ethnic Albanian representation in the Yugoslav government notwithstanding, economic goals are generally determined for Yugoslavia as a whole. And, as results indicate, the economic system structure adopted by the League of Communists has worked to the advantage of richer regions of the country. Under these circumstances, it is as unreasonable to be critical of Kosova's performance as it is to suggest that, because the rate of growth of social product over the period 1976-80 was higher in Kosova than in Albania, economic development in the former has been more "successful" than in the latter. Only a politician in Enver Hoxha's position can afford to draw decisive conclusions.

* * * * *

NOTES

1.   For a detailed discussion, see A. Schnytzer, *Stalinist Economic Strategy in Practice,* Oxford, 1982.

2.   This "creative development," unique in the socialist world is discussed in ibid., Appendix C.

3.   See M. Kaser, "Trade and Aid in the Albanian Economy," in *East European Economies Post-Helsinki,* Joint Economic Committee, U.S. Congress, 1977, pp. 1325-1340.

4.   For a general discussion, see International Bank for Reconstruction and Development, *Yugoslavia: Development with Decentralization,* Baltimore, 1975.

5.   L. D. Tyson, "The Yugoslav Economy in the 1970s: A Survey of Recent Developments and Future Prospects," in *East European Economies Post-Helsinki,* op. cit., p. 945.

6.   See J. P. D. Wiles, *Economic Institutions Compared,* Oxford, 1977, Chapter 3.

7.   Belgrade domestic radio broadcast, October 15, 1981.

8.   *Statistički Godišnjak SFRJ 1979,* Belgrade.

9.   M. Shehu, *Report on the Sixth Five-Year Plan (1976-1980),* Tirana, 1977, p. 42.

10.   See M. Kaser and A. Schnytzer, "The Economic System of Albania in the 1970s: Developments and Problems," in A. Nove et al., *The East European Economies in the 1970s,* London, 1982.

11.   E. Hoxha, *Report to the Seventh Party Congress,* Tirana, 1976, p. 45.

12.   J. V. Stalin, *Economic Problems of Socialism in the USSR,* Peking, 1972, pp. 40-41.

13.   See A. Schnytzer, "The Impact of the Sino-Albanian Split on the Albanian Economy," in J.E.C., U.S. Congress, *East European Economic Assessment,* Part 1, Washington, 1981.

14.   E. Hoxha, op. cit., p. 33.

15.   L. D. Tyson and G. Eichler, "Continuity and Change in the Yugoslav Economy in the 1970s and 1980s," in *East European Economic Assessment,* op. cit., pp. 164-167.

16.   Ibid., p. 166.

17.   Ibid., p. 167.

18.　See, for example, *Privredni Pregled,* 11 March 1981.

19.　M. Popovis, *Über die wirtschaftlichen Beziehungen zwischen sozialistischen Staaten,* Mainz, 1950, cited in P. J. D. Wiles, *Communist International Economics,* Oxford, 1968, pp. 14-15.

20.　L. D. Tyson and A. Eichler, op. cit., p. 166.

21.　See A. Schnytzer, "The Impact of the Sino-Albanian Split on the Albanian Economy," op. cit.

22.　L. D. Tyson and A. Eichler, op. cit., p. 165.

23.　*Ekonomska Politika,* 24 August 1981, p. 16.

24.　L. D. Tyson and A Eichler, loc. cit.

25.　J. Reuter, *Die Albaner in Jugoslawien,* Vienna, 1982. I am indebted to A. Pipa for this reference.

Anton Logoreci

A CLASH BETWEEN TWO NATIONALISMS
IN KOSOVA

The political, military and judicial shock waves of the riots that broke out of Kosova in the spring of 1981 were felt throughout that year and the next. The state of emergency—which in the eyes of many local Albanians was tantamount to a Serbian military occupation of their province—remained in force. Hundreds of Albanians from Kosova as well as from Macedonia and Montenegro were tried and sentenced to terms of imprisonment ranging from one to fifteen years, charged with hostility to the government and irredentism. Yugoslav official sources gave somewhat confused and occasionally conflicting reports about the number of people involved. It is therefore difficult to be quite sure how accurate such figures are.

According to the federal secretary of internal affairs, a total of seven hundred people had been arrested by the end of September 1982. Of these, three hundred and twenty were tried by district courts. Yet another 1,300 were dealt with by magistrates' courts.[1] The senior party official of Kosova said that magistrates' courts had passed prison sentences ranging from thirty to sixty days.[2]

Apart from the many trials there were also very sweeping purges and dismissals of Albanians in every walk of life throughout 1981 and 1982. The first of these were carried out immediately after the riots. They affected party and government officials; television, radio and press journalists; university and secondary school teachers. However, no sooner had these drastic changes taken place than there were repeated demands for further "differentiation"—the slimy official weasel word for purges. Such

185

demands came mainly from the leaders of the Serbian republic, of which Kosova is one of two autonomous provinces. They alleged that the local authorities had been unwilling to punish all those involved in the disturbances, and that there had also been a good deal of passive resistance to the political cleansing campaign. Strong pressure was brought to bear on the provincial authorities to pursue this campaign to the bitter end. In order to bring this lesson home, several federal and Serbian republican leaders visited Kosova between June and September 1982. They included the federal prime minister, the federal secretary of internal affairs and his Serbian counterpart, the president of the Yugoslav League of Communists, the president of the Serbian assembly, and the commander of the Serbian territorial defence units.

The principal target of this pressure was the provincial university which was regarded not only as the power-house of Albanian nationalism but also as the mainspring of the 1981 disturbances. The political situation in the university was discussed at a meeting of the Prishtina municipal party committee in September. It divided university teachers into three main groups. The first comprised those who had taken an active part in hostile activities. The second was made up of people who had merely condemned the demonstrations verbally, but had done nothing to oppose various nationalistic manifestations. Members of the third group had maintained complete silence about what had happened. Six professors belonging to the first group, together with nineteen students, were expelled from the university and the League of Communists.[3] One of those dismissed was Professor Ali Hadri, a well-known Albanian historian. A few days later he was asked to report to a university party meeting at which he was accused of having failed to condemn Albanian nationalism and irredentism. Another charge against him was that his writings were based on Tirana's historical interpretation of the post-war period. In reply, Professor Hadri said that his interrogators had resorted to inquisitorial methods, and that the Yugoslav press had waged against him a fiercer campaign than the French press had waged against Dreyfus in the last century.[4]

The purges did not spare even Kosova's security forces. One-fifth of their members, it was alleged, had joined various illegal organizations. Consequently several police officials employed at different levels of the security administration lost their jobs.[5]

* * * * *

What steady accumulation of feelings of frustration and bitterness, of humiliation and anger was it that finally caused the eruption of Albanian street demonstrations in the towns and villages of Yugoslavia's southern region early in 1981? I do not think it is possible to begin to understand these events without a brief examination of Serbian-Albanian relations since 1913, the year when large Albanian areas were ceded to Serbia and Montenegro by the European great powers of the time. During most of the 1913-1941 period these areas formed part of the Yugoslav state which came into being at the end of the First World War. Unlike many other national minorities in Europe, the Albanians of Yugoslavia were given no specific international protection in the 1919 peace settlement.[6] So they became a minority cast in limbo, completely at the mercy of their Serbian rulers. They had no voice in the local administration; no schools or publications of any kind in their own language. Harsh police methods were used to subjugate them and deprive them of all vestiges of their national identity. In addition, several thousand were forced to emigrate to Turkey and Albania, their land being taken over by new Serbian and Montenegrin settlers.[7] This was indeed the time when the seedbed of Serbian-Albanian hostility was well and truly cultivated.

The Second World War introduced new political complications as well as more human suffering into the situation. Following Yugoslavia's defeat in 1941, the greater part of Kosova and the Albanian-inhabited areas of Montenegro were annexed to Albania by the Italian fascists who were then in control of Albania. As a result of the annexation, the future of the Albanian regions of Yugoslavia became a burning political issue for both the Yugoslav and the Albanian wartime communist resistance movements. The Yugoslav communist party had made certain vague promises, before the war, that it would grant the right of self-determination to all national groups if it achieved power. This was done in the hope of attracting the greatest possible support for its cause. For similar reasons, the Albanian communist partisans were also in favor of the proposition that the Albanians of Yugoslavia should be given the right to decide their own future after the war. However, when it came to shaping a joint Yugoslav-Albanian policy on the issue in 1943, the Yugoslav communist party went back on its earlier promises and rejected the idea of self-determination in Kosova. This caused the first serious rift between the two communist parties, making the future of the Albanian regions of Yugoslavia more uncertain and precarious than ever. Whatever lingering illusions there may have been in people's minds about self-determination, these were brutally destroyed when the Yugoslav communist partisan forces launched, towards the end of 1944 and the beginning of 1945, a large-scale military campaign in Kosova. The campaign seems to have been designed to achieve two things: to deal with all those suspected of collaboration with the enemy during the Italian-Albanian occupation of the province; to establish firm communist rule in the area. There were numerous clashes between the local Albanian inhabitants and the Yugoslav partisan forces in which a large number of Albanians were killed.[8]

When the Albanian territories reverted to Yugoslavia after the war, they were partitioned between Serbia, Macedonia and Montenegro. Kosova, the largest of them, became part of the republic of Serbia. Despite the unpropitious circumstances resulting from the war, the position of the Albanians began to improve after 1945. They were recognized for the first time as a distinct national group. Schools in their own language were opened in some areas. But this slow improvement in their wretched lot came to an abrupt end in 1948, when Tito's communist regime was expelled from the Soviet bloc and Tirana broke off relations with Belgrade. The main victims of these events were the Albanians living in Yugoslavia. Some of the old Serbian-Albanian mutual suspicions and hatreds were revived, together with many of the cruel persecutions and injustices which the Albanians had suffered between the two wars. The Serbian communist authorities also introduced the prewar policy of forced emigration. As a result, between 1953 and 1966 some 230,000 Albanians left Yugoslavia.[9]

The removal from office in 1966 of Alexander Ranković, the Yugoslav vice-president and head of the security police, led to a gradual improvement in the situation of the Albanians. This in turn opened the gates to a powerful nationalist revival as well as to new demands for greater freedom and equality in all fields. The Albanians began to argue that their rights could not be properly secured unless Kosova was detached from the republic of Serbia, under whose despotic rule it had remained for so long, and became a separate republic. These demands were voiced publicly for the first time in the street demonstrations which broke out in several towns of the province in November 1968. The demonstrations were quelled by the police; several young Albanians were subsequently tried and sentenced to imprisonment. Although the authorities responded to the disturbances by making some concessions which will be discussed below, political agitation and unrest, in one form or another, became almost an annual feature between 1968 and 1981. The long series of trials of young people, who were imprisoned from one to fifteen years, added more fuel to the simmering pool of discontent, frustration and anger that already existed in the province. The situation was, in fact, close to the one described by Alexis de Tocqueville when he writes that it is often when a people which has put up with an oppressive rule for many years without protest will suddenly rise in anger when the government decides to relax its pressure.

Apart from the often severe sentences given at the Albanian trials, the official publicity surrounding them and the allegations that political prisoners are tortured have also caused great resentment. According to an Amnesty International report on prisoners of conscience in Yugoslavia, press coverage of political trials is usually either very brief when the accused is relatively unknown, or selective, if the trial has aroused public interest. In the latter case, press reports tend to imply that the accused is guilty even before court conviction. Public statements by Yugoslav politicians attacking the accused before trial or conviction have also led to allegations that verdicts in political trials are decided in advance by the authorities. Regarding torture, the report says that Amnesty International has received allegations of people in Kosova being tortured after the 1981 demonstrations. But because of insufficient evidence, the report neither confirms or denies such allegations.[10] During the trial of nine Albanians in Prishtinë in July 1982, one of the main defendants (Halil Alidema) said in court that he was beaten during the interrogations, and had sustained injuries as a result.[11]

After the 1968 demonstrations, the authorities decided to make a number of important concessions to Albanian opinion. In constitutional changes introduced in 1969, 1971 and 1974, Kosova was given greater autonomy and was enabled to forge direct links with the federal authorities. An Albanian university was also set up in the provincial capital in 1969. But perhaps the most important concession of all, the one that finally provided the driving forced behind the upsurge of Albanian nationalist feelings and aspirations of the 1970s and early 1980s, was the decision that Kosova could establish the closest possible cultural ties with Albania across the border. A series of agreements concluded in 1968,

1969 and 1970 provided that Albania should supply the province with textbooks and other educational facilities as well as with visiting university teachers. Apart from satisfying some of the most pressing demands of the young Albanians of Yugoslavia, these cultural exchanges were also regarded by President Tito and his colleagues as a kind of bridge or channel of communication along which Yugoslavia would be able to exert a benign political and ideological influence on isolationist and Stalinist Albania. In point of fact, however, such exchanges proved to be a one-way traffic, benefitting Tirana and Albanian nationalism in Yugoslavia far more than it ever did the hopes and ambitions of Belgrade. The main reason that things turned out the way they did was because, having been denied for many generations everything that helped to nourish a people's national consciousness and identity, the Albanians living in Yugoslavia, especially the post-war generation, were by the 1960s like a very parched sponge, immensely avid to absorb anything that helped to illuminate their past history and made some sense of their contemporary situation.

Two of the most common charges made at political trials of Albanians since 1968 are hostile activity against the state and irredentism. These were made by the news media and politicians both before and after convictions. After the 1981 disturbances, official propaganda maintained fairly consistently that the ultimate goal of the demonstrators was nothing less than to achieve political union between the Albanian territories of Yugoslavia and the republic of Albania. A fairly typical example of such propaganda is this statement by the Yugoslav federal secretary of internal affairs, Stane Dolanc:

> Albanian irredentists are now showing their true face. They no longer talk about the republic of Kosova, but say 'Long live Enver Hoxha.' It's quite clear that what was really involved was the integrity of Yugoslavia. This is why we call it a counter-revolution.[12]

What truth is there in the official claim that the many Albanians convicted in political trials were in fact irredentists? The simple answer is that no hard evidence has been produced to sustain such a charge. As most political trials were held either *in camera* or else in open court in which access is severely restricted to selected individuals issued with official passes, no independent observers could be satisfied that the charge of irredentism was actually proved in a fair trial. The Albanian government has also been accused by Yugoslav official sources that it encouraged irredentist aspirations in Kosova and elsewhere. Here again no evidence was forthcoming in support of the contention. For his part, the Albanian communist leader, Enver Hoxha, said in November 1981 that his country had made no territorial claims on Yugoslavia nor asked for any frontier changes.[13]

But even if, for argument's sake, one were to assume that the Yugoslav charges were true, what power or influence could a weak Albania (weaker than ever after losing China's protection in 1978) possibly exert to bring about a change in the frontiers of a country not only much larger than itself but also one which enjoyed a good deal of international support for its independence and policy of non-alignment? In view of all this, many Albanian dissidents and their supporters may have come to regard the blanket charges of irredentism levelled against them as yet another one of those official propaganda slogans, like "brotherhood and unity," which are designed, not to inform, but to gag people, and so prevent them from expressing their own views on the many problems of their society.

When the political powers and functions of Kosova's provincial government were increased by the constitutional amendments enacted after 1966, President Tito began to take a close personal interest in the affairs of the province. He established direct channels of communication with its leaders. This suggested that he was conscious of his government's heavy collective responsibility for imposing on the Albanians two decades of draconian rule, and would do all he could to protect them from the pressures of hard-liners in the Serbian government. There were, however, signs that these developments were resented by some Serbian politicians who tried to assert their old power and authority in Kosova after Tito's death in 1980, and particularly after the explosion of Albanian unrest a year later. But the Serbian claim that Kosovo was a purely Serbian problem was challenged by some Croat and Slovene politicians. For instance, Milja Ribičić, the Slovene who was prime minister of Yugoslavia from 1969 to 1974, said a few months after the riots that Kosova was essentially an economic and political problem that could not be dealt with by judges and lawyers. He believed it was pointless to send young demonstrators to prison for declaring in public that they wished to have a republic of their own.[14] Vladimir Bakarić, a senior Croat politician, regarded

regarded the status of Serbia's two provinces—Kosova and Vojvodina—as "Yugoslavia's greatest political problem." Although he thought the Serbian republic had a right to have a say in Kosova's domestic affairs, it could only do so within the general framework of the Yugoslav federation.[15] In short, the perdurable though latent political tension between Serbs, on the one hand, and Croats and Slovenes, on the other hand, came to the surface over the Kosova crisis.

The centralist policies of the Serbian republic came under attack from another unexpected quarter—from the Serbs of the province of Vojvodina who make up 54 percent of its population. Addressing the party central committee of Serbia in December 1981, Bosko Krunić, the provincial leader, complained that the republican leaders in Belgrade had tried to make the Kosova riots an excuse for limiting the constitutional powers of both autonomous provinces. In any case, he said, the troubles of Kosova had stemmed, not from the degree of autonomy it enjoyed, but rather from the mistaken policies its government had pursued in the past. Speaking at the same meeting, Iljaz Kurtezi, the representative of Kosova, said it looked as if certain people had in fact been hoping that something awful like the 1981 riots would take place sooner or later so that they could demand drastic political changes.[16]

But the Serbian leadership swept aside such criticisms and relentlessly pursued throughout 1982 the repressive policies it had introduced in the spring of 1981. The state of emergency remained in force. Purges continued unabated. Political trials went on giving out heavy prison sentences to more young men and women. Yugoslav politicians spoke of their determination to stamp out Albanian nationalism, apparently unaware of the invisible, mined demarcation line between pristine national consciousness and the political ideology of nationalism. By the end of 1982 Kosova was in a state of frozen political deadlock, having in effect forfeited many of the constitutional and political gains it had made since 1966. And the fact that these policies had to be executed by Albanian local politicians, party and government officials, judges and policemen—all acting under orders from the Serbian republican leaders—added to the general anger, dismay and friction.

According to the official census taken in March 1981, there are 1,730, 000 Albanians in Yugoslavia. Most of them live in Kosova where they constitute 77.5 percent of the population. Albanians have the highest annual rate of population increase in Europe. If it wants to avoid the kind of political and social turmoil that has affected Kosova and parts of Macedonia in recent years, the Yugoslav leadership will have to seek a genuinely federal ·and democratic solution—as opposed to the Soviet solution it had chosen—to the Albanian problem, one based on a continuous procedure of discussion and consultation, of compromise and conciliation.

* * * * *

NOTES

1. Stane Dolanc, federal secretary of internal affairs. Tanjug, 29 September 9182.

2. Sinan Hasani, communist leader of Kosova. Belgrade radio, 16 June 1982.

3. Prishtinë radio, 18 September 1982.

4. Tanjug, 23 and 24 September 1982.

5. Mehmet Maliqi, secretary of internal affairs of Kosova, Tanjug, 13 July 1982.

6. C. A. Macartney, *National States and National Minorities.* London, 1934, p. 240.

7. H. Islami, "Kërkimet antropogjeografike në Kosovë," *Gjurmime Albanologijike: Seria e Shkencave Historike* (Prishtinë), 1971, pp. 134-44; H. Hoxha, "Politika e eliminimit të Shqiptarëve nga trualli i Jugosllavise së vjetër," *Përparimi* (Prishtinë), No. 5, 1970, p. 432; both quoted in S. K. Pavlowitch and E. Biberaj, *The Albanian Problem in Yugoslavia: Two Views,* Institute for the Study of Conflict, No. 137/138, London, 1982, p. 25; R. Marmullaku, *Albania and the Albanians,* London, 1975, p. 138.

8. A. Hadri, "Shqiptarët në Mbretërinë e Jugosllavisë prej vitit 1918 deri më 1941 dhe pjesëmarrja e tyre ne LNÇ të Jugosllavisë" in *Historia e Popullit Shqiptar,* Vol. 2, Prishtinë, 1969, p. 811; R. R. King, *Minorities under Communism,* Harvard University Press, Cambridge, Massachusetts, 1973, p. 283, quoted in P. R. Prifti, *Socialist Albania since 1944: Domestic and Foreign Developments,* MIT Press, Cambridge, Massachusetts, 1978, p. 229.

9. H. Islami, "Kërkimet antropogjeografike në Kosovë," p. 141, quoted in Pavlowitch and Biberaj, op. cit., p. 29.

10.   Amnesty International, *Yugoslavia: Prisoners of Conscience,* London, 1982, pp. 26-28.

11.   *Times* (London), 23 July 1982.

12.   Tanjug, 29 September 1982.

13.   *Zëri i Popullit* (Tirana), 2 November 1981.

14.   *Vjesnik* (Zagreb), 19 September 1981.

15.   *Vjesnik* (Zagreb), 31 December 1981, 1-3 January 1982.

16.   S. Stanković, *The Serbian Question, One of Yugoslavia's Major Internal Problems,* Radio Free Europe Research, Munich, 26 January 1982.

Sami Repishti

THE EVOLUTION OF
KOSOVA'S AUTONOMY WITHIN THE
YUGOSLAV CONSTITUTIONAL FRAMEWORK

During the months of March, April and May 1981, a series of massive student demonstrations shook the foundations of the Socialist Autonomous Province (SAP) of Kosova,[1] the southern region of Yugoslavia inhabited predominantly by Albanians. The Yugoslav government used special police forces and the Army to disperse them. In the clashes that followed, scores of Albanians were killed and several hundreds were wounded. Several thousands were arrested.[2]

The demonstrations which started at the University of Kosova in Prishtinë over a seemingly unimportant incident—a protest against poor food and poor living conditions at the University dormitories—soon took a political turn. Antigovernment slogans were used by students who were later joined by large numbers of workers and farmers. The most frequently used slogan, and the most persistent one, was the demonstrators' demand that the SAP of Kosova, a component of the Socialist Republic (SR) of Serbia, be elevated to the rank of a republic. The demand implied a change in the present constitutional arrangements of the Socialist Federal Republic (SFR) of Yugoslavia. Thus far, the Yugoslav official reaction has been a flat and uncompromising denial, accompanied by massive arrests and heavy jail sentences for Albanian protesters.

One may well ask what is the constitutional position of the SAP of Kosova in the SFR of Yugoslavia today? How did it originate and evolve? Is there a basis for constitutional changes to allow the elevation of the SAP of Kosova to the status of a full-fledged republic? The entire state and social order of the country rest upon the concept of a "working class" ruling sovereign, as a sole representative of the general will. This representation is entrusted to the Yugoslav Communist Party (YCP), now known as the Yugoslav Communist League (YCL). This avant-garde of the working class is the *sole* organized group committed to correctly interpreting the interest of the working masses.

Chronology of Constitutional Developments

Historically, Yugoslav constitutionalism began with a political act, the Declaration of Corfu (1917). The document indicated that the liberation of the South Slav lands should lead to the establishment of a common democratic South Slav state.[3] In 1921, the Vidovdan Constitution and its concept of Great Serbian hegemony over a single "national" state violated the principles of Corfu. The new state was defined as "one nation" with "three names,": The Kingdom of Serbs, Croats and Slovenes. Ethnic, religious and language differences were intentionally neglected.

In 1929, the Vidovdan Constitution was subverted by the military dictatorship that produced the 1931 Constitution. The state's official name was changed to the Kingdom of Yugoslavia (the Kingdom of the South Slav peoples). In 1939, an agreement was reached granting limited autonomy to Croatia. The Kingdom of Yugoslavia was destroyed by Nazi Germany in the spring of 1941.

The state of Yugoslavia was reconstituted after World War II, as a result of an armed struggle from which the Communists came out victors. "The embryo of the new state, which was born during the struggle, has been the National Liberation Councils, local administrative units in the liberated areas of the country, and the people's army," wrote J. B. Tito.[4] First in Serbia, then in Montenegro, the first general assemblies of these organs deliberated as provisory legislative bodies. In February 1942, the High Command of the Communist Armed Forces released its first legislative document concerning the power structure of the new Yugoslavia. According to this document, the National Liberation Councils were authorized to act as full representatives of the new administration except for matters within the competency of the army. Other legislative acts concerning organizational matters followed until the First Anti-Fascist Council of the National Liberation Front for Yugoslavia (AVNOJ) was formed on November 26, 1942.

This Council, however, was constituted neither as the highest people's authority (parliament) nor as the central body of the new state organization (government), but it retained the character of the political organ of the general party organization. Only the Jajče Resolution of November 29, 1943 constituted AVNOJ into Yugoslavia's "highest representative body, both legislative and executive," declaring that "Yugoslavia will be constructed on the democratic federative principle, as a state community of equal peoples."[5]

A second resolution on the nature of the new Yugoslavia stresses:

> . . . the rights of each people to self-determination, including the right to secession or union with other peoples, and, in accordance with the genuine wishes of all peoples of Yugoslavia . . . (Preamble). Yugoslavia is being constructed and will continue to develop on the federative principle, which will provide for full legal equality of Serbs, Croats, Slovenes, Macedonians, and Montenegrins, respectively the peoples of Serbia, Croatia, Slovenia, Macedonia, Montenegro, and Bosnia-Herzegovina (Article 2).[6]

The Albanians, numerically larger than the Macedonians, and the Montenegrins, are not mentioned in this document, where only people of Slavic stock appear. However, Article 4 of the above resolution states: "All national rights of the national minorities are guaranteed."[7]

From the wording of the resolution it was apparent that, except for the peoples listed in it, all others were to be treated as "national minorities." During 1944, the Jajče Resolution was approved by the AVNOJ Regional Councils, with the exception of the Regional Council of Kosova-Metohija.

The establishment of the Anti-Fascist National Liberation Council of Yugoslavia, and the formulation of the principle of federation signified a break with the pre-war Monarchist state. The federal principle became the legal basis for the new state structure, which was named the Federal Democratic Yugoslavia. The federal trend was reinforced with the formation of supreme courts in all the federal units, including Vojvodina, but excluding Kosova-Metohija. In August 1945, these two units were constituted as an autonomous province and an autonomous region respectively, within the framework of the People's Republic of Serbia. By that time, the new Federal Democratic Yugoslavia had recovered all of the territories of pre-war Yugoslavia, and expanded them with the annexation of the formerly Italian region of Venezia Giulia.[8]

In July and August 1945, the Third Session of AVNOJ confirmed the decisions taken since November 1943. The Council itself was transformed into a Provisory People's Assembly and enlarged with the inclusion of a number of representatives of the 1938 Yugoslav Parliament.[9] The November 1945 elections brought the Constituent Assembly, which approved the Declaration on the Proclamation of the Republic, and the new name, The Federative People's Republic of Yugoslavia. The final act in the formation of the new Yugoslavia—composed of six republics and two autonomous units—is the Constitution of January 31, 1946.[10] This Constitution explicitly stated the principle of self-determination and the right of secession as the basis of the federation.

Since its foundation, the new state of Yugoslavia has promulgated three constitutions, in 1946, 1963, and 1974, as well as a Constitutional Law in 1953. The 1946 Constitution, an almost identical copy of the 1936 Soviet Union's Constitution, was meant to serve a highly centralized state structure dominated by the Communist Party of Yugoslavia (CPY).[11] The strong centralization of power, and the forceful socialization of the means of production and distribution resulted in an "increase of state violence in economy and society at large, and the split between government and people, especially peasantry," due to the massive collectivization of the village.[12] The state-party relationship was abnormal, with the Party as an authority about the state. This gave rise to the Party bureaucracy dominating the entire state structure, what Milovan Djilas was to call later "the new class." This development reached its peak by the end of 1949, when the need for change became imperative, thus generating the reforms of the 1950s.[13]

The introduction of the "Workers' Councils" for economic control was confirmed by the 1953 Cosntitutional Law, mainly as an attempt to discard Stalinism (after the 1948 break) by taking a strong anti-Soviet stand.[14] In principle, the change meant the workers' participation in the state structure and, potentially, its control. Henceforth, the term "social" began to parallel the term "state." The new development contained the seed of an important trend: state ownership became social ownership, an indication of a democratization process, although in economy alone, with far-reaching consequences. It was the beginning of the movement towards administrative decentralization.

The 1963 Constitution also presents a novelty. The first part stated the ideological "Basic Principles," whose spirit and content reflected the course taken by Yugoslav society. The second part laid down the political and socio-economic state structures, the "juridical norms." Here, the socio-political system, known as "the socio-political communities," and their organization were defined.[15] Such were the federation, the republics, the autonomous provinces, and the communes, as separate communities, but interrelated through common functions.

To counterbalance these radical changes, the 1963 Constitution stressed the permanent nature of the principles and relationships defined by it. Two were especially important in this regard: 1) the protection of the sovereign rights and equality of the peoples and the socio-political organizations of the Republics, and 2) the unity of the system of the socialist self-management. From the smallest administrative-territorial unit to the highest federal body, delegates of the working masses would be elected to all representative bodies of the country, on behalf of the "sovereign will of the people." The 1963 Constitution changed the name of Yugoslavia to Socialist Federal Republic of Yugoslavia (SFRY). The use of the term "Socialist," and its place before "Federal" was indicative of the new ideological turn.

Introduced after the Constitutional Amendments of 1967, 1968 and 1971, the 1974 Constitution confirmed many major changes that took place after the 1966 Brioni Plenum and the expulsion of Alexander Ranković. In many of its provisions pertaining to the organization of the socio-economic and political system, mainly in the workers' self-managing mechanism, in the delegate system, and in the field of federal system, the changes were brought "into accord with the level attained in the development of self-management, and in social decentralization of decision-making."[16]

This Constitution, too, had a long introductory part of Basic Principles. "The peoples of Yugoslavia" of the 1963 Constitution was changed into "the nations of Yugoslavia" . . .

> in conformity with their historical aspirations . . . together with the nationalities with whom they live, united in a federal republic of free and equal nations and nationalities, and founded as a socialist federal community of working people, the Socialist Federal Republic of Yugoslavia . . . .[17]

No mention is made of the historical aspirations of "the nationalities," a term used more as a nominal than a sociological one, and designating those "members of the national whose native countries border on Yugoslavia, and for members of other nations living permanently in Yugoslavia."[18] A new principle, however, specified that:

> the working people, and the nations and nationalities, shall exercise their *sovereign rights* in the Socialist Republics, *and* in the Socialist Autonomous Provinces in conformity with their constitutional rights, and shall exercise these rights in the Socialist Federal Republic of Yugoslavia when in their common interest it is so specified by the present Constitution (Part I, par. 2).[19]

Decisions on the federal level were now being made ". . . according to the principle of agreement among the Republics and Autonomous Provinces . . . [and] equal participation by the Republics and Autonomous Provinces . . . (Part I, par. 3).[20]

Evolution of the Federal-State Concept

The evolutionary aspects of the federal-state concept in the constitutional development from 1946 to 1974 took the following course.

The 1946 Federal Constitution proclaimed the Federal People's Republic of Yugoslavia as:

> . . . a federal people's state, republican in form, a community of peoples equal in rights who, on the basis of the right to self-determination, including the right to secession, have expressed their will to live together in a federal state (Part I, Ch. 1, Art. 1).[21]

The new Federation was made of six People's Republics, the PR of Serbia including "the Autonomous Province of Vojvodina, and the Autonomous Region of Kosova-Metohija" (Art. 2). The sovereignty of the People's Republic was limited only by the prerogatives, which this Constitution bestowed upon the Federation itself (Art. 9). The republics had their own constitutions, which had, however, to reflect and be in conformity with the Constitution of the FPR of Yugoslavia (Art. 11). The rights and their scope defining the autonomy of the AP of Vojvodina and the AR of Kosova-Metohija were determined by the constitution of the PR of Serbia. Their statutes (not constitutions) had to be confirmed by the People's Assembly of the PR of Serbia.

The 1953 Constitutional Law defined Yugoslavia as ". . . the socialist democratic federal government of sovereign and equal peoples" (Art. 1). The state structure in the federation-republic and (Serbian) republic-autonomous unit's domain remained formally unchanged. The "self-managing rights" of these two units were confirmed (Art. 13) and reaffirmed in the Constitution of the PR of Serbia (Art. 2).[22] However, although no move was made to change formally the 1946 social and political order of the FPR of Yugoslavia concerning the two autonomous units, a change occurred by a continuous practice of pretermission. The Federation stopped referring to the institution of autonomy as a federal matter, tacitly delegating the constitutional-juridical powers of the provinces to the constitutional-juridical system of the PR of Serbia. The two autonomous units were reduced, for all practical purposes, to the status of two ordinary districts of Serbia. This trend was sanctioned by the 1963 Constitution of the SFR of Yugoslavia and that of the SR of Serbia.

In 1961, a major qualitative change in the 1943 Jajče Resolution took place: the Moslems of Bosnia and Herzegovina were formally recognized as a "nation" (*narod*) of Yugoslavia.[23]

The 1963 Constitution inaugurated the trend of polycentrism, with the states as the essential components of the Federation. The nominal right to secession was reinstated, but it was given to the "peoples" of Yugoslavia—not the republics—a right that was assumed to have been exercised in November 1943, when the peoples of Yugoslavia gave their consensus to join in the Yugoslav federal state. In 1963, the SFR of Yugoslavia was described as a ". . . federal state of voluntarily united and equal peoples . . ." (Art. 1), and it comprised the same six republics.[24] Stress was laid on the concept of equality among the six republics by naming them in alphabetical order (since 1943, Serbia, the largest republic, had always come first). The socialist republics were ". . . socialist democratic state communities based on the power of the working people, and on self-management" (Art. 108). Unlike the 1946 Constitution which recognized the *original* right of existence of the autonomous provinces, the 1963 Constitution transferred to the socialist republics ". . . the right to establish autonomous provinces in areas with distinctive national characteristics, or other distinguishing features, on the basis of the expressed will of the population of these areas" (Art. 111). Thus, the status of the autonomous provinces was demoted. From constituent elements of the Federation constitutionally recognized, they became "socio-political communities within the republic [of Serbia]" (Art. 112) or "juridical creations" of the Republican constitution.

The 1963 Constitution was revised three times by three sets of constitutional amendments: six in April 1967, thirteen in December 1968, and twenty-three in June 1971. The spirit and the letter of these amendments reflected the new atmosphere created in Yugoslavia, after Ranković's removal, by national outbursts all over the country, especially in the SAP of Kosova in 1968, and in Croatia in 1971.

The 1974 Constitution has considerably narrowed the powers of the Federation while extending those of the republics and autonomous provinces. It has especially reinforced and extended the various forms of representation and participation by its eight constitutive elements in the exercise of federal functions. Its Basic Principles which are ". . .both the basis of, and a directive for, the interpretation of the Constitution and laws, and for the action of all and everyone," brought to the new definition of the Federation:

> The Socialist Federal Republic of Yugoslavia consists of the Socialist Republic of Bosnia-Herzegovina, the Socialist Republic of Croatia, the Socialist Republic of Macedonia, the Socialist Republic of Montenegro, the Socialist Republic of Serbia, the Socialist Autonomous Province of Vojvodina and the Socialist Autonomous Province of Kosova which are constituent parts of the Socialist Republic of Serbia, and the Socialist Republic of Slovenia (Part I, Art. 2).[25]

For the first time since their inception, the two autonomous provinces were integrated as primary constituents of the Federation, although their dependency on the SR of Serbia was maintained.

The double dependency, on the Federation *and* on the SR of Serbia, requires, for the purpose of our study, a short review of the related republican dispositions.

Evolution of Serbia's Republican-State Concept

The first (1947) Constitution of the People's Republic of Serbia[26] defined her as ". . . the people's state of a republican form" (Art. 1), united with ". . . other peoples of Yugoslavia, and their people's republics . . . in a common, federative state, the Federal People's Republic of Yugoslavia" (Art. 2). The PR of Serbia included (*"obuhvata"*): 1) seventeen districts, 2) the Autonomous Region of Kosovo-Metohija, and 3) the Autonomous Province of Vojvodina (Art. 3). The AP of Vojvodina and the AR of Kosova-Metohija had their autonomous rights guranteed by the Republican Constitution, with their own *statutes* (not constitutions) confirming these rights. The statutes, originated by these two units, had to be approved by the People's Assembly of the PR of Serbia (Art. 13). National minorities enjoyed ". . . the right to protect their cultural development, and the freedom to use their languages" (Art. 14). The publication of the Constitution of the PR of Serbia included the two sets of statutes of the autonomous units, thus reinforcing the concept of unity in the republic.

> The 1953 Constitutional Law defined Serbia as the . . . socialist democratic state of the working people of Serbia, united on her free will with the working people of other people's republics in the Federal People's Republic of Yugoslavia as a federative state of equal and sovereign nations" (Art. 1).[27]

All powers went to the working people and were:

> . . . exercised through their representatives and people's councils, the People's Council of the Autonomous Region of Kosova-Metohija, the People's Assembly of the Autonomous Province of Vojvodina, and the People's Assembly of the People's Republic of Serbia . . . " (Art. 2).[28]

The PR of Serbia included (*"ima u svom sastavu"*) the AP of Vojvodina and the AR of Kosova-Metohija. The rights of these two units were guaranteed within the framework of rights prescribed by the constitution, and the laws issued by republican authorities (Art. 14). The statutes of the two autonomous units were written by their respective "assembly" and "council," in conformity with the Constitution of the PR of Serbia (Art. 15). The organs of the AP of Vojvodina and of the AR of Kosova-Metohija could exercise their rights and duties on the basis of, and within the framework of, the Federal Constitution, the Constitution of the PR of Serbia, and laws promulgaged by the republican assembly, and their own statutes. In case of a disagreement, the republican laws would prevail (Art. 16). The Serbian secretary of state also had the right and the duty to call to the attention of the Executive Council the illegal acts of the People's Assembly of Vojvodina and the People's Council of Kosova-Metohija, as well as of their Executive Councils (Art. 91, par. 1). The twelve major fields of activities falling within the jurisdiction of the autonomous units (economics, education, culture, health, and social services, among others) were clearly defined (Art. 104).

The 1963 Serbian Constitution, reinstating the right to secession, defined the republics as follows:

> The Socialist Republic of Serbia is a democratic socialist state, and a socialist community of the peoples of Serbia based on self-management and the power of the working people (Art. 1).[29]

The territory of the Republic included "the present-day communes and districts" (Art. 4). No mention was made of the two autonomous provinces as territorial divisions of the Republic. The rights of national minorities were guaranteed to ". . . Albanians, Hungarians, Slovaks, Bulgarians, Rumanians, Turks, Russians, and members of other national minorities who live within the Republic of Serbia, as citizens of the Socialist Republic of Serbia . . ." (Art. 82).

The minorities also enjoyed the freedom to use their languages, the expression and the development of their cultures, and the right to establish the organs needed to enjoy these rights. For the first time, the Republic was also given the right to establish new autonomous units and to eliminate the existing ones, although final approval of the measure had to be confirmed by the Federal Constitution. As a result of this provision, the existence of the autonomous units became a republic prerogative, thus ceasing to be constitutive elements of the Federation. In fact, the autonomous provinces were defined as simple administrative units just like the ordinary communes and districts. They became simply juridical creations of the SR of Serbia. Their role, ". . . to take care of the economic development and other social activities, as well as furthering the socialist self-management system within the borders of their respective provinces," and their rights were defined by the Republican Constitution and by laws promulgated by Serbia's Assembly (Art. 135).[30]

As a result of the constitutional amendments of 1967, 1968 and 1971, the 1974 Serbian Constitution reiterated the notion that the SAP of Vojvodina and the SAP of Kosova were components of the SR of Serbia, but unlike the 1963 Constitution, it reaffirmed that they were:

> . . . established during the common struggle of the nations, and the nationalities of Yugoslavia, in the national-liberation war and socialist revolution, and on the basis of the freely expressed will of the population, the nations and nationalities of the Provinces and of Serbia, are associated (*"udružila su"*) with the Socialist Republic of Serbia, within the framework of the Socialist Federal Republic of Yugoslavia (Basic Principles, Part I).[31]

With their original right to exist thus redefined, the two autonomous provinces were recognized as ". . . autonomous socialist self-managing democratic socio-political communities with their two national compositions and other characteristics. . ." (Art. 291). Their territories were guaranteed not to be changed without prior approval by the respective provinces (Art. 292). Their rights and duties were to be exercised by them independently, except for those concerning the Republic (and, by extension, the Federation), as a whole.

The Serbian Republican Assembly remained the highest organ of the republic, invested with the sovereignty of Serbia, and the symbol of the unity of the republic.

Evolution of Kosova's Provincial Autonomy Concept

The course of the present autonomy for the predominantly Albanian inhabited region of Kosova was chartered for the first time in July 1937. The Regional Committee of the YCP for Kosova-Metohija (then a branch of the YCP for Montenegro, Boka, and Sandžak) requested to become an autonomous unit of the Yugoslav Communist Party. The jurisdiction of the Regional Council would extend ". . .from here [Pejë] to the vicinity of the town of Shkup (Skoplje)."[32] In September 1939, the First Conference of the Regional Committee for Kosova, ". . .explaining the importance of the national composition of the [Region's] population and the specific economic and cultural characteristics, proposed for the first time that autonomous status be requested for Kosova-Metohija."[33]

In the first few days of August 1939, the Second Conference of the Regional Committee for Kosova-Metohija, meeting near the town of Pejë (Peć) passed a resolution instructing that ". . .the main duty of the Regional Committee, as well as of all members of the YC Party is the mobilization of the Albanian element around the YCP. This can be done," continued the resolution, "only if each party member takes a correct attitude towards the national question, and expresses it in his relations with the large masses of the population. . . ." Furthermore, the resolution requested that ". . .the party materials be published in the Albanian language, too."[34]

On August 8, 1940, the Eighth Regional Conference of the YCP for Montenegro, Boka, Sandžak and Kosova-Metohija rejected the latter's request for autonomy. Due to the direct intervention of J. B. Tito, then the secretary general of the YCP, this question was left for discussion at the Fifth Conferences of the YCP to be held in Zagreb, two months later. The Fifth Conference met between October 19 and 23, 1940. Its resolution declared:

> 5) The Fifth Conference accepts the proposal of the comrade delegates from Metohija and Kosova that the party organization of that Region be separated from Montenegro, and that the Regional Committee of Metohija and Kosova establish direct ties with the Central Committee of the Yugoslav Communist Party.[35]

The Fifth Conference went even further. Its resolution spoke also of

> . . .the struggle for freedom and equality of the Albanian minorities in Kosova-Metohija and Sandžak. . . , and the war against the colonization methods of the Serbian bourgeoisie in these regions, including the expulsion of all settlers who are being used by the Serbian bourgeoisie to oppress the Macedonians, Albanians and other peoples. . . .[36]

From 1940 to the establishment of the Autonomous Region of Kosova-Metohija in 1945, the direct contact of the Regional Committee of the YCP for Kosova-Metohija with the Central Committee of the YCP became an established practice. "During the war years (1941-45) besides the Regional Committee of the YCP for Kosova-Metohija and the Regional Committee of the Young Communists' League, there also existed the Headquarters of the People's Liberation Army and Partisan Units for Kosova-Metohija, as well as the regional leadership in this Region."[37] Albanians in Yugoslavia were acting as a "nation" in a territory of their own.

In a frequently referred to article on the national question in Yugoslavia, published in *Proleter* (December 1942), the YCP chief, J. B. Tito, while defining the Party's line on this problem, write openly against the oppression of ". . . Croats, Slovenes, Macedonians, Albanians, Montenegrins and others." He added:

> Each people has the right to decide its own future . . . . The National Liberation War phrase would be meaningless, even a deception, if it did not have, besides its general meaning, also a national meaning that included not only the liberation of Yugoslavia, but at the same time, the liberation of the Croats, Slovenes, Serbs, Macedonians, Albanians, Moslems, etc.[38]

In this text, Albanians are twice referred to as a separate people of Yugoslavia.

One year later, the Second Session of AVNOJ proclaimed the principle of federation, enumerating the main constitutive "nations" of the future federation. Albanians were not included. They were treated as one of the many "national minorities" by an assembly that did not include any Albanian representatives.

One month later, December 31, 1943-January 2, 1944, meeting at the village of Bujan (in Albania), the Founding Regional Conference of the Anti-Fascist National Liberation Council of Kosova-Metohija, enthused by the formal party promises they had received, and unaware of the politically motivated stand of the AVNOJ Resolution at Jajče, resolved unanimously:

Kosova and the Dukagjin Plateau is a region predominantly inhabited by Albanians who, now as always before, desire to unite with
Albania. Therefore, we consider it our duty to show the correct way
which the Albanians must take in order to fulfill their aspirations.
The only way for the union of Albanians living in Kosova and the
Dukagjin Plateau with Albania is through a joint struggle with the
other peoples of Yugoslavia, against the invader and its lackeys, because that is the only way to regain freedom, when all the peoples,
including the Albanian people, will have the opportunity to decide
their fate, exercising their right to self-determination, including the
right to secession.[39]

The YCP and the Yugoslav Army Headquarters were quick to answer.
Two letters, one by Marshal J. B. Tito, secretary general of the YCP, and
the other by S. V. Tempo, Tito's military lieutenant for Southern Yugoslavia, strongly criticized the Bujan Resolution,[40] which ever since has
been treated by Yugoslav official propaganda as a political blunder.[41] As
a result of this uncompromising intervention, the wartime Albanian
sentiments of indepedence from Serbian tutelage were dealt a severe blow.
The Albanians of Kosova-Metohija were reluctantly compelled to accept
a mere regional atuonomy within the PR of Serbia. Albanian discontent
grew. In November 1944, a general insurrection broke out, which was sub-
dued in May 1945.[42] On February 8, 1945, Marshal Tito declared Kosova-
Metohija a "war zone," and a Military Directorate took over the administration and the pacification of the Region.[43]

In an underhanded effort to exploit the critical situation in Kosova-
Metohija, the Montenegrin delegation at the Third Session of the Presidium of AVNOJ, held in Belgrade on February 24, 1945, formally requested the annexation of Kosova-Metohija to the PR of Montenegro.[44]
The stratagem (Sandžak had just been dismembered between Serbia and
Montenegro) failed.[45] On June 10, 1945, the Anti-Fascist National Liberation Council for Kosova-Metohija, reversing itself, decreed that a Regional
Representative Council be called, "on behalf of the people," for the
union of the Region with the PR of Serbia. One month later, on July 10,
1945, a convocation of delegates in Prizren, orchestrated by the Communist Party organizations, passed the following Resolution:

> The Regional People's Council of Kosova-Metohija expresses its satisfaction that the situation in the Region has calmed down, and it is sufficiently stable to permit satisfactory activities in the various fields of economic, cultural, and social life. . . . The Regional People's Council of Kosova-Metohija unanimously declares that the population of this Region, just as all the other peoples of Yugoslavia, has accepted neither the dismemberment of the Region by the invader, nor the dismemberment of Yugoslavia. Therefore, it expresses the desire of the entire population living in this Region in requesting that this Region become a constituent part of Federal Serbia. . . . [46]

No Albanian delegate participated in the Second Session of AVNOJ at Jajče in 1943, nor did any Regional Council of Kosova-Metohija approve the AVNOJ's decision, as it has been the case with other political units of Yugoslavia. Nonetheless, the July 1945 Resolution, taken by delegates hurriedly assembled shortly after the crushed popular insurrection, has been consistently and officially maintained to be the fundamental legal act of Kosova-Metohija's "expressed free will" for union with Serbia and, through Serbia, with the new state of Yugoslavia. The July 1945 Resolution was accepted by the Presidium of AVNOJ on July 23, 1945, and by the Presidium of the Serbian Assembly on September 3, 1945.[47] The final act of the performance was the 1946 Constitution of the FDR of Yugoslavia, followed by the 1947 Constitution of the PR of Serbia, as well as the Statute of the AR of Kosova-Metohija, in May 1948. The administrative division of the territories inhabited predominantly by Albanians in Yugoslavia left them dispersed in the three people's republics of Serbia, Macedonia and Montenegro. Only the Albanians living in the Kosova-Metohija Region were given autonomous status.[48]

The 1946 Federal Constitution did not *establish* the autonomous region, as had been the case with the republics; it simply *participated* in its establishment (which was seen as a republican function) by defining its position and form within the socio-political and constitutional system of the republic of Serbia and of Yugoslavia, as well.

The Autonomous Region of Kosova-Metohija, as it was formally called, promulgated its statute, instead of its constitution, a prerogative of the republican-state. Her status was defined as follows:

The Autonomous Region of Kosova-Metohija is an autonomous
region and a constituent part of the People's Republic of Serbia
(Art. 1).[49]

The rights of this autonomy were guaranteed by ". . . the Constitution of
the People's Republic of Serbia, in conformity with the Constitution of
the Federal People's Republic of Yugoslavia" (Art. 2, par. 2). The nationalities of the Region were specified as Serbs, Montenegrins, Albanians, and
after 1949, Turks. The Serbo-Croatian and Albanian languages enjoyed
equal treatment in administrative services only inside the territory of the
AR of Kosova-Metohija (Art. 3, par. 2).

The position of the AR of Kosova-Metohija was squarely defined to be
under the direct scrutiny of the PR of Serbia, which held the authority to
invalidate each and every decision taken by the regional authorities, whenever it was thought to be not in agreement with the republican law. The
statute itself became effective only "after its approval by the People's
Assembly of the People's Republic of Serbia" (Art. 44), the Assembly
being, as we have seen, the highest authority of the Republic as a whole,
and the symbol of unity of the PR of Serbia. The main organs of the AR
of Kosova-Metohija were the Regional Council, and the Executive Council. The word "Council" was used to differentiate it from "Assembly," a
prerogative of the republic, as well as of the AP of Vojvodina. The rights
and duties of the Executive Council were listed in eighteen categories
which included matters related to the regional statute (with the approval
of the People's Assembly of the PR of Serbia), local statutes, administrative local divisions, application of laws, economic organization and
development, budgetary problems, communications, transportation,
education and culture, social welfare, and (state) security. The Regional
People's Council was the highest organ of the Region. All these prerogatives were, in essence, of a juridical and economic, not political, order.

The differentiation between the AP of Vojvodina and the AR of
Kosova-Metohija, and the inferior position of the latter, was due "to the
ways of thinking" of those days. They were "similar to those in the Soviet
Union, where the less-developed nationality enjoyed autonomy, and the
economically less-developed territory where this autonomy is established,
are invested with a lower degree of autonomy."[50] As a result, the AR of
Kosova-Metohija's delegation in the Federal Assembly had only 15 members

compared to 20 for the AP of Vojvodina, and 30 for the republics. In general, the government structure in Vojvodina was similar to that of a republic, whereas in Kosova-Metohija it resembled that of a local government. No higher court was allowed in Kosova-Metohija, although there was one for the AP of Vojvodina.

Even more important was the fact that the Federal and/or republican authorities were able, with a stroke of the pen, to nullify or suspend any and all functions of the legislative and executive branches. The 1953 Yugoslav Federal and Serbian (republican) Constitutional Laws were reflected in the Statute of the AR of Kosova-Metohija, adopted by the People's Council, and authorized by the Federal Constitutional Law (Art. 114), and the Serbian Constitutional Law (Art. 104, item 1). The AR of Kosova-Metohija was defined as:

> . . .an autonomous region, and a constituent part *of the socialist democratic state* of the People's Republic of Serbia (Art. 1).[51]

A qualitative omission was noticeable in Article 2: "The working people of the Autonomous Region of Kosova-Metohija elects the regional organs of authority, and through them executes its own autonomous rights which are granted by the Constitution of the People's Republic of Serbia." Omitted was the 1946 provision, "in conformity with the Constitution of the People's Federal Republic of Yugoslavia." The omission left the authority for the institution of autonomy to the juridical system of the PR of Serbia. The main organ of the Region remained the Council. The Executive Committee exercised its functions on matters of "general interest for the Region in the fields of economy, education, culture, people's health, and social welfare," as well as "the juridical aspects related to those matters" (Art. 4). No higher court was established for the Region, as items pertaining to that organ were referred to the Supreme Court of the PR of Serbia in Belgrade.

The short Preamble of the 1963 Autonomous Province of Kosova-Metohija Statute indicated that the new document was being issued "on the basis of the authorization deriving from the Constitution of the Socialist Republic of Serbia, and in conformity with the special conditions of the economy, education, culture, and social development, as well as with the specific national composition of the population of Kosova-Metohija."[52]

Even more damaging to the concept of the autonomy were the defini-
tions of the status of the Region (now called Province):

> The Autonomous Province of Kosova-Metohija is a socio-political
> community within the Socialist Republic of Serbia, based on the
> power of the working people, and self-management . . . . The auto-
> nomous Province of Kosovo-Metohija has been established as an
> autonomous unit in 1945 with the decision of the People's As-
> sembly of the People's Republic of Serbia, based on the freely ex-
> pressed will of the population of Kosova-Metohija (Art. 1).[53]

Within this framework, the AP of Kosova-Metohija became a formal creation of Serbia, namely an administrative autonomous unit without any
direct relationship with the Federation.

According to the 1963 Statute of Kosova-Metohija, the self-management of the working people of the Province consisted in taking care of:

> . . .the development of socialist relations *in its own district* and for
> this purpose its exercises its rights, and fulfills its duties as defined
> by the Constitution of the Socialist Republic of Serbia, within the
> framework of the rights and duties of the Socialist Republic of
> Serbia as a whole . .which derive from the specific development of
> economy, education, culture, and social welfare of the Province, as
> well as the national composition of its population (Art. 2).[54]

The territory of the Province was defined as a "district" and included
"the existing districts and communes" (Art. 8). The Regional Council became the Provincial Assembly—an upgrading to the status enjoyed by
Vojvodina—the number of delegates to the House of Peoples was raised
from 4 to 5, as it was for Vojvodina, and in Prishtinë, a section of Serbia's
Supreme Court was established. However, the delegations of the autonomous units to the House of Peoples lost their independence, and became
an integral part of the Serbian republican delegation.

From the right to self-determination, promised during the war years,
and the freely expressed will to unite with Albania, proclaimed by the
Bujan Resolution of January 1944, to the Military Dicectorate of February 1945 and then the July Resolution of 1945 to incorporate the

Region in the Republic of Serbia, the Albanian population of Kosova-Metohija experienced a downhill spiral of decreasing political power, which reached its lowest point with the 1963 Federal and Republican Constitutions, as well as with the Provincial Statute. The AP of Kosova-Metohija became a simple unit of the SR of Serbia.

After the Brioni Resolution of 1966, as a result of the drive to strengthen the principle and the practice of workers' self-management (of both nations and nationalities), the position of the autonomous provinces was redefined. Therefore, it was reaffirmed that the autonomous provinces:

a) were born in the common struggle of nations and nationalities during the national-liberation war and the following socialist revolution (the historical argument);

b) were actually established and confirmed constitutionally by the expressed will, not only of the nations and nationalities inhabiting them, but *also* of the entire people of Serbia (the argument of Serbian sovereign rights);

c) had joined with the SR of Serbia, an equal and federated member of the Yugoslav Federation, with the approval and the expressed will of the nations and nationalities of Serbia and the provinces themselves (the asymmetric structure of the Federation).

The resulting effect of this redefinition was the autonomy's treatment as a feature of Yugoslav federalism and its original concept as a sociopolitical institution. The redefinition rejected the existing and prevalent interpretation of the autonomous provinces as territorial-political communities *integrated* within the framework of a republic state structure. Yet, the redefinition did not go so far as to extend to the state-juridical domain. All this meant that Yugoslavia was based on a dualistic federalism:

1. The *community of all* nations and nationalities, based on the *socialist* element (living in both republics and autonomous provinces), and

2. The federal *state,* constituted into republican states, based on the *national* element (Amendment XVIII).

The concept of the new amendments was embodied in the 1969 Constitutional Law of Kosova, following the student unrest in the Province.[55] This Law was prepared and approved to reflect ". . .the new conditions permitting the initiation of due process of law for a further development of the Socialist Autonomous Province of Kosova as a socialist democratic socio-political community" (Preamble). In a long introductory Basic Principles section, the reasons for its existence were described as being the historical conditions, a common existence, and the joint aspirations for freedom and social progress of the Montenegrins, Serbs, Albanians, and Turks of Kosova during the common struggle of the nations and nationalities of Yugoslavia. The Province was recognized as a territorial unit originally established during the war and the revolution, ". . . later attached to the Socialist Republic of Serbia, within the framework of the Socialist Federal Republic of Yugoslavia, on the basis of the expressed will of the local population, as well as of the will, freely expressed, of the peoples of Federal Serbia. . . ."[56] The rights of the SAP of Kosova were limited to, and had to be consistent with, the rights that ". . . in the common interests of the working people, and of all nations and nationalities of Yugoslavia and Serbia are defined as rights and duties belonging to the Federation, and the Republic" (Basic Principles, Part I). Now, the SAP of Kosova was:

> a socialist democratic socio-political *community* based on the power of the working people and of self-management, as well as the community of equal nations and nationalities: Montenegrins, Serbs, Albanians, Turks, and others (Art. 43).[57]

The SAP of Kosova remained within the framework of both the SR of Serbia and the SFR of Yugoslavia (Art. 1, par. 2). Its rights and duties were ". . . defined by this Constitutional Law (of Kosova) in accordance with the principles of the Constitution of the Socialist Federal Republic of Yugoslavia, and the Constitution of the Socialist Republic of Serbia" (Art. 4). The territory of the Province was composed of the territories of the existing communes and could not be changed ". . . without the approval of the Provincial Assembly" (Art. 7). Albanians and Turks won the right to use their national flags (Art. 11). The highest organ of the Province remained the Provincial Assembly which now was authorized *to make laws,* as opposed to the prior practice of "decrees" based on federal and republican laws. When dealing with exclusively federal laws, ". . . the Province can apply them when a republican law authorizes it." And, ". . . if a republic law (affecting the Province) has been enacted without prior consent from the Provincial Assembly, the republican law is applicable in the territory of the Province until such time as a Provincial law will be enacted" (Art. 66). The constitutionality and the legality of the rights and duties of the SAP of Kosova were entrusted to the Supreme Court of Kosova, established for the first time in this Province (to which a constitutional-juridical branch was attached). For the defense of the Province's rights, as defined by the Constitution, the Provincial Assembly, the Executive Committee and the Supreme Court of Kosova were authorities to "initiate procedures with the Constitutional Court of Yugoslavia" (Art. 78, par. 2). In case of conflicting views "the federal, or the republican, laws are applied until a decision, by the competent Federal law, is reached" (Art. 79).

The Provincial Executive Committee applies the provincial, republican, and federal laws in the territory of the SAP of Kosova: however, it decrees on the execution of republican laws only when it is expressly authorized by law, and "it decrees on the execution of federal laws only when it is expressly authorized by the Republican Executive Committee" (Art. 133, item 5). The provincial representation of the Chamber of Nations and Nationalities of the Federal Assembly was fixed to ten delegates, and the provincial delegation became, again, independent from that of the SR of Serbia.

In 1971, a relatively new definition was brought in with Amendment XX. The provinces were now:

> . . . socio-political democratic *self-managing* autonomous communities, in which the *working people, the nations and nationalities fulfill* their rights, and whenever in the common interest of the working people, of nations and nationalities of the Republic as a whole, as defined by the Constitution of the Socialist Republic of Serbia, also in the republic.[58]

Thus, the province became similar, but not identical to the republic. It still remained an ill-defined "community;" it was given greater autonomy, however, extracting it from the prior "regional self-administration" or "administrative autonomy" concepts. The province's rights and obligations were also extended and defined by the provincial authorities themselves, but always "limited and relative" within, and depending on, the federal and republican constitutional provisions.[59] It was denied recognition as a "state."

The new arrangements, according to a Yugoslav constitutionalist, confirmed:

1. The historical development that brought the SAP of Kosova to its establishment, based on its national composition, and socio-economic elements.

2. The rights, and the means, of its participation in the formulation and execution of policies as well as the solution of social relations in the Federation.

3. An autonomy in dealing with social relations and national rights and equality in the province through autonomous legislation.

4. The autonomous organization of the government, complete with a judicial branch, in dealing with economic and constitutional questions, socio-political organizations and institutions, as well as their autonomous activities.[60]

The Present Constitutional Status of the SAP of Kosova

The last constitutional document, the 1974 Constitution of the SAP of Kosova,[61] is the first to be called "constitution" (*"ustav"*) rather than "statute," or "constitutional law," a privilege heretofore granted to the republics. The new document contains a section of Basic Principles in ten chapters and another, General Norms, in nine chapters and two hundred-ninety-nine articles. The Basic Principles closely follow the language used in the Federal and Republican Constitutions, as well as in the Constitutional Law of Kosova (1969). The province is described as the territory were:

> United by their common past, and joint existence, as well as by their struggle for freedom and social progress, Albanians, Moslems, Serbs, Turks, Montenegrins, and members of other nations and nationalities, and ethnic groups. . .have found, for the first time, freedom, equality and brotherhood in the Socialist Autonomous Province of Kosova, which. . .on the basis of the freely expressed will of its population—nations and nationalities of Kosova—and the freely expressed will of the peoples of Serbia, is associated with (*udružila se*)

the Socialist Republic of Serbia, within the framework of the Socialist Federal Republic of Yugoslavia.[62]

Unlike the 1969 Constitutional Law, the 1974 Constitution of the SAP
of Kosova recognizes that the working people of the Province exercise
their "sovereign" rights in the uniform Yugoslav socio-economic and political system, "on the basis of the power of the working class, and other
working people" (Art. 1) and *not* by the authority of the Constitution of
the SFR of Yugoslavia, and the Constitution of the SR of Serbia.[63] Also,
unlike the 1969 Constitutional Law, but in agreement with Amendment
XX (1971), the 1974 Constitution of the SAP of Kosova recognizes the
province as "an autonomous" and "self-managing" community (Art. 1).

Having defined the status of the SAP of Kosova as deriving from its
historical conditions, national composition, and "freely expressed will,"
the 1974 Constitution determines its position and prerogatives, as follows:

> The working people, and the nations and nationalities of Kosova shall
> exercise their sovereign rights in the Socialist Autonomous Province
> of Kosova, and when this is in the common interests of workers,
> nations and nationalities of the Republic as a whole, also in the Re-
> public as prescribed by the Constitution of the Socialist Republic
> of Serbia, and in the Socialist Federative Republic of Yugoslavia
> too, whenever this is in the common interests of, and prescribed by,
> the Constitution of the Socialist Federative Republic of Yugoslavia
> (Basic Principles, Chapter I, par. 3).[64]

This cooperation includes problems of common concern, general economic and social interest, participation in the federal and republican organs,
relations with socio-political organizations in other republics and the autonomous province of Vojvodina, the establishment of common bodies to
administer items of joint interest, coordination of fiscal policies (especially whenever these policies affect the uniformity and the stability of
the Yugoslav market), and the obligation to accept the principle that
decisions and other government measures, taken by the republics and the
autonomous province of Vojvodina, have the same validity in the SAP of
Kosova (Articles 294, 295, 296 and 297).[65]

The extension of sovereign rights outside the province, namely, in the
Federation and the Serbian republic, gives the SAP of Kosova the right

"to decide" on a federal level. Within the framework of the foreign policies of the SFR of Yugoslavia and the international agreements, the SAP of Kosova also ". . . pursues cooperation, and develops relationships with organs and organizations of other governments, as well as international organs and organizations" (Art. 293).[66]

The highest organ of the SAP of Kosova remains the Provincial Assembly, which has the authority to directly deliberate, within its own territory, on the most important issues of the province, including two very important ones: *constitutional* and *territorial* changes. The Provincial Assembly has the last word on both issues.

A Presidency of the SAP of Kosova is instituted—imitating the Federation and the republics—as the body representing the SAP of Kosova with rights and duties defined by the Constitution, including relations with the international community.

The Social Council (*Pleqësia*) of the SAP of Kosova is also a new institution in the structure of the political organization of the province. Its function is only consultative, and its opinions are presented to the Provincial Assembly and the Presidency of the Province. The executive authority rests with the Provincial Executive Committee which is responsible before the Provincial Assembly for its policies, the application of the enacted legislation, and other fields of social life.

A new Provincial Attorney for Self-Management, appointed by the Provincial Assembly, is in charge of social defense, self-management rights, and social property. The former constitutional-juridical branch of the Supreme Court—called, since 1972, the Constitutional Court of Kosova—is confirmed as an independent body, in charge of defending constitutionalism and legality in the province.

The new element of *participation* and *representation* in performing joint federal functions has taken two forms:

1. The process of direct participation in common decision-making in the Federal Assembly (the Federal Chamber and the Chamber of Nations and Nationalities were voting is done by delegation);

2. The process of representation: *equal* for republics, and *adequate* for the autonomous provinces. The exact meaning of "*adequate*" representation for the autonomous provinces has not been defined, "but the Constitution has defined the ratios according to which the provinces do not have the same representation as the republics; these ratios as 3 to 2, and 2 to 1 in favor of the republics."[67]

The rotating Presidency of the Federation has one representative for each republic and autonomous province, but the Federal Executive Committee and other federal bodies do not respect this parity principle. An "adequate" representation is also taken into consideration for the Coordinating Commission of the Federal Executive Committee, the inter-republican committees, and the Federal Social Councils.[68] In the Supreme Court of Yugoslavia, the ratio between representatives of republics and those of provinces is 2 to 1.

On the republican level, the participation of the SAP of Kosova is exercised in three ways:

1. Through the inclusion in the SAP of Kosova's Constitution of the constitutional principles of the SR of Serbia of the essential elments of the socio-economic and socio-political system which ensure the unity of the SR of Serbia.

2. Through republican jurisdiction pertaining to questions clearly defined in the Constitution of the SR of Serbia which are uniformly applied in the entire republic.

3. Through procedures provided in the Constitution of the SR of Serbia to integrate *additional* subject-matters in all fields of socio-economic and political life. However, for new provisions to be applied, the consent of the Provincial Assembly is required.

Provincial participation and representation in the republic are elaborated by the by-laws of the Assembly of the SR of Serbia, and other laws of executive decrees of an administrative, and social council's nature. As of now, the process has not advanced smoothly, because of ". . .subjective and objective flaws. . .There have been different interpretations of the constitutional provisions concerning both the essence and the degree of the uniform arrangements between the Republic and the Province."[69]

Legislation emanating from the Assembly of the SR of Serbia includes all laws uniformly applied in the entire republic. To this effect, this Assembly includes the two provincial delegations of Vojvodina and Kosova.[70] Furthermore, the Serbian Assembly, in cooperation with the two Assemblies of the Autonomous Provinces of Vojvodina and Kosova, can enact additional laws uniformly applied to the entire republic. In this direction, the process has been slow, ". . .mainly because the legislative bodies have been little mobilized, and the initiative has been taken over by administrative and executive bodies."[71]

The Presidency of the SR of Serbia exercises its rights of representing the autonomous provinces in all activities that are uniformly applied to the entire republic. The chair people of the provincial presidencies are members of the republican presidency.

The Republican Executive Committee is responsible for the entire all-republican administration. However, the uniformly applied republican laws in the Provinces are executed by the provincial authorities, unless otherwise specified by law. The Constitutional Court of Serbia, as the Republican Assembly, is in a unique position. Since its competencies derive from the republic as a whole, this Court examines the cases of republic-province relationships, the application of republican laws, and other republican decrees that are uniformly applied in the entire republic. The Supreme Court of Serbia and those of the autonomous provinces act independently. For a joint coordination of the activities a special chamber with equal representation is established. The public prosecutors cooperate in their activities of defending their respective public. However, the Serbian Public Prosecutor may intervene in the Autonomous Provinces in cases described by republican law as republican organs is not yet fully settled, except for cases of the Republican Assembly and Presidency. At present, the Republican Executive Committee and the Constitutional Court of Serbia each have one member from each of the two provinces. The Supreme Court and the General Public Prosecutor's Office do not have representatives "because the volume of the activities uniformly applied in the entire republic is small, and in some organs, the Constitution does not provide for representation."[72] And finally, the Republican constitution cannot be changed without prior Provincial approval, whenever the changes contemplated involve the interests of the Autonomous Provinces.

Summary and Conclusions

The entire state structure of the SFR of Yugoslavia is organized to reflect the ideological leadership of the Yugoslav Communist League (YCL) assisted by the Socialist Alliance of the Working People (SAWP), the Yugoslav equivalent of all-comprehensive trade union organizations.

It is within this framework that all organized socialist groups achieve the political and operational unity of the socialist forces. They also determine the moral and political suitability of each citizen and, consequently, of each candidate.[73] These groups ensure "democratic" nominations for their candidates, elect entire delegations, issue guidelines for the selected delegates in the assemblies, and draw programs for social activities. Delegates to a lower assembly send delegates, elected among themselves, to the appropriate chamber of a higher assembly, a procedure which culminates, stepwise, in the election of the Federal Assembly.

Assembled through a strictly partisan selection process, these legislative bodies of the commune, province, republic, and federation select the executive bodies and, at the Federal level, the Presidency of the SFR of Yugoslavia, the judges of the Supreme Court and of the Constitutional Court, and the Federal Public Prosecutor. The Assembly becomes, in this way, the supreme organ of power within the framework of the enumerated rights and duties of a socio-political community.

The legislative branch, being ultimately harnessed to the political program of the YCL and the SAWP, necessarily produces legislation that codifies the political orientation of the YCL. In the case of the SAP of Kosova, we have seen how the political orientation has functioned in a progress-regress cycle of constitutional amendments, according to the political climate of the day. Having been promised equality during the wartime years, but reduced to a mere appendage of the SR of Serbia at the end of the war, the former AR of Kosova-Metohija managed, by 1963, to reach the status of a mere district of the Serbian republic. It is only after the disclosure of the Ranković crimes against the Albanians and the massive demonstrations of 1968 that the juridical position of the Province improved. The improvement, however, had no bearing on the lamentable situation of the Albanians outside the SAP of Kosova. To this day, that situation remains basically unchanged.

The 1968-1971 constitutional amendments that brought the SAP of Kosova back to the fold of the Federation were confirmed with the Constitution of 1974, which recognized its right to exist as an original political entity, namely, not derived or emanating from another otuside source of authority, but established on her own rights and merit. Due to her double dependency on the Federation and the Serbian republic, the SAP of Kosova can only *indirectly* exercise her freedom of action. In this respect, two tendencies are discernible:

1. To increase the rights of the autonomous provinces as much as possible, by bringing them *de facto* as near as possible to the status of a republic.

2. To maintain *de jure* the principle of *state and territorial integrity* of the SR of Serbia.

Clearly, this arrangement would satisfy the adamant Serbian demand for sovereignty over the SAP of Kosova, but would leave Albanians in a constitutionally inferior position.[74] A Serbian official publication explains:

> While increasing the rights of the autonomous provinces in this sphere, such relations prompted the need to enact republican laws so that every possibility of a legal vacuum is avoided, and the function of the Republican Assembly of Serbia, as a *unified* general-political body of the Republic is assured.[75]

The formal differentiation of the two terms, *nation* and *nationality,* entitled to their own *republic* and *autonomous province* respectively, is of paramount importance in the Yugoslav constitutional system. In treating Albanians as a "nationality"—a euphemism for national minority—Yugoslavia cannot escape criticism for its inconsistent behavior.[76] In granting republican status to six components of the Federation, where there are in fact eight, Yugoslavia cannot seriously claim the principle of equality. The denial of a nation's status to Kosovars is an untenable tenet. Montenegrins were granted a nation's status, although they are mainly people of Serbian stock. Moslems in Bosnia-Herzegovina were granted the nation's status as late as 1961, because of their *religious* differentiation, although they are also mainly people of Slavic stock. Macedonians were granted a nation's status (as a Serbian answer to Bulgarian claims) although, until 1945, to be Macedonian meant, to a large extent, to be Bulgarian. After thirty-eight years, these new "nations" have developed a certain "national identity" of their own. So have the Albanians presently living in Yugoslavia.

Although divided between the three republics of Serbia, Macedonia and Montenegro, Albanians share the feeling of belonging to a single people, different from that of the neighboring Slavs, but identical to those who speak the same tongue. In Yugoslavia, they speak a non-Slavic language and they are not being assimilated, or absorbed by other Slavic peoples. With the elaboration and advancement of their language and national culture, their prewar identity crisis, a direct consequence of their long oppression and persecution, has altogether disappeared. They now feel and think of themselves as a separate nation, with its own history and cultural heritage on which they can build a meaningful present and future.

The denial of a nation's status seems to be grounded on the argument that "Albanians" have their own national state, the present-day Albania, and that Albanians in Yugoslavia cannot have a second one.[77] Here, we have a case of discrepancy between party imposed legislation and sociopolitical reality, which is even more disturbing since it deals with rights and aspirations of people constantly victimized in the past.

To an impartial observer, the present-day demand of the Albanians in Yugoslavia for a nation's status *within* the Yugoslav federation does not warrant the mainly Serbian psycho-emotional syndrome resulting from the fear of a possible secession, a political act of this nature being only a remote possibility, due to the present constitutional arrangements. To begin with, Kosova cannot claim secession without first obtaining a republican status. But if the Province were to ask for a republican status, it would be necessary for it to go through an amending of the Constitution of the SFR of Yugoslaiva, a process which is very intricate in its legal aspects. "A motion to initiate proceedings for amending the Constitution of the SFR of Yugoslavia could be introduced by no less than thirty delegates to the Federal Chamber,"[78] and the SAP of Kosova has only twenty. Supposing now that the SAP of Kosova will eventually be elevated to the status of a republic, its delegation to the Federal Chamber would contain an insufficient number to initiate the proceedings for amending the Constitution leading to secession. And even if a motion would be presented for such a purpose, it is the Federal Chamber that may decide to initiate proceedings, and *only* when the motion for initiating it ". . .has been agreed upon by the Assemblies of *all* Republics. . ."[79] i.e., including the SR of Serbia. The Constitution of the SFRY specifies that ". . .if the Assembly of *one or more* Republics. . .has not agreed with the text of the motion, . . .the motion fo the amendment. . .may not be placed on the agenda before the expiration of one year from the day the Federal Chamber ruled that no agreement has been reached."[80] Furthermore, a fundamental principle of that Constitution states: "The frontiers of the Socialist Federal Republic of Yugoslavia may not be altered without the consent of *all* the Republics and Autonomous Provinces."[81]

Theoretically, secession could occur only if the SR of Serbia, the largest republic in the Federation, decided to leave it. Since the SAP of Kosova joined the Yugoslav federation through its incorporation by the PR of Serbia in 1945, the Province will remain a constituent member of the Federation for as long as the SR of Serbia does, with no freedom of choice of its own.

In conclusion, the least that can be said is that the tortuous progress-regress cycle of the constitutional status of Kosova does not bear out a principled policy of the Yugoslav government. The latest Spring 1981 riots in the SAP of Kosova and the ensuing persecutions must be seen in this light. The constitutionally inferior status of the SAP of Kosova remains a structural defect of the SFR of Yugoslavia's federation, a permanent source of friction between Kosovars and their Slavic neighbors, and a potentially explosive issue for the SFR of Yugoslavia.

A new approach to the Albanians' demands seems to be imperative. Yet, the Yugoslav willingness to do so is still lacking. Whenever that willingness appears, the following data will have to be taken into consideration:

1. The division of the Albanian population presently living in Yugoslavia among the three republics of Serbia, Macedonia and Montenegro, has engendered in them a credibility gap towards the official Yugoslav intentions, fostering a deep-rooted antagonism against the Slavic ruling elites of those three republics.

2. The "autonomous" status of the SAP of Kosova is not the "sovereign" position that most of its local population have been yearning for many long years; it falls considerably short of it. To reach the degree of "sovereignty" that the other six constituent republics of the federation have remains a major strategic aim for the Albanians in Yugoslavia.

3. There are about two million Albanians presently living in Yugoslavia. They make for about forty percent of the Albanian nation in the Balkans. With the rapid demographic growth, Albanians will soon be the third largest ethnic group in Yugoslavia, after the Serbs and the Croats.

The insistence on and the intensity of the demand "Kosova-Republikë," which to many outside observers seems to be a logical one, will eventually force the Yugoslav rulers to make a choice under more inauspicious conditions. They will either have to initiate peaceful constitutional changes elevating the status of the two autonomous provinces of

Vojvodina and Kosova to that of the other six republics, or accept the risks brought into being by a constant denial of constitutional equality.

As things now stand, there are no incentives for the Albanians in Yugoslavia to cooperate in perpetuating their present constitutionally inferior status.

* * * * *

NOTES

Titles of articles in Serbocroatian and Albanian periodicals published in Yugoslavia are usually given in English translation.

1. The SAP of Kosova is a territorial unit with an area of 10,880 km² and a population of 1,650,000 according to the 1982 Yugoslav census.

2. For a detailed account of the Spring 1981 riots, see two articles by Stevan K. Pavlowitch and Elez Biberaj in *Conflict Studies* (London, England: Institute for the Study of Conflicts) 1982, No. 137/138. For they Yugoslav official view, see "What Happened in Kosova?," *Socialist Thought and Practice*, 21 (1981) 8. Interview with Sinan Hasani, Vice-president of the Assembly of the SFR of Yugoslavia. For a wider view of the problem of Kosova see Cathérine Verla, "Une question nationale explosive," *Inprécor* (Paris), June 1981; and Pedro Ramet, "Problems of Albanian Nationalism in Yugoslavia," *Orbis*, 25 (1981) 2. The events received worldwide coverage. See also *The New York Times*, April 4, 5, 6, 7, 19 and 22, 1981.

3. Jovan Djordjević, *Constitutional Law* (Prishtinë: University of Prishtinë, 1972), p. 75.

4. Josip B. Tito, "The Special Character of the National Liberation Councils," *Komunist* (1948) 1, p. 6.

5. A detailed account of the legislation's process during the war years can be found in J. Djordjević's book mentioned in note 3.

6. "The Second Session of AVNOJ," *Flaka e Vëllazërimit*, December 16, 1982, p. 14 (Albanian version). Also, *Drugo Zasedanje AVNOJ 1943 god.* (Kultura: Belgrade, 1953), p. 20.

7. Ibid.

8. Stevan K. Pavlowitch, *Yugoslavia* (Praeger: New York, 1971), p. 195.

9.   Tito-Šubašić Agreement (1945). The November 1945 elections, however, were characterized by political intimidation of the "opposition." Typical of this attitude is the slogan "Ballots for Tito—Bullets for Grol." Milan Grol was one of the leaders of the opposition.

10.   *Službeni List FNRJ* (Belgrade), February 1946.

11.   Vladimir Dedijer et al., eds., *History of Yugoslavia* (McGraw-Hill: New York, 1974), p. 698.

12.   J. Djordjević, op. cit., p. 91.

13.   The predominance of the Yugoslav Communist Party can be only partially explained by the break with the Soviet Union, and Stalin's avowed aim to overthrow the Tito government.

14.   *Službeni List FNRJ*, No. 3, January 13, 1953.

15.   A "socio-political community" is a territorial community containing elements of a constitutional socio-economic and political unit (the commune, district, republic, federation, and since 1963, the autonomous province). In practice, it stands for the common activity of the working people using society's means of production, and "freely" disposing of its own income. (See J. Djordjević, op. cit., p. 107).

16.   Smiljko Sokol, "Introduction to the Constitution of the SFR of Yugoslavia," *Constitutions of the Communist World,* William B. Simons, ed. (Sitjhoff and Nordhoff: Germantown, USA, 1980), p. 424.

17.   *The [1974] Constitution of the Socialist Federal Republic of Yugoslavia* (Crosscultural Communications: Merrick, 1976), p. 13.

18.   Ibid., p. 165.

19.   Ibid., p. 13.

20.   Ibid., p. 14.

21.   "The 1946 Constitution of the Federative Democratic Republic of Yugoslavia," *Official Gazette of the FDRJ,* Belgrade, 1946.

22.   "Ustav Narodne Republike Srbije," *Službeni Glasnik NRS* III, January 22, 1947.

23.   The 1961 census added the category of "Moslems by ethnic affiliation," in which were registered nearly one million people who had previously registered as "Yugoslav unspecified." *Statistički Godišnjak FNRJ 1961* (Federal Statistički Zavod: Belgrade, 1962), p. 53.

24.   *Constitution of the Socialist Federative Republic of Yugoslavia* (Secretariat for Information of the Federal Executive Committee, Belgrade, 1963), Part I, Ch. 1, Article 2.

25. See note 17.

26. See note 22.

27. "Ustavni Zakon od 1953 god," *Službeni List NRS*, February 21, 1953, p. 1.

28. Ibid.

29. *Constitution of the Socialist Republic of Serbia,* Ch. I, General Dispositions (Albanian version in *Rilindja,* April 11, 1963—*Rilindja* is the official organ of the Socialist Alliance of the Working People of the SAP of Kosova, and the major newspaper in Albanian).

30. Ibid., Ch. V (Autonomous Provinces) Art. 135.

31. "Ustav Socialistićke Republike Srbije," *Službeni List NRS*, April 1974, Introductory Party, Basic Principles, I, par. 14.

32. Miodrag Nikolić, "Miladin, Tito's Comrade-in-Arms," *Rilindja,* February 26, 1983.

33. Ibid., February 28, 1983, p. 17.

34. Ibid., March 3, 1983, p. 17.

35. Ibid., March 4, 1983, p. 12. "The delegates from Kosova-Metohija returned very happy and enthusiastic from the Zagreb Conference. . . . The physionomy of Kosova was now being defined fully. With the decisions of the [Zagreb] Conference the specific status of Kosova as a separate region inhabited predominatly by Albanians, and its autonomy were fully approved." (Nikolić, "Miladin," March 5, 1980, p. 20.)

36. Ibid.

37. *Socialist Republic of Serbia* (Beogradski Grafički Zavod: Belgrade, 1970), p. 210.

38. From the Albanian text in *Rilindja,* January 9, 1981, p. 14.

39. "Resolution of the First Conference of the National-Liberation Council of Kosova," *The People's Council of the Autonomous Region of Kosova-Metohija, 1943-1953* (Rilindja: Prishtinë, 1955), p. 45.

40. The two letters were published in the *Annals of the Belgrade Law School,* No. 3 (1969). Quoted by Ramadan Marmullaku, *Albania and the Albanians* (Bourst: London, 1965), p. 152, note 1.

41. "We expected the national problem to be solved after the liberation, in the spirit and nature of our revolution. The frontiers, we were told, were not to be the essence of the problem. . . . There were perhaps some erroneous stands, but due to the contact with the Supreme Headquarters of the Army and the Central Committee of the Yugoslav Communist Party

attention was drawn to these stands." Sinan Hasani, "What happened in Kosova? " (See note 1).

42.   Paul Shoup, *Communism and the Yugoslav National Question* (New York: Columbia University Press), pp. 104-105.

43.   Ali Hadri, *A Brief History of the Albanians* (Rilindja: Prishtinë, 1966), pp. 102-104.

44.   Speech by Marko Vujacić, delegate from Montenegro, in the Minutes of the Third Session of AVNOJ, February 24, 1945. Published in *Treće Zasedanje AVNOJ 1945 god.* (Kultura: Belgrade, 1955), p. 55.

45.   "It was only then that the Yugoslav leadership took a different attitude towards the border region with Albania. In recognition of its mixed ethnic character, Kosova was declared an autonomous province in the constitutional settlement, and Albanian was introduced as one of the official languages. . . ." (S. K. Pavlowitch, op. cit., p. 197).

46.   See: *The People's Council of the Autonomous Region of Kosova-Metohija 1943-1953* (Rilindja: Prishtinë, 1955), p. 55.

47.   "Zakon o ustavnovljenju i ustrojstvu Kosovsko-Metohijske Oblasti," Article 2, *Službeni Glasnik NRS,* No. 28, September 8, 1945.

48.   By the end of 1982, there were about 400,000 Albanians concentrated in eight communes of Macedonia: 100,000 in three communes of Serbia and 40,000 in five communes of Montenegro. According to S. K. Pavlowitch, ". . . [Macedonians] could not afford to give way to their own Albanians in Macedonia, as Serbs had in Serbia, and were ready to oppose any attempt to limit their national rights or to divide them." Op. cit., p. 337.

49.   "The Statute of the Autonomous Region of Kosova-Metohija," *Official Gazette of ARKM,* May 28, 1948.

50.   Kurtesh Salihu, *The Origin, Position, and Development of the SAP of Kosova* (Center for Marxist Studies: Prishtinë, 1982), p. 12.

51.   "The 1953 Statute of the AR of Kosova-Metohija," *Službeni List AKMO,* Ch. 1, General Provisions. The underlined words indicate the changes introduced in this Statute.

52.   Resolution on the Proclamation of the Statute of the AR of Kosova-Metohija," *Rilindja,* Arpil 11, 1963, p. 2.

53.   Ibid. Ch. 1, General Dispositions.

54.   Ibid. Emphasis added.

55.   *The Constitutional Law of the Socialist Province of Kosova-*

Metohija (Fletorja Zyrtare of SAPKM: Prishtinë, 1969). For a detailed account of the unrest, see Peter R. Prifti, "Kosova in Ferment" (Center for International Studies, MIT: Cambridge, Mass., 1969).

56.   The word "freely" in the expressed will of the local population is curiously missing.

57.   Emphasis added to stress the difference between "community" (for autonomous provinces) and "state" (for republics).

58.   Emphasis added.

59.   "Our national question has been solved within the framework of the republics. In the future, as we are contemplating constitutional amendments within the republics, we will see mainly internal rearrangements, which means that essentially there will be a further development of self-management, and not any political decomposition." J. B. Tito to YCL organizations in Zagreb (1971). Quoted by Ivan Kristan, "The Constitutional Status of the Autonomous Provinces: Autonomy and Its Specifics," *Rilindja,* June 16-22, 1982.

60.   Mihajlo Maletić, *Kosova: Yesterday and Today* (Borba Publishing House: Belgrade, 1973), p. 502. The redefinition of the Province "might have resolved the juridical contradictions, but the autonomy itself has not gained a new and qualitative form," according to Jovan Djordjević. He sees the harmonization of "the contradictory elements" in the establishment of the autonomous provinces as specific and logical socio-political and constitutional entities to be "neither simple nor easy." To Djordjević, the "autonomous republics" of the 1936 Soviet Constitution are the closest model to the autonomous provinces as defined in 1971. This theory, he adds, has influenced those trends of thoughts which see the process of the autonomous provinces reaching over to "quasi-republic" and even to "special republic" status. This fluid situation, brought in by an "empirical and political practicality" approach has engendered "frictions affecting the international relations." Djordjević advises a "democratic solution, that would be based on the respect of the various demands and interests, as well as on being aware of the political rationalities, and equality of nations and peoples." (J. Djordjević, op. cit., pp. 661-663).

61.   "Constitution of the SAP of Kosova 1974," *Ustav SR Srbije* (1974), pp. 393-521. For the first time, Albanians are mentioned first in the list of nationalities presently living in Kosova.

62.   Ibid., Basic Principles, Ch. 1.

63.   M. Maletić, op. cit., p. 496.
64.   "Constitution of the SAP of Kosova," see note 61.
65.   Ibid., pp. 520-521.
66.   Ibid., p. 519.
67.   Enver Rexhepi, "Aspects of the Autonomy in the SAP of Kosova," *Rilindja,* February 27, 1982, p. 6. See Table:

Representation of the SAP of Kosova in the Federal Assembly

	1946			1953		
	Rep.	Vojv.	Kos.	Rep.	Vojv.	Kos.
a) Federal Chamber		1/50,000		10	5	4
b) Chamber of National-ities (Chamber of Producers)	30	20	15	1/70,000		

	1963			1974		
	Rep.	Vojv.	Kos.	Rep.	Vojv.	Kos.
a) Federal Chamber	10	5	5	30	20	20
b) Chamber of National-ities (Chamber of Producers)	10	5	5	12	8	8

(Source: The Yugoslav Constitutions of 1946, 1963, 1974; Constitutional Law of 1953.) See notes 20, 24, 17, and 27 respectively.

68.   There were no Albanians in the Federal Executive Committee before 1978. During that year, two Albanians were trusted to direct the departments of Information, and Domestic Trade and Prices. In 1982, the new Yugoslav government included only one Albanian, the Undersecretary for Transportation.
69.   Enver Rexhepi, "Aspects of Autonomy," *Rilindja,* March 8, 1982, p. 7.
70.   There are thirty-five delegates from the SAP of Kosova to the Serbian Republican Assembly. Twenty-eight of them are Albanians. ·

71. See note 59.

72. Enver Rexhepi, "Aspects of Autonomy," *Rilindja,* March 8, 1982, p. 7.

73. Regarding the moral and political suitability of the citizens to be elected delegates, a conflict exists between the line of the political groups and the constitutionality of the "suitability." According to the Yugoslav press, "the Constitutional Court of Yugoslavia, and the constitutional courts of the republics and provinces are in agreement concerning the definition of such a condition for election to be against the Constitution of the SFR of Yugoslavia . . . . The Constitutional Court is of the opinion that all the requirements set forth by the by-laws can be checked and verified in proper manner, or by addressing the court, but the moral-political suitability cannot be one of the requirements. . . . " "Moral-political Suitability—Unconstitutional," *Rilindja,* April 27, 1983, p. 6.

74. "The trend towards identifying the republics with ethnic groups increased the Serbian malaise, since of all ethnic groups, the Serbs had the largest proportion living outside 'their' republic . . . . In the republic of Serbia itself, Vojvodina in the north and Kosova in the south had been given special status, because of their mixed ethnic composition. The latter, however, was rapidly becoming a national home for the Albanian minority in Yugoslavia . . . . [For these reasons] Serbian opinion was not keen in giving yet more power to the republics at the expense of the federation." (S. K. Pavlowitch, op. cit., p. 337).

75. *SR of Serbia,* p. 212. See note 37.

76. "The post-war policies of nationalities started by recognizing Macedonians, then created Montenegrins (which had historical, administrative, and political raison d'être, [but] was artificial on ethnic grounds." (Pavlowitch, op. cit., p. 337.)

77. Stane Dolanc (Press Conference, Belgrade, April 6, 1981) asked rhetorically: "Do you want two Koreas, do you want two Germanies?" *Süddeutsche Zeitung,* April 9, 1981, p. 1, commented: "What Dolanc did not say, but nonetheless meant, is this: divided people seek reunification."

78. *Constitution of the SFRY* (1974), Art. 339.

79. Ibid., Art. 400.

80. Ibid., Art. 402.

81. Ibid., Art. 5.

Paul Shoup

THE GOVERNMENT AND CONSTITUTIONAL
STATUS OF KOSOVA:
SOME BRIEF REMARKS

In my presentation I would like briefly to review the constitutional development of the province of Kosova within the Yugoslav federation, as well as to comment on the significance of these developments for the future. As the conclusion suggests, the Yugoslavs find themselves in a dilemma created by their inability or unwillingness to grant the Albanian population symbolic equality with the Slav nationalities. Something approaching de facto equality has already existed since 1971, but this has not been enough to satisfy the demands of the Albanian minority in Yugoslavia for equality of treatment with the remaining Yugoslavs.

Under the provisions of the constitution of 1946 (or Kosova-Metohija, as it was then called) enjoyed a decidedly inferior status within the Yugoslav federation. Although Kosova-Metohija sent a delegation to the Chamber of Nationalities in Belgrade, she had no independent legislature, supreme court (as did Vojvodina), or provincial administration. Both the *Oblast* (province) of Vojvodina and the *Oblast* of Kosova-Metohija were administered as integral parts of the Serbian republic. Only the existence of provincial statutes, and representation in the federal Chamber of Nationalities, set these provinces apart from other local government jurisdictions in Serbia.[1] With the abolition of the Chamber of Nationalities in 1953, the significance of the autonomous regions was reduced even further. In actual practice, between 1946 and 1966 Kosova was under secret police control. Serbs and Montenegrins, not Albanians, played the dominant role in the administration and politics of the province.

233

Between 1967 and 1974 the status of the republics underwent a dramatic change. In 1967 the Chamber of Nationalities was reinstated as a separate assembly within the federal parliament. This move reflected the victory of liberal and regional interests over Ranković in 1966. In Kosova, change was slower in coming, but was finally spurred by the riots of November 1968. In January 1969, the Serbian parliament adopted a constitution for Kosova. Kosova was recognized in the federal constitution as part of the Yugoslav federation in its own right. The province received its own supreme court, and each nationality (including the Albanians) was allowed to display its own flag. These rights were incorporated into the amendments to the federal constitution adopted in 1971;[2] at this time the province also gained equal representation with the republics in the organs of the federation. From 1971 onward, the republics and provinces enjoyed equality in the eyes of the federal government. Most important in this respect was the power of the provincial delegations in the Federal Executive Council to veto or block legislation of which they did not approve. After 1974, this right of veto was extended to the decisions of the Chamber of Republics and Provinces.[3] Thus, in the 1970s, Kosova emerged as an independent actor in the federation, no longer under direct Serbian tutelage. This was a remarkable transformation, given the fact that it was paralleled by a consolidation of the power of the Albanians in the provincial government under the leadership of Mahmut Bakalli and David Nimani, presidents of the provincial party and government, respectively.

The 1974 constitution of Kosova, and the Serb constitution of the same year, presently determine the rights, duties, and powers of the province.[4] The right of the province to representation in the federal assembly and government, on an equal basis with the republics, is once again affirmed. Under the provisions of the provincial constitution, the provincial assembly can, along with the assemblies of the republics, consider and approve the foreign policy of the federation.[5] The province has its own national bank, supreme court and independent administration under the supervision of the provincial executive council and provincial presidency. Under the provisions of the provincial constitution, the presidency has the right, among other things, to determine plans for the defense of the province in time of war.[6]

Further, under the provisions of the Serbian constitution of 1974, republic legislation which could be applied to the entire republic, including the two autonomous provinces, is sharply limited in scope. Such legislation may be passed in the areas of state security, defense, property relations, the status of religious orders, and like matters.[7] In other areas, including economic policy, taxation, education and culture, the Republic of Serbia is empowered to pass legislation valid for the entire republic only with the prior approval of the assembly of the province. If only one province approves such legislation, the law will apply only to that province (as well as to the territory of Lesser Serbia).

Within the province of Kosova, the 1974 provincial constitution provided for a system of government patterned after that of the other republics and provinces; legislative power was entrusted to an assembly made up of three chambers, while executive power resided in the hands of the Executive Committee (*Izvršno Veće*). Above both bodies stood the nine man Presidency in which the President of the Assembly and the President of the party were ex-officio members.[8] The provincial constitution, like those of the republics and fedeation, placed great stress on self-management procedures, processes and principles. It is easy to see that the drafters of the constitution hoped that self-management principles would play a major role in integrating the nations and nationalities of the province.

These constitutional changes mirror quite accurately the actual shift of political, governmental and administrative power to the province between 1968 and 1981. Evidence of this cannot be detailed here. We know, however, that Serbian legislation for the entire republic was often blocked by provincial action, even in those areas under Article 300 of the Serbian constitution where prior approval of the provinces was not required. The Kosova delegation in the federal Chamber of Republics and Provinces, while it was not under as tight control as some other republic delegations, was capable of standing up for the interests of the province, as the lengthy debate over the supplementary financing of Kosova in 1976 demonstrated. The provincial leadership had, by the late 1970s, begun to look tolerantly on expressions of Albanian nationalism, and would not permit criticism of developments in the province on the part of other republics—for example, in the case of the "Blue Book" of 1977 cataloging Serbian grievances, which was suppressed, in part, due to the objections of the Kosova provincial leadership.

This is not to say that the Kosova leadership always got its way. Economic policy, in particular, seemed to reflect a compromise with outside interests as well as a fascination with prestige projects which were of little intrinsic value to the province. Still, all the evidence suggests that the Kosova government and party operated with minimal restraints, either from the side of the Serbian republic or the federal government, between the years 1971 and 1981.

Today the situation is far more complex. The constitution of 1974 remains in force. The martial law powers exercised after the riots of April 1981, have brought the police back into Kosova, however, and even the army may be playing a role in the administration of the province. The new Kosova leadership under Sinan Hasani, President of the LC, and Ali Šukrija, the power behind the scenes, is heavily dependent on outside support. Yet it appears that this same leadership is continuing to defend Albanian interests in the province, as evidenced by the interesting developments in September 1981, when Dušan Ristić resigned from the Kosova Executive Council, and barely veiled illusions were made concerning the need to enhance the constitutional status of the province.[9]

As we are all aware, there is little hope that the province will attain the status of a republic. Under the provisions of the 1974 provincial constitution, Kosova is not a state (as are the republics), but only a "socio-political community" within the state of Serbia.[10] Although now constituting more than 77 percent of the population, the Albanians in the province are technically a "nationality," in theory enjoying a lesser status that the Serb and Montenegrin minorities in the province, these groups being part of their respective "nations." While granting Kosova the status of a republic would result in only slight changes in her role in the federation (the representation of Kosova in federal organs would increase while Serb laws now in effect in the provinces would be rescinded) the symbolic effect of elevation to republic status would be immense. (Whether this would be enough to satisfy nationalist feeling among the Albanians is another question.)

How is one to evaluate the history of the province, and its evolution to a position of de facto equality with the republics, but without de jure recognition of republic status? Could any other approach have been more successful in integrating Kosova into Yugoslavia while protecting the rights of the Albanian population in the province?

In retrospect, one can point to the importance of the failure to create a republic in Kosova in 1946. As an equal member of the federation from the start, the Albanians might have escaped the excesses of police terror inflicted by the Ranković forces prior to 1966, and might have come to associate their own future more closely with Yugoslavia. Again, after the riots of 1968, an opportunity to declare Kosova a republic was lost. Today it is no longer possible to take this step without creating a crisis among the Slav nationalities. The reaction of the Serbs to events in Kosova, which has been nationalistic in the extreme, has seen to that.

Nevertheless, the constitutional innovations of 1971 and 1974 were a step forward, and resulted in an unprecedented degree of autonomy for Kosova. Nowhere in Europe have such far-ranging concessions to national rights been granted in regions considered as potentially separatist. Why, then, did not these concessions work?

Others in this volume will have more to say on this subject. In respect to the constitutional solutions sought by the Belgrade government, one senses an effort to bow to political expediency without, however, attacking the problem of underlying national outlooks and emotions, especially among the Serbs, among whom opposition to republic status for Kosova was greatest. The resulting situation not only did not satisfy the highly aroused feelings of the Albanians, who had set their sights on republic status, but led to concealment and prevarication concerning the problems of the provinces. The true state of relations among the nationalities was never frankly discussed, and little effort was made to inform either the Serbs or the Albanians of the legitimate interests and concerns of the other community. In brief, no effort was made to allow reasonable discussion to replace emotion, or for all concerned to adjust their demands and expectations to the existing situation. This does not mean that a dialogue between Serbs and Albanians would have produced agreement over the constitutional status of Kosovo, and prevented the April 1981 riots. But the fact remains that the pragmatic solution sought for Kosova after 1971—de facto but no de jure republic status—was not followed up by a broadening of the dialogue between Serbs and Albanians which might have made this solution more palatable to the Albanian population, or convinced the Serbs that the final step—republic status for the provinces —could be accomplished without detriment to the rights of Serbs in the province or the historic interest of Serbia in Kosova.

Today, it could be argued that the element of open dialogue between the Serbs and Albanians is more necessary than ever before. The Serbian public must be better informed concerning the origins of the April riots and the desires of the Albanian population. What holds true for the Serbs holds true for the Albanian national movement also. It must seek ways to open a dialogue with the Serbs. Whether this will happen within Yugoslavia is not clear, but seems open to doubt. It remains, therefore, for some efforts to be made in a different context, perhaps within that of the democratic movement, or well-intentioned Albanian and Serb groups outside Yugoslavia. Such moves, of course, would take away the initiative for the solution of the national question in Yugoslavia from the existing government. Others, perhaps more capable of initiating a meaningful dialogue among groups who today view each other with deep suspicion and distrust might find compromise solutions in the realm of constitutional arrangements for Kosova which elude the present government.

* * * * *

NOTES

1. Paul Shoup, *Communism and the Yugoslav National Question* (New York, 1968), p. 115.

2. *Ustav Socjalističke Federativne Republike Jugoslavije* (Belgrade: 1978).

3. "Intrafederal Relations in the Socialist Federal Republic of Yugoslavia," *Yugoslav Survey*, August 1980, pp. 3-28.

4. *Ustav SR Srbije* (Belgrade, 1974).

5. Article 301 of the Kosova Constitution.

6. Article 339 of the 1974 Kosova Constitution.

7. See Articles 300, 301 and 343 of the Serbian constitution of 1974.

8. Article 339 of the Kosova Constitution.

9. See Radio Free Europe, *RAD Background Report* No. 294 (21 October 1981).

10. "Intrafederal Relations," op. cit., p. 11.

Arshi Pipa

THE OTHER ALBANIA: A BALKAN PERSPECTIVE

Kosova has been in the limelight in the last two years. The Spring 1981 demonstrations and riots in Prishtinë and other cities, followed by the Federal troops' drastic repression, have called attention to the "autonomous province." There is another autonomous province in the Socialist Federal Republic of Yugoslavia, Vojvodina, the two being integrant parts of the Socialist Republic of Serbia. The official description of the two provinces is the same. The differences between them are striking in two respects. Whereas Vojvodina is a rich province, richer than the rest of Serbia, Kosova's economy is not only poorer than that of Serbia, but the poorest in Yugoslavia. The March 1981 student protest in Prishtinë was sparked by undernourishment at the University's cafeteria and by sharing beds by shifts at the dormitories. The high rate of unemployment among university graduates was an additional cause for the riots. The main cause, however, was the pent-up feeling of frustration, universal among the Kosovars, for failing to have their province promoted to republican status. And here we come to the other important difference between the two provinces. Vojvodina is populated in greater part by Serbs (54.5%), whereas Serbs, Montenegrins, and other Slavic and Turkish ethnics make up only 22.5% of Kosova's population, the rest being Albanians. And since Kosova's population (1,584,558, i.e., 7.8 percent of Yugoslavia's whole population, according to the 1981 census) is scarcely smaller than the population of the Republic of Macedonia, but much larger than that of Montenegro, the Kosovars feel strongly that the status of their province should be raised to that of a republic.[1] The refusal of their demands is interpreted as discrimination against them as Albanians by South Slavs.

239

Their depressed economy makes them the proletarian ethnics of socialist Yugoslavia. Their second class citizenship offends their national pride; Serbian tutelage is felt as a yoke. These sentiments are shared by the leaders to a great extent, witness the extensive purges in the Party and the government after the riots.[2]

Serb reaction to Kosovar nationalism is predictable. The Serbs fear that once republican status is granted to Kosova, the province would secede and join the People's Socialist Republic of Albania. Kosova's secession would not only weaken the Yugoslav Federation, but it could also jeopardize its national security. Serbs and Kosovars have been sworn enemies in the past, and Yugoslav-Albanian relations have been bad for more than a generation. A greater Albania including Kosova would be a greater danger for Yugoslavia. The severe punitive measures against the leaders, supporters, and even sympathizers of the demonstrations and riots have been motivated by precisely that fear.[3] Many of those sentenced to high prison terms were accused of irredentism, instigated by the Albanian government. Tirana has rejected the charge.[4]

Kosova was made an "autonomous region" under the name of Kosmet (Kos[ova]-Met[ohija]) in 1945. Its autonomy was nominal for a long time, and it continued to be so even after Kosova was promoted to an "autonomous province" in 1963. The Kosovars began to feel at home in the province only after Alexander Ranković, notorious for his Albano-phobia, was expelled from the Party's Executive Committee. In 1968 demonstrators in Prishtinë voiced the request that Kosova be made a republic. From that time on, Kosova's dependence on Serbia has gradually diminished. The 1974 Constitution recognizes the autonomous province rights that are almost the same as those exercised by the six federal republics. The Kosovans have their own administration and legislature, their territorial army and police, and their courts and schools. The language in the schools is predominantly Albanian. And the Kosovars can even fly their own flag, which is the same as the Albanian flag. The Serbs feel they have been more than generous to them. Granting the province republican status too would be tantamount to inviting the Kosovars to secede, they think. And Serbia would not permit secession. The Serbs consider Kosova Serbian territory, though the population of the province is 77.5 percent Albanian and only 13.2 percent Serb (1981 census).

We have touched on a very sensitive point. According to Yugoslav historians, it was Stefan Nemanja (1168-1196), the Rašian founder of the first Serbian dynasty, who first conquered Kosova.[5] Albanian as well as some foreign historians maintain that the Serbs settled in Kosova towards the end of the thirteenth century and that Kosova was still essentially Albanian and Christian in the fourteenth and fifteenth centuries.[6] When Stefan Dušan proclaimed himself Emperor of Serbs and Greeks, he founded the independent Patriarchate of Serbia in Peć (Pejë, a city in Kosova close to the Albanian border). The treasures of Serbian religious art, the churches of Gračanica and Dečan (the Emperor was buried in the latter) are found in Kosovan territory. And it was in Kosovo Polje (Blackbird Field) that the memorable battle between Turks and Slavs (including Albanians, according to Albanian historians) took place in 1389, a date which marks the beginning of the Turkish domination of the Balkans. Serbian and Albanian princes surrendered or were defeated; Kosova became a Turkish province in the fifteenth century.

The Croat historian Milan Šufflay advanced the thesis of a Serbo-Albanian symbiosis in the Middle Ages.[7] Šufflay's thesis is confirmed by documents such as the 1416 Venetian Cadaster of Shkodër (Scutari),[8] the 1455 Turkish *defter* ('register' [of landed property]) of the Kosova region,[9] and the 1485 Turkish *defter* of the Shkodër region.[10]

In all three documents many landowners have Albanian names, usually with Slavic suffixes. To Serb historians these people were Serbs. Albanian historians maintain that they were Orthodox or Catholic Albanians whose names had been slavicized during the reign of the Serbian kings. These Albanians were autochthone descendants of the Illyrians. Illyrians, according to the Greek geographer Strabo, were also the Dardanians, who lived in an area (capital Niš, Lat. *Naissus*) bordering on Thracia.[11] Study of the Albanian language led several Albanologists to hold precisely that area as the primitive homeland of the Albanians.[12] Serb historians deny the existence of Albanians in "Stara Serbia" (Old Serbia, another name for Kosova) before the Turkish occupation of the Balkans. According to them, Albanians colonized Kosova and other parts of Jugoslavia with the strong support of the Turks, whose religion they were quick to embrace (today the Kosovars are Moslem, except for a restricted number of Catholics). Catholic ecclesiastic reports are proof that at least some Albanian Catholics lived in Kosova at the beginning of the seventeenth century.[13] During the 1690 Austro-Turkish War, a great number of Serbs who had sided with the Austrians left their lands, which were occupied

by Albanians, Yugoslav historians say. Albanian historians counter that
Albanians too fought the Turks, migrating together with Slavs into Hungary when the Austrian army was defeated. Another Serbian exodus occurred during the 1737 Austro-Turkish War. In general Albanian historians
do not deny that some Albanians occupied Serbian lands (the North-
Albanian provenience of many Kosovars is attested by their own pedigree).
But they tend to minimize the size of the colonization, while letting their
opponents read between the lines that, after all, these immigrants were
going back home, the lands they occupied having belonged to their Illyrian
ancestors, the Dardanians.

In the first half of the nineteenth century, Kosova was overwhelmingly
populated by Albanians, who had also firmly entrenched themselves in
the Novi Pazar region, reaching as far as Niš in the North. It was in Kosova
that the nationalist movement for autonomy began. After the Turkish
defeat by the Russians in 1878, the Great Powers convened in Berlin to
moderate the Russian designs to increase the territories of Russia's *pro-
tégé's* with lands carved from Turkish possessions inhabited wholly or in
part by Albanians. The Albanians at that time were living in the four
vilayets (governorships) constituting the greater part of European Turkey.
The Vilayet of Shkodër was entirely inhabited by Albanians.[14] The percentage of Albanians in the Vilayet of Kosova was 60 percent in 1910,
the rest being Serbs, Bulgarians, and Turks.[15] The Vilayet of Monastir
(Bitolje), including Central and part of Southern Albania, had a typically
Balkan population, i.e., it was composed of Albanians, Bulgarians, Greeks,
Aromunians, Turks, and Jews, the Albanians having an absolute majority
(58 percent in 1910).[16] The Vilayet of Yannina, including part of Southern
Albania and Epirus, was inhabited mostly by Albanians (62 percent in
1910), the rest being Greeks, Aromunians, Jews, and Gypsies.[17] The
Congress of Berlin assigned parts of the three former vilayets to Montenegro, Serbia, and Bulgaria respectively. The cession of the Plavë and
Gucî (Plava and Gusinje) districts to Montenegro sparked the movement
known as the League of Prizren, from the city in Kosova where the Albanian representatives met (1878). Under the leadership of Abdul Frashëri,
a South-Albanian diplomat, the League resolved to create fighting units
for the defense of the Albanian territories assigned to South Slavs. The
League summoned the Albanians, regardless of regional or confessional
differences, to unite for the creation of an autonomous Albania comprising the four vilayets—later called Greater Albania—within the frame

of the Ottoman Empire. The autonomy was restricted to an Albanian administration with Albanian schools and an Albanian army commanded by Turkish officers. The Turks, who had at the outset favored the League for their own interests, reacted against it when the League opposed a compromise solution, accepted by the Empire, to barter the Plavë and Gucî districts for other North-Albanian districts. The North-Albanians revolted. Turkey jailed the League's principal leaders and proceeded to disband it.

The Turkish defeat by the Balkan allies in the Balkan wars resulted in the further dismemberment of the Albania of the four vilayets by the victors. The 1913 Treaty of London recognized an independent Albania with an area roughly the same as the present one (10,629 square miles, about the size of the Vilayet of Kosova) and with a population that was less than half of the Albanian population in the four vilayets (close to two million in 1912). The Conference of Versailles debated the question whether even this truncated Albania was to exist as an independent state. The greater part of the Yannina Vilayet went to Greece. To the newly formed Kingdom of Yugoslavia were assigned the greater part of Kosova, the Albanian territories east of the Drin River in present-day Macedonia, and the Albanian coastal zone incorporated by Montenegro after the Congress of Berlin. The Kosovars rose in revolt. The Serbian army crushed it.[18]

In the period between the two world wars, the Yugoslav government tried to colonize Kosova with Serbs and Montenegrins by legal as well as illegal means. The plan was to clear Kosova of the Albanians. It failed, though many Kosovars families emigrated to Albania and Turkey. When, during World War II, Yugoslavia collapsed (1941) and most of the Albanian territories merged with the Italian-occupied Kingdom of Albania, the Albanians living in those territories greeted the Italians as liberators. Antifascist resistance in Kosova and the peripheral Albanian regions was consequently weak.[19] After Yugoslavia's liberation from the nazi-fascist troops by the partisans, reprisals took place against Albanian collaborators as well as individuals who had inflicted vexations on the Slav population. Soon the reprisals degenerated into a persecution of the Albanian population. The Kosovars rose in arms, an insurrection flared up in Drenica. It was ruthlessly crushed by the partisans. The Autonomous Region of Kosmet was born by Cesarean section.

This brief excursus on the history of Kosova is not meant to prove anything. It purports only to make the reader aware of the complexity of the

Kosova problem. Invoking history does not help solve it. History deals with the past, and the past cannot be erased. On the other hand, ignoring history is unwise, for history explains the present and orients toward the future. Perhaps the way to approach cases such as this is to remember and pity while being ready to go a long way on the road of persuasion based on rational discourse. To ask when the Serbs occupied Kosova and who was inhabiting it beforehand is a legitimate historiographical question. But answering that question will not solve the problems besetting Kosova today; it will only exasperate them. Calling Kosova Serbian because the Serbian nation was born there has its counterpart in calling Kosova Albanian because it was formerly inhabited by the Dardanians. The next move in this sense would be to identify the ancestors of the Dardanians. Consideration of what Strabo wrote about their dwelling would lead to calling them troglodytes.[20]

A reasonable way to avoid such pitfalls would be to shelve both *"Stara Serbia"* and "Greater Albania." One term is no better than the other. The four vilayets constituting the *Arnautluk* (Albaniandom) of the Ottoman Empire were administrative divisions corresponding to its political system, which was based on religion, not nationality. To resort to Old Serbia as a counterweight for Greater Albania, or the other way round, is to search for allies among conjured phantasms. Both Old Serbia and the Ottoman Empire are gone, and going back to them to prop up political arguments is to play politics with history.

The question is to be reversed. Kosova's location at a juncture where the road joining the Pannonian Basin to the Aegean Sea crosses the old road from the Adriatic to Constantinople, makes Kosova a "turn-table," as one geographer has called it, between Belgrade and Salonika on the one hand and Tirana and Sofia on the other hand.[21] Considering Kosova's rich agricultural and industrial potential, one can surmise that the chances that the province will became a major factor in the Balkans are as bright for the future as they are dark today. The Balkan vocation of Kosova is favored by its unique amphibious nature as an overwhelmingly Albanian province which is a constitutive part of the Yugoslav Federation.

The Albanian leaders have repeatedly declared that Albania has no territorial claims on Kosova. This is not mere rhetoric, considering the important differences in ideology and the political system between the two. An attempt by Albania to englobe Kosova would be a suicidal act.

Here the answer is cultural differentiation. So long as the Kosovars will not differentiate themselves culturally from their Albanian brothers, their chances of obtaining republican status will be slight. Differentiation does not mean discontinuation of cultural exchange. But the exchange should be, to deserve its name, on a parity basis, with the Kosovars as donors as often as recipients. Of course they should continue to develop their Albanian culture. But their contribution to the latter will be more effective if they elaborate on those national traits that are peculiar or more specific to them in fields such as language, folklore, ethnology, and history. Their own variety of Gheg presents distinct phonetic features not found in other Gheg dialects.[23] Their literary tradition goes back to the most important of the earliest Albanian writers, Pjetër Bogdani (1630-1688). A patriot and an erudite, this Catholic bishop produced a model of literary Albanian, a first *koinë* of North-Albanian dialects. Elaborating on that literary tradition would free the Kosovars from mimicking a language unsuited to them.[24] Their bilingualism is an asset for studying—not discarding, as they have been doing—the Serbocroatian epic songs sung by Albanian bards.[25] An eminent Kosovar folklorist, Shtjefën Gjeçov, did not eliminate from his Albanian name its Slavic suffix. In the field of history, one expects Kosovar scholars to study in depth the League of Prizren, a capital Kosovar achievement. But Kosovars and peripheral Albanians played a major role in shaping not only modern Albanian history, but also the history of the dying Ottoman Empire. Ibrahim Temo was a pioneer of the Young Turk movement,[26] which had among its influential members people like Nexhip Draga, Ahmed Nyazi,[27] and Dervish Hima.[28] It was the Kosovar movement of protest against Austrian interference that led to the proclamation of the Constitution which brought the Young Turks to power in July 1908.[29] And when Young Turk nationalism alienated the Albanians, the general insurrection planned by the Albanian leaders was to begin in Kosova. In 1912, Hasan Prishtina, the foremost Kosovar leader, proposed that Bulgaro-Macedonian leaders join the insurrection and create together an "autonomous Albanian-Macedonian state."[30] Led by him, the Kosovar insurgents gathered in Prishtinë in July of that year demanded—and obtained—the dissolution of the Turkish Parliament. The occupation of Skopje (Shkup) by the Kosovar insurgents in August of that same year brought down the Young Turk government.[31] The Kosovar insurrection which paved the way for the victory of the Balkan allies over the Turks during the First Balkan War (October 1912) created also the conditions for the proclamation of Albania's independence (November 1912). Kosova has played a major role in shaping the Balkan map as it stands today to its own disadvantage. It is the responsibility of Kosovar historiography to explain this phenomenon and draw lessons from it.

Considerations such as these suggest that the Kosovars have much to gain by developing their own brand of Albanian culture, adding to it a Balkan dimension. This will make them visible in the European cultural scene. International recognition of their culture will immensely help their cause. Good work has been done in this sense by organizing Albanological seminars and language courses for foreigners at the University of Prishtinë. Unfortunately, the same thing can not be said for their cultural outreach activities. If the province is not yet sufficiently prepared for instructional exchange with other countries, contacts can be established through their scholarly publications and literature. The information and propaganda services are disorganized. In the United States, for instance, no distribution agency exists for Kosovar publications—Tirana has more than one. Not even the Library of Congress receives all their important publications.[32] To compile a decent bibliography of Kosovar scholarly and literary output, one has to travel to Europe.[33] Sizable Kosovar contingents live in Turkey, the United States, and Australia. They would like to know about what has been achieved in their homeland. Have their cultural needs been met?

When even University students are poorly fed and lodged, one can imagine the plight of the economy in the province. Kosova's social productivity is by far the lowest in the Yugoslav Federation: $795 per capita income compared with $2,635 for the Yugoslav average (1979). Kosova remains a province loosely attached to the rest of the Federation, almost an appendage. The problem of integration has been a main concern of both the provincial and the central government. It has often been pointed out that not all the blame for Kosova's lag rests with the Kosovars. Foreign experts have named Serbocentrism as a main cause. Another major cause is the Federation's policy of discrimination: until the end of the 1950s, Kosova did not receive financial grants from the Federation like the other undeveloped areas. It has also been noted that lack of expertise diminishes Kosova's negotiating power with Serbia and the other republics. The

primacy of the basic industry (extractive and thermoelectric), which dates
from the period of the centralized economy, has not been seriously questioned and no alternative has been proposed.[34] In 1944-48, Albanian's
economic subservience to Yugoslavia, whic laid the ground for the planned
annexation of Albania, was mostly a question of economic naiveté on the
part of the Albanian leaders. It seems that the Kosovars have not profited
from the lesson. They continue to invest in basic industries the funds allocated to Kosova by the Federal Fund for the Development of Undeveloped areas (88 percent for 1966-1970, 66 percent of 1971-1980).[35] These
funds constitute nearly two-thirds of the Kosovan investments; part of
them could be invested elsewhere. But one should know where and how
to invest; and adequate cadres to run the economy are missing. In 1982,
the Department of Economics at the University of Prishtinë was still at
the very bottom of the scale as to number of students.[36] Of course numbers alone are not a sure criterion for judgement. Yet considering what
has been said and will be specified in the following paragraph, one won-
ders whether quality corresponds to quantity in this case. The bolstering
of a Department of Economics respected nation-wide is an absolute priority for the Kosovans.

It can be safely stated that economic progress will not be possible until
a process of economic education begins, involving large strata of the population. This means first of all determination to change the obsolete agricultural mode of production in the private sector (89.5% of arable land
producing 75 percent of the total agricultural income) while at the same
time enlarging the social sector (11.5 percent producing the rest of the
percentage).[37] Due to the province's high rate of unemployment (27 percent of Yugoslavia's unemployed and only 178,000 employed in a population of more than one and a half million) as well as to the high rate of
demographic growth (26 per 1,000 population compared with 8.6 for the
Yugoslav average) the labor force in the private sector has increased about
10 percent from 1948 to 1978—in the rest of Yugoslavia it has decreased
about 16 percent in the same period.[38] The anomaly is a result of agriculture's absorbing unemployment without substantially adding to productivity. A great deal of human energies, which could be profitably used
in industry, are thus wasted. But industry itself has been stagnating. Kosova's industrial output amounts to only 2.2 percent of the total federal
output, whereas the province's population represents 7.8 percent of the

total Yugoslav population. The industry is concentrated in two giant conglomerates. Trepça in Titova Mitrovica combines mining, metallurgy, and chemicals; Kosova in Obilić uses lignite to generate energy while also producing fertilizers. The processing industry is represented by a plant for shock absorbers in Prishtinë, another in Uroševac which makes steel tubes, and a third in Suva Reka producing rubber conveyers. Basic industry does not create new jobs as processing industry does. The latter also brings money, finished goods being an important source of income. Lacking such income, Kosova must resort to aid in the form of Federal Development Funds. But whereas the underdeveloped republics use these funds to supplement investment funds generated by their more industrial establishments, Kosova invests the greater part of the Federal funds in basic industries. True, Kosova's share of those funds has been proportionately higher than the shares of the underdeveloped republics. The Federation has been generous to its black sheep. But generosity in this case turns out to be a form of exploitation. Since 70 percent of Kosova's industry is of the basic type, the profits accrue to those members of the Federation that use Kosova's minerals and energy to generate goods and machinery. The Federal Development Funds are, moreover, subject to repayment, although after a long term and with minimal interest. Furthermore, the salaries of Kosovar workers are lower than those of the average Yugoslav worker: $180 per month compared with $235. The situation is similar to that in semicolonial countries exploited by foreign capital. The analogy becomes obvious if we add to the picture the Kosovan rate of illiteracy: 31.5 percent compared with 15.2 percent in all Yugoslavia.[39]

What can be done to remedy this deplorable situation? Expertise in the economic sector is of course a first requisite. Lack of it, however, is not totally the Kosovars' fault. The Kingdom of Yugoslavia did not allow them to have even elementary Albanian schools. Now they have their own university. But do they have enough vocational schools? They have built a majestic library in Prishtinë, of which they are deservedly proud. But they have long emphasized humanistic education, and now they are short of engineers and technicians. The sooner they acquire expertise in the various economic sectors, the closer they will be to freeing themselves from economic dependence.

But expertise alone will not solve the problem. A transformation of the still medieval mode of production in the countryside is badly needed and, together with it, a change in the Kosovar way of life, governed by traditional mores and outdated customs. The emancipation to be achieved is social no less than economic, and concerns first the still patriarchal family life. The position of a woman is that of a human being deprived of fundamental rights. Women are kept secluded at home when they do not work in the fields, get minimal education, and are totally subordinate to male authority. In extended families, economics permitting, women live in a separate wing of the house, reserved for them alone. The emancipation of women is the first and foremost task for the Kosovars to get fully emancipated. A community denying half of its members access to full education can never be a civilized community. It is also imperative that women be admitted to factories and plants. By exercising professions and participating in productive work, they will improve the economy of their families and begin to play a role in social life.

Cultural differentiation and economic expertise coupled with social emancipation will lead naturally to self-determination if wise politics are pursued. Since the Kosovars are the only large non-Slavic ethnic community in the Federation, it is extremely important that ethnic assertiveness not offend the national feelings of other ethnics and Serbs in particular. The way to avoid trouble is to abide by internationalistic sentiments. Since the dominant ideology in the Federation is Marxism, the Kosovan profession of internationalism cannot be but welcome.

The history of the Balkans in modern times has been a sequence of battles and wars, instigated by immoderate ambitions for domination and fanned by nationalism and outright chauvinism. Differences of language and religious traditions and customs have been overemphasized in order to allow social groups and classes that used nationalism as a smoke screen for satisfying their desire for power and their greed. The victims thereof have invariably been the Balkan peoples, be they Slavs or Greeks, Albanians or Turks. Ethnic and cultural differences exist; they cannot be denied. But there exists something else too, which brings these peoples together: a common layer of culture, the sediment of first Byzantine and then Turkish domination. And buried deep underneath that layer lies the abjection and suffering of whole populations who underwent those dominations.

Stressing these cultural and socio-economic elements ought to be a concern for all who care for the future of humanity. This globe of ours risks being shattered to pieces by another world war whose main arena will most likely be Europe, just as it was in the two previous world wars. And here Kosova comes into the picture again. For besides being geographically located in the heart of the Balkans, Kosova bridges Yugoslavia and Albania through three limitrophe republics: Montenegro, Serbia, and Macedonia. Administratively a component of the Yugoslav Federation but ethnically a piece of the Albanian homeland to an overwhelming degree, Kosova is in an ideal position to bring together the two countries instead of separating them. The international conjuncture favors an initiative in this sense, Yugoslavia and Albania being the only two Balkan countries not aligned with either of the two military blocs. Although no pact for reciprocal military aid exists between Yugoslavia and Albania, the Albanian leadership has more than once declared that Albania would join Yugoslavia in resisting an invasion. The declaration should not be taken lightly, considering that an invasion of Yugoslavia is at the same time an invasion of Kosova, considered by the Albanians as part of their homeland. The declaration of the Albanian leaders gives the Kosovan leaders strong leverage for diplomatic moves toward their own goal. Their diplomacy would be more effective within a Balkan perspective. Kosova's geo-political position lends itself to the role of a catalyst for Balkan integration. Precedents are not lacking.[40] And if Kosova will pledge itself to that worthy pursuit, it will elicit international support. Serbs themselves will be won over to its cause. For if Serbia has produced a Vasa Čubrilović,[41] it has also given birth to people like Dimitrije Tucović.[42] A Yugoslav-Albanian *rapprochement* would constitute an important factor for shifting the balance of power in the Balkans from the politics of war to that of nonalignment. Countries such as Greece and Romania which have shown fluctuations in their stance as members of their respective blocs could be attracted to the idea of a pact of nonaggression signed by the four Balkan countries, a decisive first step for establishing peace in the Balkans.

* * * * *

NOTES

1. According to the 1981 census, the population of Macedonia is 1,760,000, that of Montenegro, 565,000.

2. About six hundred people had been expelled from the Party at

the end of 1981. Michele Lee, "Yugoslavia's Albanian Crisis: Wrong Turn in Kosova," *Labor Focus on Eastern Europe* 5 (1982) 1-2:51.

3.   A total of more than 1,800 years in jail (until March 1982), distributed among people of various categories, mostly intellectuals and students, including workers.

4.   Groups ideologically related to Tirana have been engaged in subversive activities. One of them, The Movement for the Albanian Socialist Republic in Yugoslavia, publishes a periodical in Switzerland: *Zëri i Kosovës* (The Voice of Kosova).

5.   History of Yugoslavia by V. Dedijer, I. Božić, S. Ćirković, M. Ekmečić. McGraw Hill: New York, 1974, p. 60.

6.   Alain Ducellier, "Les Albanais et le Kosovo," *Le Monde,* June 2, 1982. See also Ducellier's article in this volume as well as "Conclusion générale" in his *La Façade maritime de l'Albanie au moyen âge.* Institute for Balkan Studies: Salonika, 1981.

7.   *Srbi i Arbanasi (njihova simbioza u srednjem vijeku).* Belgrade, 1925.

8.   First partially published by S. Ljubić, "Skadarski Zemljišnik od god. 1416" in *Starine* 14 (1882): 30-57. Fulvio Cordignano published the Cadaster together with the concessionary acts in the codex, *Catasto veneto di Scutari e Registrum Concessionum* 1, 2 (Tolmezzo-Roma, 1944, 1942) as well as a study of the names and toponyms in the former, *Onomastico del Catasto di Scutari e Registrum Concessionum* (Tolmezzo, 1945). Giuseppe Valentini made a new edition of the codex, which constitutes vol. VIII of *Acta Albaniae veneta saeculorum XIV et XV* (Trofenik, Munich, 1970). Vol. IX of the series (Trofenik, March 1970) is an index of the cadaster, provided with statistics. An Albanian translation and edition of the codex was made by Injac Zamputi, *Rregjistri i Kadastrës dhe i koncesioneve për rrethin e Shkodrës 1416-1417.* Institute of History, Albanian Academy of Sciences: Tirana, 1977.

9.   H. Hadžibegić, A. Handžić, E. Kovačević, *Oblast Brankovica* I, II. Sarajevo, 1972.

10.   Selami Pulaha, *Le Cadastre de l'an 1485 du Sandjak de Shkodër* I, II. Présentation, introduction, translittération, traduction et commentaire. Institute of History, Tirana, 1974.

11.   Edith Durham quotes Strabo describing the Dardanians as "an entirely savage people, so much so that they dig caves beneath dung-heaps,

in which they dwell." Durham adds that most probably the dwellings of the Dardanians had been reduced to ashes by the Romans when Strabo visited the province (*Some Tribal Original Laws and Customs of the Balkans*. Allen & Unwin: London, 1928), p. 13.

12.   Among others: Norbert Jokl, "Rumänisches aus Albanien" in *Studia albanica* (1964) 2:75-79; Henrik Barić, *Istorija arbanškog jezika*. Balkanološki Institut: Sarajevo, 1959; Vladimir Georgiev, "Sur l'ethnogenèse des peuples balkaniques. Le Dace, l'Albanais et le Roumain," *Studi Clasice* 3(1961) 1:3-62.

13.   See Peter Bartl's article in this volume.

14.   238,106 in 1910, according to Turkish statistics. Antonio Baldacci, *L'Albania* (Instituto per l'Europa Orientale: Rome, 1930), p. 199.

15.   742,509 in 1910, according to Turkish statistics. Ibid., p. 200.

16.   599,582 in 1910, according to Turkish statistics. Ibid., p. 201.

17.   340.477 in 1910, according to Turkish statistics. Ibid., p. 200. About 400,000 in 1912, according to Antonio San Giuliano, *Briefe über Albanien*. Leipzig, 1913, p. 143.

18.   In his book, *Serbs and Albanians* (in Serbocroatian), Dimitrije Tucović protested against the cruel repression: "The bourgeois press called for merciless annihilation and the army acted upon this. Albanian villages, from which the men had fled on time, were reduced to ashes. At the same time, there were barbarian crematoria in which hundreds of women and children were burned alive. . . . It was once again confirmed that the popular revolt of the most primitive tribes is always more humane than the practices of standing armies used by modern states against such revolts." Quoted in *History of Yugoslavia* (see note 5), p. 436.

19.   By peripheral Albanian regions are meant the Albanian regions in Montenegro and Macedonia.

20.   See note 11.

21.   Michel Roux, "Le Kosovo; développement régional et integration nationale en Yugoslavie," *Hérodote* (1982) 26 (2nd quarter), p. 13.

22.   Albanian is an indoeuropean language with two main dialects, the Gheg, spoken in the North, and the Tosk, spoken in the South of the country. The differences are mostly in phonology and, to some extent, in morphology. See note 24, p. 101.

24.   *Rilindja* (17 November 1980, p. 13), published an article by Academician Idris Ajeti, President of the Society of Teachers of Albanian

Language and Literature in the Autonomous Socialist Province of Kosova, on the situation of the teaching of the Albanian (Tirana) language in the elementary and secondary schools, which was described as "not at all good" and "disturbing." The main causes for this situation were, according to the findings of the Society, "the lack of an organized social activity for the appropriation of the Albanian literary language on a vast social level," and "the low level of knowledge of the literary language by the teachers" themselves. The document is proof of the general lack of interest in a language which is not germane to the spoken Kosovar and results in artificial writing—Kosovar literature has lost its impetus and flavor.

25.   The Kosovars have been strangely silent about this important sector of their oral poetry. Two Harvard professors, Milman Perry and Albert B. Lord collected epic songs from Albanians. A first volume, *Serbocroatian Heroic Songs,* was published in 1954. The first article, to my knowledge, on this volume is dated 2 April 1983, published in the Kosovar newspaper *Rilindja.*

26.   Peter Bartl, *Die albanische Muslime zur Zeit der nationalen Unabhängigkeitsbewegung* (1878-1912) (Harrassowitz: Wiesbaden, 1968), p. 153.

27.   Stavro Skendi, *The Albanian National Awakening* (Princeton University Press: Princeton, 1967), p. 335.

28.   Hima was sympathetic to the idea of a Balkan Federation. See Hasan Kaleshi, *Biographisches Lexikon zur Geschichte Südosteuropas,* vol. II (Oldenbourg: Munich, 1976), p. 163. Hima and a Vlach (Aromunian), Dimitri Papazoglou, founded what seemed to have been a joint Albanian-Vlach Committee in Paris in 1902 (Skendi, *The Albanian National Awakening,* p. 325).

29.   Ibid., pp. 342-43.

30.   Ibid., p. 427.

31.   Bartl (see note 26), p. 182.

32.   The Acting Chief of the European Division at the Library of Congress told me (Spring 1981) that purchases of Kosovar publications have been conducted through dealers, direct contact having failed. The situation is even worse at the British Museum, where Kosovar publications are not even listed in the catalogues. The person in charge of Albanian in the Slavonic and East European Branch there explained to me that they are now receiving the more important publications (not yet calalogued in Spring 1983).

33.   In this respect a case is particuarly telling. The Modern Language Association of America publishes a yearly *MLA International Bibliography* in many volumes, covering books and articles on the language, literature, and folklore of practically all the countries in the world. The compiler of the bibliography of Albanian literature and folklore in that periodical has more than once written to the University of Prishtinë asked for their contribution to a venture which is in the interest of Kosovar and Albanian culture in general. His letters have not been answered and no attempt has been made to correct this unfortunate situation.

34.   M. Roux (see note 21), p. 38.

35.   Ibid., p. 35.

36.   *Politika,* 18 May 1982.

37.   M. Roux (see note 21), p. 30.

38.   Ibid., p. 30.

39.   Catherine Verla, "Après les émeutes due Kosovo. Une question nationale explosive," *Inprecor,* June 1981, p. 10.

40.   See for this L. S. Stavrianos, *Balkan Federation. A History of the Movement Toward Balkan Unity in Modern Times.* Archon Books: Hamden, Conn., 1964.

41.   Academician Vasa Čubrilović wrote a memorandum to the Royal government in Belgrade in March 1937, "The Expulsion of the Arnauts"— Arnaut is the Turkish name for the Albanians.

42.   Dimitrije Tucović was the founder of the Serbian Social Democratic Party. See note 19.

APPENDIX

Jens Reuter

EDUCATIONAL POLICY IN KOSOVA

After the break between Yugoslavia and Albania in the wake of the Cominform crisis, a competitive situation developed between Kosova and Albania in an area which was of the utmost importance for the future development of both regions. It dealt with the problem of illiteracy among the population. In both regions conditions were similar. Right after World War II eighty percent of the population in Albania as well as in Kosova was illiterate. Today one could say that this race has resulted in a tie, although both sides intended from the very beginning to accuse the ideological opponent of mistakes and failures in educational policy. In Albania as in Kosova, illiterates are found primarily among the members of the older generation, the youth can be considered virtually as literate. However, if one compares the school education of both populations, Albania has the advantage. In Albania there is compulsory school education for all children between the ages of seven and fifteen, just as in Kosova. While compulsory school education is realized in Albania, in Kosova it is very often only on paper. Many children among Kosova Albanians—primarily girls—leave school after completing the fourth grade of elementary school.[1] In the first postwar years the schools in Kosova were organized according to the "language principle," i.e., there were "Serbian," "Albanian" and "Turkish" schools. Since 1953 the schools have been organized according to the territorial principle, i.e., the pupils of all nationalities were concentrated respectively in one school and there they received, according to

259

their nationality, instruction in the Serbo-Croatian, Albanian and Turkish languages. At first there were great difficulties in regard to the instruction in the Albanian language, because there was a lack of qualified teachers. Such problems no longer exist today. Already in the school year 1973-74 more than seventy percent of all teachers in all schools of Kosova had Albanian nationality.[2]

The network of high schools (*srednje škole*) in Kosova was grossly un-derdeveloped during the postwar years. Even at the beginning of the 1970s, official Yugoslavian sources admitted that pupils of Albanian nationality were markedly underrepresented in the high schools. This situation chang-ed during the following years very rapidly. More and more Kosovars com-pleted high school and thronged to the only university of the province in Prishtinë. In 1981 there were 47,000 students at Prishtinë University, three-quarters of whom were Albanian nationals. While in all Yugoslavia on the average for every 10,000 inhabitants there were 200 students, in Kosova there were 299. Even the Yugoslavian media admitted that this unusually high number of students was motivated by a policy of promot-ing employment. A large number of young people were allowed to study as a way of poorly covering up the alarming high rate of youth unemploy-ment in the province. Under these circumstances it was clear that a gradu-ate of Prishtinë University hardly had job opportunities. In Kosova, the positions which came in question were already filled; in the other parts of Yugoslavia graduating from Prishtinë University is considered second class quality. Moreover, there are language problems, because in the mean-time there were only a few young Kosovars who have a command of written and spoken Serbo-Croatian.[3] Kosova's incontestable achievements in the fields of education and culture were effusively praised by the Yugo-slav press and other official publications. Towards the end of the 1970s numerous magazine articles glorified the cultural progress of Kosova, which was manifested in increased pupil and student enrollment, stepped-up book production, as well as more television and radio programs in the Albanian language.

After the bloody riots in the spring of 1981, however, there was a radi-cal change in the public opinion in Yugoslavia. Just because the youth had taken part in the violent demonstrations in such great numbers, Ko-sova's educational system became one of the main targets of criticism. The Yugoslav mass media discovered that this system was essentially formed in an *Albanian* way, considering its spiritual, historical and cultural background, and therefore this system handed down values, which were hardly compatible with the collective Yugoslav ideals of "brotherhood and unity." The cultural cooperation between Kosova and Albania, strongly intensified toward the end of the 1970s, was very sharply criticized. This cooperative effort consisted in the exchange of certain television and radio programs as well as in the usage of certain school books and textbooks from Tirana, their reproduction in Kosova being justified by economic motives. The fact that a series of professors had held guest lectures at Prishtinë University gave rise to particular indignation. The Yugoslav press gave the impression that the whole educational system of Kosova had been infiltrated by "Greater Albanian ideology." Cultural relations with Albania were frozen; top party officials of the Yugoslav Communist League of Kosova demanded that schools, universities, radio and television as well as the societies of art and culture must be thoroughly purged of all elements which had been infected by Albanian nationalism. The "ideological-political differentiation" (a synonym for purge) had led to many dismissals from office and new hirings in the YCL of Kosova. These procedures were now to be continued in the areas of education and culture. Up until July 1981 more than 260 students and pupils were expelled from the universities, vocational schools and high schools in Kosova, because direct participation in the violent demonstrations had been established. More than 210 persons employed in educational professions lost their jobs for the same reason.[4]

In no way did this mean an end to the purges in the cultural sector, they continue to this day. The center of criticism is still Prishtinë University, which from the very beginning was labeled as the "hotbed of Albanian nationalism and irredentism." This fall the magazine *Komunist,* the theoretical organ of the Yugoslav Communist League, launched a campaign with the apparent goal of effectively supporting and most likely intensifying measures against a great number of university professors. In this year's issue of September 24, *Komunist* published a "blacklist" with the names of numerous professors and assistant professors at Prishtinë University. This list was compiled by a team which consisted of the members of the Kosova party presidency, the local committee of the YCL of Prishtinë and the conference on action of the party organization of the university.[5] Already on September 18 it was reported that six professors who had engaged in "organized hostile activity contrary to our legal regulations," had been expelled from the faculty and fired from their jobs, and that as a result of "hostile activity" nineteen students were also expelled and "immediately" left the university.[6] The first name on the blacklist is that of the well-known historian Ali Hadri, who is being threatened with expulsion from the party and removal from the university. Four professors in the department of philosophy, also mentioned on the blacklist, are being called to account for their actions. In this case the sanctions range from a warning or a serious reprimand to exclusion from the party. Not only are subjects in the humanities affected by these measures, but also numerous members of the departments of science are on the blacklist.

If one investigates the background of this new campaign toward ideological-political "differentiation" at Prishtinë University, one comes to the conclusion, that it is a result of strong Serbian pressure. In September of this year the presidency of the Serbian Central Committee of the YCL passed the resolution that a "fuller ideological differentiation was necessary in cultural institutions, including Prishtinë University."[7]

It is clear that professors of Albanian nationality discredit themselves in the eyes of their students when they publicly advocate a policy whose guiding principles are laid down by the Serbian leadership in Belgrade. This is also the reason why most university teachers of Albanian nationality have kept quiet up until now on political questions. Arsem Vlasi, member of the party conference on the YCL of Kosova, made it clear that such an attitude would no longer be tolerated in the future. Vlasi stated: "We don't want to transform scholars and professors into a propaganda machine for our current political issues, but we cannot tolerate it, if individuals want to avoid clearly committing themselves to the political actions, which we carry out."[8] On another occasion Vlasi explained: "This society and this working class have invested so much—even in a material sense— in order to form a healthy socialist intelligentsia, and therefore we also have every right to demand that this intelligentsia does its utmost for the realization of the policies of the YCL."[9] The university teachers are thus faced with the alternative of either actively engaging in political issues or risking the loss of their jobs.

At the beginning of the new school year, Salih Nushi, president of the Provincial Committee for Education and Culture in Kosova, explained: "It is a fact that a considerable number of young people is indoctrinated with antagonistic ideology. Therefore it is essential that the schools as well as the whole educational system in the province be as well equipped as possible to do away with the consequences of counterrevolutionary activities."[10]

In order to more closely approach this goal, seminars in political education were held in all communities of Kosova, their special target group being young people. Pupils, who because of their involvement in violent demonstrations had been suspended from classes, may be readmitted to their schools, if the local party leadership is of the opinion that they sincerely regret their actions. The local party leadership reevaluates each and every teacher and decides whether or not he may remain in his position. In its edition of October 22, the magazine *Komunist* demanded tougher measures against teachers, who are charged with "nationalism and opportunism." In particular, all towns in Kosova are mentioned which have not yet taken assertive measures against teachers under suspicion.[11]

The 350,000 pupils at the primary and secondary school levels in Kosova may no longer use any textbooks which have been made in Albania. The "Bukvar"—that is, a spelling book for first graders—was also replaced by a new book as well as the sharply criticized grammar of the Albanian language for the seventh and eighth elementary school grades. Some of the textbooks which were produced in Kosova were purged of their "detrimental content." 648 textbooks were translated from Serbo-Croatian into Albanian and printed with a total circulation of 9.3 million copies. In this manner, according to official information, the important objective was attained that these textbooks are identical with those in the whole area of the republic of Serbia.[12]

The whole process of "political differentiation," which currently is taking place on the cultural level in Kosova, is based on the false assumption, that it is sufficient to remove "politically unreliable" professors and teachers from their positions in order to win the Albanian youth of Kosova on a long-term basis for the ideals of multinational Yugoslavia. However, this overlooks the fact that the youth in question were not "seduced" by political agitators, but that the youth themselves feel and think Albanian to a considerable extent.

The fact that the purges are a result of Serbian initiative and Serbian pressure discredits these actions altogether. This makes it all the harder for Albanian policy makers in Kosova, who are fighting for the ideals of the Yugoslav federation, to appear credible to the youth. This state of affairs is described by the most prominent politician of Kosova, Fadil Hoxha, in the following words: "We have not succeeded yet in turning the indoctrinated youth onto the road of the LCY, onto Tito's path. We must be especially vigilant in providing the correct education for the people, in explaining our ideas. And we cannot achieve this if we do not maintain frequent contact with the youth, because not only do they not listen to us, but they are even calling us traitors, [adding] that we allegedly think only about our personal interests, salaries, and so forth."[13]

* * * * *

Editor's note. This paper, read at the International Conference on Kosova, was published in German, "Bildungspolitik in Kosova," in *Südosteurpa. Zeitschrift für Gegenwartsforschung* 32(1983): 8-16. The paper has been included in this volume because of its informative value and because it updates an article by Dennison I. Rusinow, "The Other Albania: Kosovo 1979. Part I: Problems and Prospects." (*American University Field Staff* (1980) 5: 1-17), where the problem of education is amply treated.

NOTES

1. Jens Reuter, *Die Albaner in Jugoslawien,* Munich 1982, p. 76.
2. Ibid., p. 74.
3. Jens Reuter, "Konterrevolution in Kosovo?" in *Wissenschaftlicher Dienst Südosteuropa,* Nr. 4/5, 1981.
4. Reuter, *Die Albaner in Jugoslawien,* p. 90.
5. *Komunist,* 24.9.1982.
6. *Rilindja,* 18.9.1982.
7. Ibid., 10.9. 1982.
8. *Komunist,* 17.9.1982.
9. *NIN,* 26.9.1982.
10. *Politika,* 28.8.1982.
11. *Komunist,* 22.10.1982.
12. *Politika,* 28.8.1982.
13. *Rilindja,* 13.10.1982.

BIBLIOGRAPHY

Listed here are the most important publications on Kosova, including the basic works supporting the research for this volume. Titles in languages other than English, German, French and Italian are accompanied by English translation in parenthesis (except when the meaning of the title is transparent).

Abdyli, Tahir. *Zhvillimi i industrisë në Kosovë* (The Development of Industry in Kosova). Rilindja: Prishtinë, 1978.

Ajeti, Idriz, "Najstariji dokument kosovskog arbanaškog govora na arapskom pismu" (The Oldest Albanian Kosovar Document in Arabic Alphabet). *Gjurmime albanologjike* (1962) 1: 9-73.

Anamali, S. and M. Korkuti. "Les Illyriens et la genèse des Albanais à la lumière des recherches archéologiques albanaises," *Studia albanica* (1970) 1: 123-56.

Anamali, Skender et al., *L'Illyrie. La ville illyrienne.* Universiteti Shtetëror i Tiranës, 1972.

Antoni, Lorenc. "Format dhe veglat muzikore të popullit shqiptar" (Musical Forms and Instruments of the Albanian People). *Jeta e re* (1950) 2: 251-57.

——. "Këndimi populluer" (Popular Singing). *Përparimi* 9 (1959): 569-608.

Arbatski, Juri. *Beating the Tupan in the Central Balkans.* The Newberry Library: Chicago, 1953.

Artisien, F. R. P. and R. A. Howells. "Yugoslavia, Albania and the Kosovo Riots." *The World Today* 37 (1981) 11: 419-27.

Aubin, Michel. "Du mythe serbe au nationalisme albanais." *Le Monde,* April 5-6, 1981.

Barbarich, Eugenio. *Albania. Monografia antropogeografica.* Voghera-Rome, 1905.

Barić, Henrik. *Albanorumänische Studien.* Zur Kunde der Balkaninsels. 2. Quellen und Forschungen. Sarajevo, 1919.

———. *Istorija arbanaškog jezika* (History of the Albanian Language). Balkanološki Institut. Sarajevo, 1959.

Bajraktarović, Danilo. "Prilog proučavanju akcenatske sisteme kosovske govorne zone" (Contribution to the Knowledge of the Stress System in the Kosovar Speaking Zone). *Gjurmime albanologjike* (1962) 1: 75-89.

Bajraktarović, Mirko R. "Dvovjerske šiptarske zadruge u Metohiji" (Biconfessional Extended Albanian Families in Metohija). *Zbornik radova etnografskog instituta Srpske Akademije Nauka,* Belgrade (1950) 1:197-209.

Bartl, Peter. "Kryptochristentum und Formen des religiösen Synkretismus in Albanien" *Grazer und Münchner Balkanologischen Studien* Trofenik: Munich 1967, pp. 117-27.

———. *Die Albanische Muslime zur Zeit der Nationalen Unabhängigkeitsbewegung.* Albanische Forschungen 8. Harrassowitz: Wiesbaden, 1968.

———. *Der Westbalkan zwischen spanischer Monarchie und Osmanischem Reich.* Albanische Forschungen 14. Harrassowitz: Wiesbaden, 1974.

Bianconi, F. *Ethnographie et statistique de la Turquie d'Europe et de la Grèce.* Paris, 1887.

Berisha, Rrustem. "Jehona e Lidhjes Shqiptare të Prizrenit në këngët historike" (The Echo of the Albanian League of Prizren in Historical Folk Songs). *Gjurmime albanologjike. Folklor dhe Etnologji* (1978): 31-46.

Biberaj, Elez. "Kosovë: the Struggle for Recognition." *Conflict Studies* (1982) 137/138: 23-43.

———. "Albanian-Yugoslav Relations and the Question of Kosovë." *East European Quarterly* 16 (1983) 4: 485-510.

Petri Bogdani. *Cuneus Prophetarum.* Padua, 1685. Reprinted by Trofenik, Munich, 1977.

Brailsford, Henry Noel. *Macedonia. Its Races and their Future.* London, 1900.

Boué, Ami. Ethnographische Karte des Osmanischen Reichs europäischen Teils und von Griechenland. Gotha, 1847.

―――――. *Receuil d'itinéraires dans la Turquie d'Europe. Détails géographiques, topographiques et statistiques.* 2 vols. Vienna, 1854.

Buda, Aleks. (ed.). *Konferenca kombëtare për Lidhjen Shqiptare të Prizrenit (1878-1881)* (National Conference of Studies on the Albanian League of Prizren [Acts of]). Akademia Shqiptare e Shkenvave: Tirana, 1979.

Burime të zgjedhura për historinë e Shqipërisë. 1, 2, 3. (Selected [translated] Sources for the History of Albania). Universiteti Shtetëror i Tiranës: 1965, 1962, 1961, ed. by F. Prendi and S. Islami, A. Buda, and [no ed.] respectively.

Çabej, Eqrem. "Die älteren Wohnsitze der Albaner auf der Balkaninsel in Lichte der Sprache und der Ortsnamen." *Atti del VII Congresso Internazionale di Scienze Onomastiche.* Florence, 1961, pp. 241-51.

―――――. L'illyrien et l'albanais." *Studia albanica* (1970) 1: 155-70.

―――――. "Le problème du territoire de la formation de la langue albanaise." *Studia albanica* (1972) 2: 125-52.

Camaj, Martin. "I poeti albanesi della nuova letteratura della Kossova," *8 Convegno Internazionale di Studi Albanesi* [Atti del] . Palermo, 1973, pp. 73-80.

Camaj, Martin and Uta Schier-Oberdorffer. *Albanische Märchen.* Dietrichs Verlag: Düsseldorf-Köln, 1974. [Contains tales from Kosova.]

Çetta, Anton. "Edhe nji motërzim i kangës popullore shqiptare mbi Luftën e Kosovës" (Another Variant of the Albanian Folk Song on the Battle of Kosovo). *Gjurmime albanologjike* (1962) 1: 263-75.

―――――. *Tregime popullore. 1. Drenicë* (Folk tales from Drenicë). Prishtinë, 1963.

―――――. *Përralla* (Tales). Instituti Albanologjik: Prishtinë, 1979.

Çitaku, Jakup. *Nga lirika popullore e Llapit* (Lyrical Folk Songs from Llap). Rilindja: Prishtinë, 1974.

Cvijić, Jovan. *Politiko-etnografska skica Makedonije i Stare Serbije.* Belgrade, 1906. [Chart of Old Serbia and Macedonia.]

―――――. *La péninsule balkanique. Géographie humaine.* Collin: Paris, 1918.

―――――. *Osnove za geografiji i geologiju Makedonie i Stare Serbije.* Belgrade, 1919.

―――――. *Balkansko Poluostrvo i južno-slovenske zemlje* (The Balkan Peninsula and the South Slav Territories). Belgrade, 1922.

Čubrilović, Vasa. Memorandum presented to the Yugoslav Government, March 7, 1937, on the expulsion of the Albanians from Yugoslavia. An excerpt, "L'expulsion des Albanais," appeared in *Albanie* (France) 2 (1981) 13: 24-25.

Dančetović, Vojislav (ed.). *Kangë popullore të Kosovë-Metohis* (Folk Songs of Kosova-Metohija). 3 vols. Mustafa Bakija; Prishtinë, 1952.

————. *Fjalë t'urta shqipe* (Albanian Proverbs). Rilindja: Prishtinë, 1971.

Desnickaja, Agnija V. *Albanskij jazyk i ego dialekty* (The Albanian Language and Its Dialects). Akademija Nauk SSSR: Leningrad, 1968.

————. "Mbi lidhjet boshnjake-shqiptare në lëmin e poezisë epike" (On Bosnian-Albanian Relations in Epic Poetry). *Gjurmime albanologjike. Folklor dhe etnologji* (1977): 41-62.

Dobroshi, Sokol. *Fjaluer serbokroatisht-shqip* (Serbocroatian-Albanian Dictionary). Prishtinë, 1953.

Ducellier, Alain. "Les Albanais ont-il envahi le Kosovo?" *Albanie* 2 (1981) 13: 10-14.

————. "Les Albanais et le Kosovo." *Le Monde*, June 2, 1982.

Durham, Mary Edith. *Some Tribal Origins and Customs and Laws in the Balkans.* Allen and Unwin: London, 1928.

Elezović, G. "Jedna arnautska varianta u boju na Kosovu" (An Albanian Variant of the Battle of Kosovo). *Arhiv za arbanašku starinu, jezik i etnologiju* 1 (1923): 54-67.

Ermenji, Abas. See Kokalari.

Faensen, Johannes. *Ethnogenese und Staatsbildung in Südosteuropa.* Vandenhoeck and Ruprecht: Göttingen, 1974.

Fazlija, Asllan. *Autonomija e Kosovës e Metohisë në Jugosllavinë socialiste.* Rilindja: Prishtinë, 1966.

Fishta, Filip. "Njoftime historike mbi argjipeshkvit e Shkupit" (Historical Observations on the Skople Archbishops). *Hylli i dritës* (1934) 9, 10, 11.

Frashëri, Kristo. *Lidhja Shqiptare e Prizrenit* (The Albanian League of Prizren). 8 Nëntori: Tirana, 1979. [An illustrated publication.]

Galanti, Arturo. Carta etnografica della penisola balcanica, *L'Albania. Notizie geografiche, etnografiche e storiche.* Rome, 1901.

Garašanin, Draga. "Les tombes tumulaires préhistoriques de la péninsule balkanique et leur attribution ethnique et chronologique." *Studia albanica* (1973) 1: 179-84.

Georgief, Vladimir. "Sur l'ethnogenèse des peuples balkaniques. Le Dace, l'Albanais et le Roumain." *Studi clasice* 3 (1961): 23-37.

Gopčević, Spiridion. *Oberalbanien und seine Liga.* Leipzig, 1881.

―――. *Madkedonien und Altserbien.* Vienna, 1889.

Haberlandt, Arthur. "Kulturwissenschaftliche Beiträge zur Volkskunde von Montenegro, Albanien und Serbien. . . ." *Zeitschrift für österreichische Volkskunde.* Supplementary issue 12. Vienna, 1917.

Hadri, Ali. "Pozita dhe gjëndja e Kosovës në mbretërinë e Jugosllavisë (1918-1941)" (The Position and Status of Kosova in the Kingdom of Yugoslavia). *Gjurmime albanologjike* (1968) 2: 163-94.

Hahn, Johann Georg von. *Croquis des westlichen Gebietes der bulgarischen Morava.* Vienna, 1861.

―――. *Reise durch die Gebiete des Drin und Wardar.* Denkschriften der k. Akademie der Wissenschaften, Phil. Cl. 15 (1867), 16 (1869).

Halimi, Kadri. "Tabački zanat u Prizrenu" (Leather Trade in Prizren). *Glasnik Muzeja Kosova i Metohiji* 1 (1956): 71-116.

Handžić, A. "Nekoliko vijesti o Arbanasima na Kosovu i Metohiji v sredinom XV vijeka" (Some Notes on the Albanians in Kosovo-Metohija in the Middle of the 15th Century). *Simpoziumi për Skenderbeun.* Prishtinë, 1969, pp. 201-209.

Hasani, Sinan. Interview with. "What Happened in Kosovo?" *Socialist Thought and Practice* 21 (1981) 8.

Haxhihasani, Qemal. "Questions d'étude comparée de l'épopée héroïque légendaire de la region N.O. des Balkans." *Studia albanica* (1966) 2: 215-21.

Hecquard, Hyacinthe. *Histoire et description de la haute Albanie ou Guégarie.* Paris, 1858.

Helm, Jesse. "The Balkans Today: Yugoslavia and the Prospects for Freeing the Albanian Nation." *Congressional Record* 129 (June 7, 1983). Speech at US Senate, followed by texts of two articles on Kosova by V. Meier and M. Baskin (*Problems of Communism,* March-April 1983) and four reports from *Wall Street Journal* and *Washington Post.*

Hoxha, Hysni. *Struktura e vargut shqip* (Structure of the Albanian Verse). Rilindja: Prishtinë, 1973.

Ippen, Theodor A. M. *Novibazar und Kossovo (das alte Rascien).* Hölder: Vienna, 1892.

Islami, Hifzi. "Kërkimet anthropogjeografike në Kosovë" (Anthropogeographic Research in Kosova). *Gjurmime albanologjike. Seria e shken-* *cave historike* (1971) 1: 134-44.

————. *Popullsia e Kosovës: studim demografik.* Rilindja: Prishtinë, 1981.

Ismaili, Rexhep. *Shumësia e tekstit* (Plurality of the Text). Rilindja: Prishtinë, 1977.

Jastrebov, J. S. *Stara Serbija i Albanija.* Srpska Akademija. Spomenik 41. Belgrade, 1904.

Jokl, Norbert. "Zur Vorgeschichte des Albanischen und der Albaner." *Wörter und Sachen* 12 (1929): 63-91.

————. "Slaven und Albaner." *Slavia* 13 (1935): 281-325, 609-45.

Kabrda, Josef. "Kodet turke (*kanunname*) në lidhje me Shqipërinë dhe rëndësia e tyre për historinë kombëtare" (The Turkish *kanunname* related to Albania and Their Importance for the History of Albania.) *Buletin i Universitetit Shtetëror rë Tiranës. Seria shkencat shoqërore* (1958) 4: 171-212.

Kajtazi, Halil. *Nga lirika popullore e Drenicës.* (Lyrical Folk Songs from Drenicë). Prishtinë, 1972.

————. *Proza popullore e Drenicës.* 1, 2. (Folk Tales from Drenicë). Prishtinë, 1970, 1972.

Kaleshi, Hasan. "Prilog poznavanju arbanaške književnosti iz vremena preporoda (Arbanaška književnost na arapskom alfabetu)" (Contribution for the Knowledge of Albanian Literature of the Resurgence Period: Albanian Literature in Arab Alphabet). *Godišnjak Balkanološkog Instituta* 1 (1956): 352-88.

————. "Prizren kao kulturni centar za vreme turskog perioda" (Prizren as Cultural Center in the Ottoman Period). *Gjurmime albanologjike* 1 (1962): 91-118.

————. "Die Albaner in Kosovo im 15. Jahrhundert." *Akten der Internationalen Albanologischen Kolloquiums Innsbruck 1972.* Innsbruck, 1977, pp. 513-24.

Kiepert, Heinrich. *Die Bulgaren in ihren historischen, ethnographischen und politischen Grenzen.* Berlin, 1917.

Kokalari, Hamit. *Kosova–djepi i Shqiptarizmit* (Kosova, the Cradle of Albaniandom). Mesagjerit Shqiptare: Tiranë, 1943. [The reprinted edition by Lidhja Kosovare contains an introduction by Abas Ermenji, pp. 11-56.]

Kolsti, John. "The English Queen and the Queen of Bagdad." *Actes du IIe Congrès International des Etudes du Sud-Est Européen,* Tome V. Athènes, 1978, pp. 623-30. [Comparison of two songs, one from the Parry Collection and the other from the Lord Collection.]

Krasniqi, Mark. "Kula u Metohiji" (Fortified Houses in Metohija). *Glasnik etnografskog instituta Srpske Akademije Nauka* 3 (1958): 47-70.

————. "La communauté familiale albanaise dans la région de Kosovo et de Metohija," *Glasnik Muzeja Kosove i Metohije* 4/5 (1959-60): 137-71.

Kretschmer, Paul. "Die Illyrische Frage." *Glotta* 30 (1943): 99-134.

Lee, Michele. "Yugoslavia's Albanian Crisis: Wrong Turn in Kosovo." *Labour Focus on Eastern Europe* (1982) 1-2: 49-52.

Lejean, Guillaume. Carte ethnographique de la Turquie d'Europe et des états vassaux autonomes/Ethnographie der europäischen Türkei. *Petermanns Mitteilungen.* Supplementary issue 4. Gotha, 1861.

Lleshi, Qazim. *Qytetet e Kosovës* (The Cities of Kosova). Rilindja: Prishtinë, 1977.

Logoreci, Anton. "Riots and Trials in Kosovo." *Index on Censorship,* April 1982, pp. 23-24, 40.

————. "A Year of Great Political Turmoil and Confusion." *Dielli* (The Sun) April 16, 1982.

Makušev, Vikentij. "Istoričeskija rozyskanija o slavjanach v Albanii v srednie veka" (Historical Inquiry on the Slavs in Albania in the Middle Ages). *Varšavskija Universitetskija Izvestija* (1871): 5-6.

Maletić, Mihajlo (ed.). *Kosovo nekad i danas/Kosova dikur e sot.* (Kosova: Yesterday and Today). Borba Publishing House: Belgrade, 1973.

Marmullaku, R. *Albania and the Albanians.* Archon Books: Hamden, Conn., 1975.

Mbi ngjarjet në Kosovë (About the Events in Kosova). 8 Nëntori: Tirana. 1981. [Contains articles published in *Zëri i popullit.*]

Meier, Viktor. "Ein Dolch im Rücken Jugoslaviens?" *Frankfurter Allgemeine Zeitung,* October 22, 1981.

————. "Yugoslavia's National Question." *Problems of Communism,* March-April 1983, pp. 47-60.

Mirdita, Zef. "Les origines des Dardaniens." *Studia albanica* (1973) 2: 117-49.

————. *Studime dardane* (Dardanian Studies). Rilindja: Prishtinë, 1979.

Mladenov, S. "Bemerkungen über die Albaner und das Albanische in Nord-Makedonien und Altserbien." *Balkan-Archiv* 1 (1925): 43-70.

Mulaku, Latif. "Kangë kreshnike nga Shala e Bajgorës" (Heroic Songs from Shalë in Bajgorë). *Glasnik Muzeja Kosova i Metohije* 9 (1964): 587-615.

————. "Über die albanischen Mundarten von Kosovo." *Akten des Inter. Alban. Kolloquiums Innsbruck 1972.* Innsbruck, 1977, pp. 557-62.

Munishi, Rexhep. "Të kënduarit dyzërash në disa fshatra të rrethit të Kaçanikut" (Singing in Two Voices in Some Villages of the Kaçanik District). *Gjurmime albanologjike. Folklor dhe etnologji* (1977): 115-36.

Nikolić, Vidosava. "Siptarska narodna nošnja u okolini Peći (Metohija)" (Popular Albanian Costumes in the Surroundings of Pejë). *Glasnik etnografskog instituta Srpske Akademije Nauka* 8 (1959): 15-44.

Oakes, John B. "Yugoslavia—Strains, Rivalries, Disparities." *New York Times,* June 24, 1982.

Obradović, Milovan. *Agrarna reforma i kolonizacija na Kosvou (1918-1941).* Priština, 1981.

Pavlowitch, Stevan K. *Yugoslavia.* Praeger: New York, 1971.

————. "Kosovo: An Analysis of Yugoslavia's Problems." *Conflict Studies* (1982) 137/138: 7-21.

Pllana, Shefqet. "Puna në kangët popullore shqiptare" (Work in Albanian Folk Songs). *Gjurmime albanologjike* (1962)1: 149-98.

————. "Kalendarske majske pesme Albanaca na Kosovu i Makedoniji" (Albanian May Songs in Kosova and Macedonia). *Makedonski Folklor* 2(1969): 129-35.

————. "Albanologische Forschungstätten in Kosovo." *Akten der Inter. Alban. Kolloquiums Innsbruck 1972.* Innsbruck, 1977, pp. 77-84.

Pllana, Shefqet, Rrustem Berisha, Sadri Fetiu. *Këngë popullore të Rilindjes Kombëtare* (Folk Songs of the National Resurgence Period). Instituti Albanologjik: Prishtinë, 1978.

Parry, Milman and Albert B. Lord. *Serbocroatian Heroic Songs. 1. Novi Pazar: English Translation.* Harvard University Press and Serbian Academy of Sciences. Cambridge and Belgrade, 1954.

————. *Srpskohrvatske Junačke Pjesme. 2. Novi Pazar: Srpskohrvatski tekstovi.* Srpska akademija nauka i Harvard University Press. Beograd i Kembridž, 1953.

Perazić, Gavro. "International Aspects of Albanian Interference in Kosovo Events." *Socialist Thought and Practice* (Belgrade), October 1981, pp. 49-72.

Pipa, Arshi. *Albanian Literature: Social Perspectives.* Albanische Forschungen 19. Trofenik: Munich, 1978. [Contains a section on Kosovar literature.]

————. "Kosova Between Yugoslavia and Albania." Interview by Michele Lee. *Labour Focus for Eastern Europe* (1982) 3-4: 33-36.

————. "Rapsodi albanesi in serbocroato." *Atti del IX Congresso Internazionale di Studi Albanesi.* Palermo, 1982, pp. 371-408.

Pollo, Stefanaq. "La lutte du peuple albanais sous la Ligue de Prizrend pour la libération nationale." *Studia albanica* (1968) 2: 29-48.

Popović, Ivan. "Albano-Slavica. Zur Geographie und Chronologie der albanischen Spracheinflüsse auf die Südslaven." *Südost-Forschungen* 15 (1956): 512-26.

Prifti, Peter. "Kosovo in Ferment." *Monograph C/69-15.* MIT Center for International Studies: Cambridge, Mass., 1969.

————. *Socialist Albania since 1944: Domestic and Foreign Developments.* The MIT Press: Cambridge, Mass., 1978. [Includes a chapter on the Albanian minority in Yugoslavia.]

Pupovci, Syrja. "Shtjefën Konstantin Gjeçovi." *Përparimi* (1979): 701-22.

Pushkolli, Fehmi. *Lëvizja revolucionare e sindikatave dhe Lidhja e Sindikatave të Kosovës, 1919-1975.* (The Revolutionary Movement of Trade Unions and the League of Trade Unions in Kosova). Rilindja: Prishtinë, 1977.

Qosja, Rexhep. *Kritika letrare* (Literary Criticism). Rilindja; Prishtinë, 1969.

————. "Letërsia e Rilindjes dhe Lidhja e Prizrenit" (The Literature of the Resurgence Period and the League of Prizren). *Jeta e re* 29 (1978): 198-216.

Ramet, Pedro. "Problems of Albanian Nationalism in Yugoslavia." *Orbis* 25 (1981) 21: 369-88.

Reissmüller, Georg von Johann. "Aufbegehren auf dem Amselfeld." *Frankfurter Allgemeine Zeitung,* August 13, 1981.

Repishti, Sami. "Let Kosovë be Kosovë." *Dielli* (The Sun), August 16, 1981.

————. "Albanians in Yugoslavia: The Struggle for National Affirmation." *Albanian Catholic Bulletin* 3 (1982) 1-2: 59-67.

Reuter, Jens. *Die Albaner in Jugoslawien.* Oldenbourg: Munich, 1982.

Roques, Mario. *Recherches sur les anciens textes albanais*. Librairie Orient-
aliste P. Geuthner: Paris, 1932.

Roux, Michel. "Langue et pouvoir en Albanie." *Pluriel* (1980) 22.

―――. "Le Kosovo: développement régional et integration nationale en
Yugoslavie." *Hérodote* (1982) 25: 10-48.

Rugova, Ibrahim. *Vepra e Bogdanit* (Bogdani's Work). Rilindja: Prishtinë,
1982.

Rushiti, Liman. *Lëvizja kaçake në Kosovë (1918-1928)* (Armed Bands in
Kosova). Rilindja: Prishtinë, 1981.

Rusinow, Dennison I. "The Other Albania: Kosovo 1979. I and II. *American Universities Field Staff* (1980) 5: 1-17, and (1980) 6: 1-11.

Sadiku, Riza. "Hasan Kaleshi (1922-1976). Leben und Werk." *Münchner
Zeitschrift für Balkankunde* (1978): 1-13.

Sax, Carl Ritter von. *Ethnographische Karte der europäischen Türkei. Mitteilungen der k. geographischen Gessellschaft Wien* 21 (1978).

Schmaus, Alois. "Volksepik in der Umgebung von Kosovska-Mitrovica
(Ibarski Kolašin, Kosovo, Drenica")". *Zeitschrift für slavische Philologie*
11 (1934): 432-39.

―――. "O Kosovskoj tradiciji kod Arnauta." *Prilozi proučavanju narodne poezije* 3 (1936): 73-90.

―――. "Kosovo u narodnoj pesmi muslimana" (Kosova in Moslem Folk
Songs). *Prilozi proučavanje narodne poezije* 5 (1938): 102-21.

Shala, Demush. *Këngë popullore legjendare* (Legendary Folk Songs). Enti
i teksteve: Prishtinë, 1972.

―――. *Këngë popullore historike* (Historical Folk Songs). Enti i teksteve: Prishtinë, 1973.

Shoup, Paul. *Communism and the Yugoslav National Question*. Columbia
University Press: New York, 1968.

Shtypi botëror rreth ngjarjeve në Kosovë (World Press on the Kosova
Events). 8 Nëntori: Tirana, 1981. [Reports in *Zëri i popullit* on articles
and reports published in different countries.]

Skendi, Stavro. *Albanian and South Slavic Oral Poetry*. American Folklore
Society: Philadelphia, 1954.

―――. *The Albanian National Awakening (1878-1912)*. Princeton University Press, 1967.

―――. *Balkan Cultural Studies*. East European Monographs 72. Columbia University Press: New York, 1980.

Skok, Petar. "Slave et albanais." Arhiv za arbanašku starinu, jezik i etnologiju 2 (1924): 107-26.

Soule, Véronique. "Les disputes nationales Yugoslaves quittent la coulisse.
Kosovo: les Albanais son là." *Libération,* March 15, 1983.

Šta se dogadjalo na Kosovu. Mala Biblioteka Politike: Belgrade, 1981. [Col-
lection of articles on the Kosova events in the Yugoslav press.]

Statistical Pocket Book of Yugoslavia. Belgrade, 1980.

Statistički Godišnjak SFRJ 1979. Belgrade.

Stipčević, Alexander. *Gli Illiri.* Il Saggiatore: Milan, 1966.

Šufflay, Milan. *Srbi i Arbanasi (njihova simbioza u srednjum vijeku).* (Serbs
and Albanians. Their Symbiosis in the Middle Ages). *Biblioteka za
arbanašku starinu, jezik i etnologiju,* Belgrade, 1925.

Svane, Gunnar. "Slovensko-arbanaške izoglosse." *Gjurmime albanologjike*
(1965) 2: 15-34.

Tagliavini, Carlo. "Le parlate albanesi del tipo ghego orientale (Dardania e
Macedonia nord-orientale)." *Le terre albanesi redente.* Reale Accademia
d'Italia: Rome, 1942, pp. 1-80.

Thalloczy, Ludwig (ed.). *Illyrisch-albanische Forschungen.* 2 vols. Munich-
Leipzig, 1916. [Thalloczy, Šufflay, Jireček, Ippen et al. contributors.]

Tomić, J. N. *O Arnautima u Staroj Srbije i Sandžaku.* Belgrade, 1913.

Trareup, Birthe. "Rhythm and Meter in Albanian Historical Folk Songs
from Kosovo (Drenica) Compared with the Epic Songs of Other Balkan
Peoples." *Makedonski Folklor* 4 (1971): 247-60.

Tucović, Dimitrije. *Srbija i Arbanija.* Kultur: Belgrade, 1946.

Truman, Ivan. "Yugoslav Myth after Tito." *The Month,* June 1982, pp.
191-95.

Ulaj, Idriz Xh. *Kéngé popullore nga Gucia.* (Folk Songs from Gucî (Gusinje)). Prishtinë, 1978.

Ustav SR Srbije (Constitution of the Socialist Republic of Serbia). Belgrade, 1974.

Ustav socjalističke Federativne Republike Jugoslavije (Constitution of the
Socialist Federal Republic of Yugoslavia). Belgrade, 1978.

Verla, Catherine. "Après les émeutes du Kosovo. Une question nationale
explosive." *Inprecor,* June 1981, pp. 9-15.

Yugoslavia: Development with Decentralization. International Bank for
Reconstruction and Development, Baltimore, 1975.

Yugoslavia: Prisoners of Conscience. Amnesty International: London, 1982.

Zajmi, Tahir. *Lidhja e II e e Prizrenit dhe lufta historike e popullit për mbrojtjen e Kosovës.* (The Second League of Prizren and the Popular Historical Struggle for the Defense of Kosova). Bruxelles, 1964.

Zamputi, Injac. "Shënime mbi kohën dhe jetën e Pjetër Bogdanit." (Notes on Bogdani's Era and Life). *Buletini për shkencat shoqërore* (1954) 3: 39-75.

———. "Pjetër Mazrreku dhe fjalorthi i tij i vjetit 1633" (P. Mazrreku and his 1633 vocabulary). *Studime filologjike* (1964) 2: 167-74.

Zmajević, Vincentius (ed.). *Concilium Provinciale, sive Nationale habitum anno 1703* . . . . Rome, 1705. [Albanian translation as *Kuvendi i Arbënit,* Rome, 1868.]

CONTRIBUTORS

Hartmut Albert, Coeditor of *Wörterbuch der Vergleichenden Bezeichnungs-lehre. Onomasiologie. Region Mittel- Ost- und Südosteuropa* (1979) and author of articles on Albanian lexicography and oral Slavic poetry.

Peter Bartl, Professor of History and Director of Albanien-Institut at the University of Munich. Author of *Die albanische Muslime zur Zeit der Nationalen Unabhängigkeitsbewegung* (1968), *Der Westbalkan zwischen spanischen Monarchie und osmanischem Reich* (1974). *Quellen und Materialen zur albanischen Geschichte der 17. und 18. Jahrhundert (1979)* as well as numerous articles on modern Albanian history. Editor of *Albanische Forschungen,* and *Münchner Zeitschrift für Balkan-kunde.*

Martin Camaj, Professor and Chair of Albanian at the University of Munich. Author of four volumes of poems and four of fiction in Albanian as well as *Il Messale di Buzuku* (1960), *Albanische Wortbildung* (1966), *Lesebuch der albanischen Sprache* (1969), *La parlata albanese di Greci in provincia di Avellino* (1971), *Die albanische Mundart von Falconara Albanese in der Provinz Cosenza* (1977) and many articles on Albanian language, folklore and literature. Editor of *Shêjzat* (Le Pleiadi) (Rome).

Alain Ducellier, Professor of Byzantine and Islamic History at the University of Toulouse (Le Mirail). Author of *Les Byzantins* (1970), *Le Miroir de l'Islam* (1971), *Le Drame de Byzance: essai d'histoire mentale* (1976), *La Façade maritime de l'Albanie au Moyen Age* (1981) and co-author of *Le Proche-Orient Médiéval* (1978). Numerous articles on medieval Albania.

Gerhard Grimm, Professor of History and Co-Chairman of Institut für Ge-schichte Osteuropas und Südeuropas at the University of Munich. Author of *Johann Georg von Hahn* (1964) and *Nationalsozialismus* (1981) as well as articles on East European and Albanian history.

277

Eric P. Hamp, Professor of Linguistics, and Albanian, at the University of Chicago. Author of *A Glossary of American Technical Linguistic Usage, 1925-1950* (1957) and many articles on linguistics; editor of *Themes in Linguistics* (1966), and co-editor of *Reading in Linguistics* (1966). PhD thesis (Harvard) on Italo-Albanian dialects and several articles on Greco-Albanian dialects.

Anton Logoreci graduated from London School of Economics. Author of *The Albanians, Europe's Forgotten Survivors* (1977) and numerous political and literary articles.

Albert B. Lord, Emeritus Professor of Slavic and Comparative Literature at Harvard University. Author of *Beginning Serbo-Croatian* (1958), *The Singer of Tales* (1960) and articles on Slavic folklore. Coauthor of *Serbo-Croatian Folk Songs,* 6 vols. (1951-1980) and *A Bulgarian Literary Reader* (1968). Editor of *Russian Folk Tales* (1970) and co-editor of *Yugoslav Folk Music* (1978).

Arshi Pipa, Professor of Italian, and Albanian, and Director of Italian Graduate Studies at the University of Minnesota. Author of four volumes of poems in Albanian and *Montale and Dante* (1968), *Hieronymus De Rada* (1978), *Albanian Folk Verse: Structure and Genre* (1978), *Albanian Literature: Social Perspectives* (1978) and articles on Italian literature and philosophy, and on Albanian and Italo-Albanian literature and folklore. Editor of *Kritika letrare* (Tirana).

Peter Prifti graduated from Pennsylvania University. Former coeditor of *Dielli* (The Sun) and Research Associate at MIT Center of International Studies. Consultant for Project on Albanian Language Studies at the University of California, San Diego. Author of *Socialist Albania since 1944: Domestic and Foreign Developments* (1978) and articles and chapters in books on Albanian politics and culture. Co-author of *Spoken Albanian* (1980) and *Standard Albanian: Reference Grammar* (1982).

Sami Repishti graduated from City University of New York (PhD in French). He is Chairman of Foreign Languages Department for Public Schools, Malverne, and Adjunct Assistant Professor of French at Adelphi University. Author of numerous articles on Kosova. An essay, "Human Rights in Yugoslavia," is a chapter in a forthcoming book.

Jens Reuter, a researcher at Südost-Institut, Munich, is author of *Die Albaner in Jugoslawien* (1982).

Adi Schnytzer, Lecturer in Economics at the University of Griffith, Australia, graduated from Oxford University (PhD thesis on Albanian economy). Author of *Stalinist Economic Strategy in Practice: The Case of Albania* (1982) and numerous articles on Albanian economy (some of them in collaboration with Michael Kaser).

Paul Shoup, Professor of Government and Foreign Affairs at the University of Virginia. Author of *Communism and the Yugoslav National Question* (1968) and *The East European and Soviet Data Handbook: Political, Social and Developmental Indicators* (1981).

EAST EUROPEAN MONOGRAPHS

The *East European Monographs* comprise scholarly books on the history and civilization of Eastern Europe. They are published under the editorship of Stephen Fischer-Galati, in the belief that these studies contribute substantially to the knowledge of the area and serve to stimulate scholarship and research.

1. *Political Ideas and the Enlightenment in the Romanian Principalities, 1750–1831.* By Vlad Georgescu. 1971.
2. *America, Italy and the Birth of Yugoslavia, 1917–1919.* By Dragan R. Zivjinovic. 1972.
3. *Jewish Nobles and Geniuses in Modern Hungary.* By William O. McCagg, Jr. 1972.
4. *Mixail Soloxov in Yugoslavia: Reception and Literary Impact.* By Robert F. Price. 1973.
5. *The Historical and Nationalist Thought of Nicolae Iorga.* By William O. Oldson. 1973.
6. *Guide to Polish Libraries and Archives.* By Richard C. Lewanski. 1974.
7. *Vienna Broadcasts to Slovakia, 1938–1939: A Case Study in Subversion.* By Henry Delfiner. 1974.
8. *The 1917 Revolution in Latvia.* By Andrew Ezergailis. 1974.
9. *The Ukraine in the United Nations Organization: A Study in Soviet Foreign Policy. 1944–1950.* By Konstantin Sawczuk. 1975.
10. *The Bosnian Church: A New Interpretation.* By John V. A. Fine, Jr., 1975.
11. *Intellectual and Social Developments in the Habsburg Empire from Maria Theresa to World War I.* Edited by Stanley B. Winters and Joseph Held. 1975.
12. *Ljudevit Gaj and the Illyrian Movement.* By Elinor Murray Despalatovic. 1975.
13. *Tolerance and Movements of Religious Dissent in Eastern Europe,* Edited by Bela K. Kiraly. 1975.
14. *The Parish Republic: Hlinka's Slovak People's Party, 1939–1945.* By Yeshayahu Jelinek. 1976.
15. *The Russian Annexation of Bessarabia, 1774–1828.* By George F. Jewsbury. 1976.
16. *Modern Hungarian Historiography.* By Steven Bela Vardy. 1976.
17. *Values and Community in Multi-National Yugoslavia.* By Gary K. Bertsch. 1976.
18. *The Greek Socialist Movement and the First World War: the Road to Unity.* By George B. Leon. 1976.
19. *The Radical Left in the Hungarian Revolution of 1848.* By Laszlo Deme. 1976.
20. *Hungary between Wilson and Lenin: The Hungarian Revolution of 1918–1919 and the Big Three.* By Peter Pastor. 1976.

51. *Czechoslovakia: The Heritage of Ages Past*. Edited by Ivan Volgyes and Hans Brisch. 1979.

52. *Prime Minister Gyula Andrassy's Influence on Habsburg Foreign Policy*. By Janos Decsy. 1979.

53. *Citizens for the Fatherland: Education, Educators, and Pedagogical Ideals in Eighteenth Century Russia*. By J. L. Black. 1979.

54. *A History of the "Proletariat": The Emergence of Marxism in the Kingdom of Poland, 1870–1887*. By Norman M. Naimark. 1979.

55. *The Slovak Autonomy Movement, 1935–1939: A Study in Unrelenting Nationalism*. By Dorothea H. El Mallakh. 1979.

56. *Diplomat in Exile: Francis Pulszky's Political Activities in England, 1849–1860*. By Thomas Kabdebo. 1979.

57. *The German Struggle Against the Yugoslav Guerrillas in World War II: German Counter-Insurgency in Yugoslavia, 1941–1943*. By Paul N. Hehn. 1979.

58. *The Emergence of the Romanian National State*. By Gerald J. Bobango. 1979.

59. *Stewards of the Land: The American Farm School and Modern Greece*. By Brenda L. Marder. 1979.

60. *Roman Dmowski: Party, Tactics, Ideology, 1895–1907*. By Alvin M. Fountain, II. 1980.

61. *International and Domestic Politics in Greece During the Crimean War*. By Jon V. Kofas. 1980.

62. *Fires on the Mountain: The Macedonian Revolutionary Movement and the Kidnapping of Ellen Stone*. By Laura Beth Sherman. 1980.

63. *The Modernization of Agriculture: Rural Transformation in Hungary, 1848–1975*. Edited by Joseph Held. 1980.

64. *Britain and the War for Yugoslavia, 1940–1943*. By Mark C. Wheeler. 1980.

65. *The Turn to the Right: The Ideological Origins and Development of Ukrainian Nationalism, 1919–1929*. By Alexander J. Motyl. 1980.

66. *The Maple Leaf and the White Eagle: Canadian-Polish Relations, 1918–1978*. By Aloysius Balawyder. 1980.

67. *Antecedents of Revolution: Alexander I and the Polish Congress Kingdom, 1815–1825*. By Frank W. Thackeray. 1980.

68. *Blood Libel at Tiszaeszlar*. By Andrew Handler. 1980.

69. *Democratic Centralism in Romania: A Study of Local Communist Politics*. By Daniel N. Nelson. 1980.

70. *The Challenge of Communist Education: A Look at the German Democratic Republic*. By Margrete Siebert Klein. 1980.

71. *The Fortifications and Defense of Constantinople*. By Byron C. P. Tsangadas. 1980.

72. *Balkan Cultural Studies*. By Stavro Skendi. 1980.

73. *Studies in Ethnicity: The East European Experience in America*. Edited by Charles A. Ward, Philip Shashko, and Donald E. Pienkos. 1980.

74. *The Logic of "Normalization:" The Soviet Intervention in Czechoslovakia and the Czechoslovak Response*. By Fred Eidlin. 1980.

75. *Red Cross, Black Eagle: A Biography of Albania's American Schol*. By Joan Fultz Kontos. 1981.

76. *Nationalism in Contemporary Europe*. By Franjo Tudjman. 1981.

77. *Great Power Rivalry at the Turkish Straits: The Montreux Conference and Convention of 1936*. By Anthony R. DeLuca. 1981.

78. *Islam Under the Double Eagle: The Muslims of Bosnia and Hercegovina, 1878–1914*. By Robert J. Donia. 1981.

79. *Five Eleventh Century Hungarian Kings: Their Policies and Their Relations with Rome.* By Z. J. Kosztolnyik. 1981.

80. *Prelude to Appeasement: East European Central Diplomacy in the Early 1930's.* By Lisanne Radice. 1981.

81. *The Soviet Regime in Czechoslovakia.* By Zdenek Krystufek. 1981.

82. *School Strikes in Prussian Poland, 1901–1907: The Struggle Over Bilingual Education.* By John J. Kulczychi. 1981.

83. *Romantic Nationalism and Liberalism: Joachim Lelewel and the Polish National Idea.* By Joan S. Skurnowicz. 1981.

84. *The "Thaw" In Bulgarian Literature.* By Atanas Slavov. 1981.

85. *The Political Thought of Thomas G. Masaryk.* By Roman Szporluk. 1981.

86. *Prussian Poland in the German Empire, 1871–1900.* By Richard Blanke. 1981.

87. *The Mazepists: Ukrainian Separatism in the Early Eighteenth Century.* By Orest Subtelny. 1981.

88. *The Battle for the Marchlands: The Russo-Polish Campaign of 1920.* By Adam Zamoyski. 1981.

89. *Milovan Djilas: A Revolutionary as a Writer.* By Dennis Reinhartz. 1981.

90. *The Second Republic: The Disintegration of Post-Munich Czechoslovakia, October 1938-March 1939.* By Theodore Prochazka, Sr. 1981.

91. *Financial Relations of Greece and the Great Powers, 1832–1862.* By Jon V. Kofas. 1981.

92. *Religion and Politics: Bishop Valerian Trifa and His Times.* By Gerald J. Bobango. 1981.

93. *The Politics of Ethnicity in Eastern Europe.* Edited by George Klein and Milan J. Reban. 1981.

94. *Czech Writers and Politics.* By Alfred French. 1981.

95. *Nation and Ideology: Essays in Honor of Wayne S. Vucinich.* Edited by Ivo Banac, John G. Ackerman, and Roman Szporluk. 1981.

96. *For God and Peter the Great: The Works of Thomas Consett, 1723–1729.* Edited by James Cracraft. 1982.

97. *The Geopolitics of Leninism.* By Stanley W. Page. 1982

98. *Karel Havlicek (1821–1856): A National Liberation Leader of the Czech Renascence.* By Barbara K. Reinfeld. 1982.

99. *Were-Wolf and Vampire in Romania.* By Harry A. Senn. 1982.

100. *Ferdinand I of Austria: The Politics of Dynasticism in the Age of Reformation.* By Paula Sutter Fichtner. 1982.

101. *France in Greece During World War I: A Study in the Politics of Power.* By Alexander S. Mitrakos. 1982.

102. *Authoritarian Politics in a Transitional State: Istvan Bethlen and the Unified Party in Hungary, 1919–1926.* By William M. Batkay. 1982.

103. *Romania Between East and West: Historical Essays in Memory of Constantin C. Giurescu.* Edited by Stephen Fischer-Galati, Radu R. Florescu and George R. Ursul. 1982.

104. *War and Society in East Central Europe: From Hunyadi to Rakoczi—War and Society in Late Medieval and Early Modern Hungary.* Edited by János Bak and Béla K. Király. 1982.

105. *Total War and Peace Making: A Case Study on Trianon.* Edited by Béla K. Király, Peter Pastor, and Ivan Sanders. 1982

106. *Army, Aristocracy, and Monarchy: Essays on War, Society, and Government in Austria, 1618–1780.* Edited by Wayne S. Vucinich. 1982.

107. *The First Serbian Uprising, 1804–1813.* Edited by Wayne S. Vucinich. 1982.

108. *Propaganda and Nationalism in Wartime Russia: The Jewish Anti-Fascist Committee in the USSR, 1941–1948.* By Shimon Redich. 1982.

109. *One Step Back, Two Steps Forward: On the Language Policy of the Communist Party of Soviet Union in the National Republics.* By Michael Bruchis. 1982.

110. *Bessarabia and Bukovina: The Soviet-Romanian Territorial Dispute.* by Nicholas Dima. 1982

111. *Greek-Soviet Relations, 1917–1941.* By Andrew L. Zapantis. 1982.

112. *National Minorities in Romania: Change in Transylvania.* By Elemer Illyes. 1982.

113. *Dunarea Noastra: Romania, the Great Powers, and the Danube Question, 1914–1921.* by Richard C. Frucht. 1982.

114. *Continuity and Change in Austrian Socialism: The Eternal Quest for the Third Way.* By Melanie A. Sully. 1982

115. *Catherine II's Greek Prelate: Eugenios Voulgaris in Russia, 1771–1806.* By Stephen K. Batalden. 1982.

116. *The Union of Lublin: Polish Federalism in the Golden Age.* By Harry E. Dembkowski. 1982.

117. *Heritage and Continuity in Eastern Europe: The Transylvanian Legacy in the History of the Romanians.* By Cornelia Bodea and Virgil Candea. 1982.

118. *Contemporary Czech Cinematography: Jiri Menzel and the History of The "Closely Watched Trains".* By Josef Skvorecky. 1982.

119. *East Central Europe in World War I: From Foreign Domination to National Freedom.* By Wiktor Sukiennicki. 1982.

120. *City, Town, and Countryside in the Early Byzantine Era.* Edited by Robert L. Hohlfelder. 1982.

121. *The Byzantine State Finances in the Eighth and Ninth Centuries.* By Warren T. Treadgold. 1982.

122. *East Central European Society and War in Pre-Revolutionary Eighteenth Century.* Edited by Gunther E. Rothenberg, Beia K. Kiraly and Peter F. Sugar. 1982.

123. *Czechoslovak Policy and the Hungarian Minority, 1945–1948.* By Kalman Janics. 1982.

124. *At the Brink of War and Peace: The Tito-Stalin Split in a Historic Perspective.* Edited by Wayne S. Vucinich. 1982.

125. *The Road to Bellapais: The Turkish Cypriot Exodus to Northern Cyprus.* By Pierre Oberling. 1982.

126. *Essays on World War I: Origins and Prisoners of War.* Edited by Peter Pastor and Samuel R. Williamson, Jr. 1983.

127. *Panteleimon Kulish: A Sketch of His Life and Times.* By George S. N. Luckyj. 1983.

128. *Economic Development in the Habsburg Monarchy in the Nineteenth Century: Essays.* Edited by John Komlos. 1983.

129. *Warsaw Between the World Wars: Profile of the Capital City in a Developing Land, 1918–1939.* By Edward D. Wynot, Jr. 1983.

130. *The Lust for Power: Nationalism, Slovakia, and The Communists, 1918–1948.* By Yeshayahu Jelinek. 1983.

131. *The Tsar's Loyal Germans: The Riga German Community: Social Change and the Nationality Question, 1855–1905.* By Anders Henriksson. 1983.

132. *Society in Change: Studies in Honor of Bela K. Kiraly.* Edited by Steven Bela Vardy. 1983.

133. *Authoritariansim in Greece: The Metaxas Regime.* By Jon V. Kofas. 1983.

134. *New Hungarian Peasants: An East Central European Experience with Collectivization.* Edited by Marida Hollos and Bela C. Maday. 1983.